PAYING THE PRICE
OF FREEDOM

PAYING THE PRICE OF FREEDOM

Family and Labor among Lima's Slaves
1800–1854

CHRISTINE HÜNEFELDT

Translated by Alexandra Stern

UNIVERSITY OF CALIFORNIA PRESS
BERKELEY   LOS ANGELES   LONDON

University of California Press
Berkeley and Los Angeles, California

University of California Press, Ltd.
London, England

© 1994 by
The Regents of the University of California
Library of Congress Cataloging-in-Publication Data

Paying the price of freedom : family and labor among Lima's
slaves, 1800–1854 / Christine Hünefeldt.
    p.   cm.
Includes bibliographical references and index.
ISBN 978-0-520-30234-1 (pbk. : alk. paper)
1. Slavery—Peru—Lima—History—19th century.
2. Slaves—Peru—Lima—Family relationships—History—
19th century.   I. Title.
HT1148.L56H87 1994
306.3'62'098525—dc20   94-4507
                                                    CIP

Contents

	List of Figures and Tables	vii
	Acknowledgments	ix
	Introduction	1
1.	Major Events and Everyday Life	9
2.	From Rural to Urban Life	37
3.	In the City	97
4.	Matrimonial Alliances and Conflicts	129
5.	Slaves and Their Owners: Property and Freedom	167
	Conclusion	199
	Abbreviations	217
	Notes	219
	Glossary	247
	Bibliography	251
	Index	261

Figures and Tables

Figures

1. Slave ownership in five Lima valleys: 1837 — 41
2. Slave ownership per household in Santa Ana: 1808 — 108

Tables

1. Methods of Manumission in Lima: 1830, 1840, 1850 — 24
2. Population of San Lázaro (Guia and Amancaes): 1813 — 39
3. Slave Population in Magdalena: 1813 — 42
4. Slave Population in Surco and Chorrillos: 1790 and 1813 — 43
5. Slave Population of Miraflores: 1813 — 44
6. Distribution of Land in the Lima Region: 1825–1840 — 45
7. Slave Children on Haciendas in 1790 and in 1813 — 48
8. Methods of Manumission in Rural Areas: 1830, 1840, 1850 — 51
9. Distribution of Slaves in Santa Ana: 1808 — 107
10. Marriages among Slave and Free Population of Lima: 1810–1850 — 145
11. Marriages between Slaves or between Slaves and Free Persons, Santa Ana and San Lázaro: 1800–1820 — 146
12. Ethnic Origins in Marriages within the Black Population of Santa Ana: 1800–1820 — 146
13. Owners' Consent and Status of Partners in Slave Marriages: 1810, 1815, and 1820 — 154
14. Reason for Placement in the *Panaderías* of Lima's Fourth District: 1803 — 189
15. Origin of Slaves and Free Persons in the *Panaderías* of Lima's Fourth District: 1803 — 189

Acknowledgments

I cannot quite fix the moment when slaves became a focus for my research. Somehow the topic was there all the time, though not as an explicit and independent project. And so my gratitude goes first to colleagues and friends who showed interest along the way by reading the small pieces of work that began this book. Financial support was never altogether absent. In 1980 the Ford Foundation in Lima and the Consejo Latinoamericano de Ciencias Sociales in Buenos Aires supported my research into peasant communities and family history. Paralleling the official research of Indians' complaints within the archives of Lima's Audiencia Real and Cabildo was an accumulation of information about Lima's slaves. Between 1983 and 1986 the Deutsche Forschungsgemeinschaft in Bonn sponsored a research project on conjugal conflict and on women in Lima that allowed me to work in the archbishopric archives and to consult parish registers of marriages for information on quarrels among spouses who were domestic servants—slaves. The topic caught my interest and full attention: here is the place to acknowledge the chance encounters and indirect courses that contributed to the book.

Heraclio Bonilla was one of the persons in Lima who convinced me that the information I was gathering was both rich and important; my first published pages on this topic resulted from his insistence. The support and interest of many colleagues in Lima in the department of economics at the Catholic University and at the Instituto de Estudios Peruanos, during conferences, coffee conversations, and debates, have helped clarify my ideas for this and other projects. Especially significant was a seminar I taught in 1986 at the Catholic University's anthropology department, on the black population's experiences in different geographical and historical settings. The eight students and I set out to gather information from interviews with Lima's black inhabitants and presented the results at a public conference that same year. Among the people we interviewed were members of the

Movimiento Congo, who work to improve the conditions of Peru's black population. Talks and other conferences followed this contact, and their views have shaped my account of Lima's past, though it may not be the story they had hoped to hear.

I regret not having the opportunity to discuss my account with the late Alberto Flores Galindo, whose genial presence *limeños* will miss for a long time to come. Carlos Aguirre is now an intellectual companion on the same route, and the similarities in our conclusions encourage me.

Over long searches through the archives, I incurred many debts to individuals there who were unfailingly helpful and courteous. Despite working conditions that were often difficult, such as the lack of detailed catalogues (or the absence of catalogues, in some cases), their memories were critical resources for my research. Mario Ormeño in the Archivo Arzobispal, and Mario Cárdenas and Yolanda Bisso in the Archivo General de la Nación were sources of help and encouragement through strikes, threats of flood and fire, and bureaucratic regulations.

A welcoming intellectual environment here at the University of California, San Diego, has helped me finish the manuscript, and my colleagues Michael Monteón and Ramón Ruiz have provided valuable comments on it. The detailed assessment of Frederick Bowser, and the thoughts of the other two anonymous readers for the University of California Press, offered good advice and suggestions that found great resonance in the final corrections of December 1991 though I did not follow all the good advice. Many thanks go to all of them.

The abundant primary sources made the task of translating the manuscript into English slow and complex, and Alexandra Stern worked hard to capture the flavor of the historical agents and moments; Nelson Altamirano helped polish and shape the tables. The efforts and patience of Eileen McWilliams and Erika Büky, my editors at Berkeley, and the detailed, sophisticated, and accurate copyediting of Edith Gladstone have contributed to the style and rigor of the arguments. I presented an earlier version of the first chapter in April 1991 at a conference in Lima organized by the Movimiento Congo and the Catholic University; the Instituto de Estudios Peruanos published it in 1992 in its Serie Mínima. I first discussed a small sample of the documents that underlie this book in 1979 and 1980, in articles for the *Revista Histórica*.

Personal acknowledgments are the most difficult to write because, lacking precise moments or expressions, they are hard to grasp. Of these, I owe the most profound debt to my parents, Helga and Joachim, for their endless support; the book is dedicated to them. Many compensating and cheerful moments at lighter levels of life have come from the generous presence of Francisco, Ximena, and Gari, my "kids"; of Nelson, my husband; of Marcela Calisto and Milagros Navarro, good friends; and of my students in Lima and San Diego. Last but not least in this list is Nelly Céspedes, who took over all domestic chores in Lima to make the project possible in the first place.

Introduction

Urban slavery was never envisaged as one of the possible important consequences of the slave trade. Nevertheless, over the course of time cities such as Lima, Buenos Aires, São Paulo, or Rio de Janeiro saw a gradual increase in their slave populations. Initially, slaves were sent to rural areas such as plantations or to mines located on coastal areas where, since the beginning of the frontier years, the indigenous population had either died or moved away, escaping Iberian encroachment. Of the approximately nine and a half million Africans who were forcibly transported to the Americas between the sixteenth and nineteenth centuries, about 98 percent were destined for plantations that raised and exported crops such as sugar, tobacco, cocoa, and cotton. More than three million slaves were deposited in the French and British Caribbean. Around one and a half million slaves, or 17 percent of the total, came to the Spanish colonies; of these, slightly more than seven hundred thousand remained in Cuba.[1]

Neither the cities in general, nor the viceroyalty of Peru in particular, became the main entrepôts for slaves: about one hundred thousand slaves came to Peru, of whom 40 percent either stayed in, or over time relocated to, Lima. In the Peruvian highlands Indians were and are the predominant labor force. But the concentration of slaves in and around the city made their presence significant, even if in absolute terms slaves were only a small percentage of the Atlantic trade. For Lima's slaves, the element that most defined their lives was the city and all that it implied. Even slaves in the rural hinterlands had expectations and social networks that were primarily urban.

The incorporation of slaves had manifold repercussions on Peruvian society. They ranged from the purely economic consequences of an occupational structure defined by race and ethnicity, to the more complicated and evasive cultural implications of the diffusion of black traditions, and of the creation of novel processes of resistance and adaptation. In the urban centers, slaves and free blacks were the backbone of day-to-day existence. Without black artisans, water carriers, muleteers, or house servants, life would have been unthinkable.

The disintegration of slavery over the course of the nineteenth century was a process that—in a global sense—radically changed the structure of human relations; it destroyed capital, reduced commercial exports from America to Europe, shifted the sites of production, transformed productive social relations, spurred Asian emigration, and reorganized the international division of labor (Klein and Engerman 1985). Such widespread effects explain the existence of a comprehensive bibliography on slavery and slave systems, which I use to compare the many trajectories of slavery and movements toward abolition and to go beyond the initial dichotomy in academic circles between the southern United States and Latin America. A growing understanding of the heterogeneity of slavery in different countries, distinct regions, and varied historical settings results from the incorporation of new methodological approaches into work on slavery, the most successful of which bring cultural and family perspectives to evaluate change at the microlevel and from the slaves' point of view. My analysis of urban slaves in Lima and of their participation in the unfolding of abolition is just one additional facet of the mosaic of research about different slave systems.

By the turn of the nineteenth century the contradictions of colonial rule had polarized Peruvian society. Indian uprisings against bureaucratic corruption, excessive work loads, and arbitrary tributary exactions, as well as *criollo* protests against royal taxes and monopolies, and scattered slave revolts: all these signs of a declining colonial relationship had been accumulating for many years. Spain's attempts to solidify its dominion through the Bourbon reforms backfired; instead of reaffirming loyalty to the ruler, the implementation of these reforms provoked sporadic outbursts that ultimately led to the viceroyalty's political separation from Spain.

In Peru, this last bastion of Spanish rule in Hispanic America, General José de San Martín declared independence on 28 July 1821. Battles persisted until 1825, however. The first incursions of rebels—who called themselves "patriots" and who opposed the "royalists"—into the Peruvian viceroyalty occurred in 1809 when forces came from the south (Chile and Argentina); the first uprising against Spain failed. The Cádiz constitution was approved in 1810 and partially implemented in the Peruvian viceroyalty starting in 1812. Yet royalist opposition to enjoining the liberal constitution caused three insurrections (in Cuzco, Huánuco, and Tacna) in which the participation and leadership of Indians were critical. Lima's *criollos*, Spaniards born in Latin America, remained on the side of the royalists or, at very least, were neutral. They feared the loosening of social control that a period of war implied and were hesitant about proclaiming their fidelity to the patriots or taking at face value the promises touted first by San Martín and later by General Simón Bolívar.

The apprehensions of the *criollos* were based on their previous encounters with rebelling blacks and Indians. Throughout the colonial period Lima's inhabitants often glanced toward the sea, awaiting the arrival of some African tribal chief who would unleash a generalized slave rebellion. Although this event never took place, such fears were deeply ingrained in the minds of *limeños*. Premonitions of uncontrollable anarchy were among the main reasons—along with growing demands for plantation labor—why slaveholders wavered so long when the time came to emancipate the slave population. For them liberalism was an idea, not a reality—one that surely did not include the participation of Indians and blacks.

The years during and following the war of independence were marked by political unrest and general uncertainty. Competing factions fought over power.[2] The contenders for power knew that one way to secure victory was to invite slaves to participate. They knew that their best strategy was to promise liberty to slaves who would fight their battles. Many slaves responded to the offers and enlisted in the army; but by the time the battles died down most of them felt they had been cheated. Again and again slave owners managed to reverse their pledges and perpetuate the slave system, until 1854 when—almost by inertia—it was finally formally abolished. Yet we must not conclude from this achievement that Peru had a strong abolitionist movement, or that liberalism gained firm ground. In Peru both elements were weak and vacillating.

Abolition of slavery in Cuba—one of the best studied areas of Latin America—had distinctive and common variables that underlay its emergence, according to Rebecca Scott's synthesis of several sources (1985, 25 ff.). One important argument is the "technological innovation argument," which contends that the use of better and more sophisticated technology was antithetical to the continuity of slavery. The abbreviated message of this approach is that when industry grows, slavery declines; in this context, decrees abolishing slavery are but footnotes to reality (Moreno Fraginals 1978, 3, 37). A second argument ascribes the abolition of slavery to the initiative of slaveholders who, pursuing the conveniences stemming from new markets and cheap free labor and perhaps influenced by moral concerns, increasingly convinced themselves that abolition's time had arrived (Genovese 1971, 69–70). A third argument asserts that abolition was the direct consequence of a worldwide diplomatic and political campaign against slavery (Corwin 1967). The three arguments have a common thread: they all locate the reasons for abolition outside the lives and world of slaves and maintain that abolition resulted from pressures originating from the elites and from transcendent humanitarian ideals. In contrast to these views, Scott suggests that "as one moves away from the invocation of internal contradictions or diplomatic pressures as explanations for abolition, and shifts the focus to the dialectic of, on the one hand, stalling and improvisation by slave owners, and, on the other, pressure and initiatives from slaves, gradual emancipation emerges as a form of social change largely controlled by planters and the state, but which nonetheless drew much of its character and timing from slaves and insurgents" (1985, 48).

From these varying arguments we can isolate one issue linked to the question of perspective—of what vantage point or whose vision allows us to see and interpret historical processes: it is the question of timing. When and under what conditions did slavery disappear? For slaveholders the answer to this question hinged on the profitability of the system. Profit was largely an ideological construct, however; the more slave owners became convinced that alternative sources of labor were less expensive, the less they supported the slave system. In Peru, slavery was abolished after decades of financial and fiscal crisis when guano revenues started to fill the state coffers and also when an alternative labor source became available through the importation of Chinese rural workers (coolies). As in other regions, slaveholders were unwilling to grant slaves freedom without some form of compensation.

My assessment of urban slavery—in all its diverse mutations—allows us to reexamine the meaning of profitability. Slave owners found means to keep profitability high despite rural decay and the massive insertion of slaves in the urban context.[3] For slaves, urban life permitted the reinforcement of familial and social ties. Some authors see slavery and family as incompatible institutions, given the precariousness and instability to which slaves were subjected. Others persuasively demonstrate that slave families did indeed exist; moreover, they gradually replace the image of the "socially dead" slave with that of a highly socially active slave—a change that apparently applies to very different slave systems.[4] Such a perspective not only challenges long-standing assumptions about differences between North American and Latin American slave systems but also enhances our understanding of slave life within the family and the larger community. In Lima, the slave family was the body around which life revolved and the combative unit through which individuals could attain freedom. The family and marriage were important realities and were also a major ingredient of a more encompassing ideological power struggle.

When President Ramón Castilla abolished slavery in Peru in 1854, slaves had already taken many steps toward emancipation. Since the beginning of the colonial era slaves had been constructing avenues to freedom; these strategies grew stronger over time. My central aim in the following chapters is to describe the myriad and diverse mechanisms that slaves created in anticipation of freedom and despite the resistance of slaveholders. There is little truth to the assertion that "in manumitting slaves, Castilla achieved in our fatherland the ideals of human equality and forever banned odious racial prejudices" (Labarthe 1955, 23). Castilla did not give slaves their freedom; they had long been purchasing it with the fruits of their own labor. Furthermore, abolition did not rise from a notion of human equality but was part of a process of domination that underwent reformulation and redirection. And last but not least, racial prejudices still play a critical role in Peruvian struggles for identity. Processes and ideologies are historically constructed; they cannot simply be erased by a decree.

As a human group smaller than the indigenous population, black slaves had profound ties to whiter societal groups. As daily wage laborers, craftspersons, and household servants, slaves shared parts of white interests and culture. Their interaction with the white population was quite different from that of the indigenous population, not only because of their distinct fiscal and legal status but also because of their steady search for social links and the manifold ways they found to insert themselves into the occupational urban structure. From the outset, blacks were a more flexible and adaptive group—to a great extent because their social and cultural connections had been disarticulated by the Atlantic passage. In order to survive, slaves had to mold themselves to the world that surrounded them; through this process they learned how to use the internal contradictions of an exploitive system to their advantage and to appropriate the tools of oppression and transform them into instruments of liberation. The moral, social, and economic inconsistencies of *limeño* society lay at the heart of the relative—yet still significant—benefits that slaves could turn to their advantage.

The complexion of Peruvian society has grown lighter over the past two centuries. Only small nuclei of blacks still exist, both in Lima and in some coastal valleys. Yet their permeation into society as a whole has been quite significant, from their cultural heritage to their racial features. How did blacks become a part of Peru's ethnic spectrum? Only an account of their day-to-day trials and tribulations, achievements, and debacles will help us answer this question.

In order to illustrate the variety of processes in which Lima's blacks were involved, I adopt a family outlook. Basing my analysis on the social microcosm of the family I explore the more intimate and emotional realms of the slave system. The archives I consulted contain episodic slices of the lives of many black and not-so-black slave families. But diaries or journals similar to those written by slaves in the United States—accounts that would have offered a look at the more subtle dimensions of slave life—are not available in Peru. For this reason the book opens with a fictive reconstruction of the life of a slave family, a combination of situations from real cases. My Lasmanuelos family history attempts to design a family biography that, beyond familiarizing us with the discordant expressions of day-to-day life (since conflict was the primary element of the legal cases we examined), helps us see and trace the development and consequences of a family's internal mechanisms of articulation. Fiction begins with the names I chose: Manuel, Manuela, and their children Manuelita, Manolo, and Manolito. During the period under discussion, someone named Manuel was almost inevitably black and, thus, a slave. With names such as these as a point of departure, I want to emphasize the homogenizing tendencies that a slave system can impose, despite the fact that a detailed analysis also reveals the actual porosity of such a system.

In the second chapter I present statistical indicators of Lima's rural hinterland and of the diversity of units of production and their development, as well as their marked differences from haciendas and plantations in Peru's other coastal areas. My primary contention is that the tenor of rural slave life, to a great extent, depended on the size of the estate, which in turn determined the mechanisms of internal social control, which in turn shaped the kind of familial and social life slaves could construct. This chapter also sets out the fluidity of relations between the rural hinterland and the city, caused both by the plans of masters and by the spatial mobility of slaves.

The third chapter examines the urban environment and reveals a diversification of slave activities in this context and different levels of slave-master interactions that shaped their relations. I pay special attention to day laborers and artisans and to how slavery and manumission affected men and women in different ways. From this perspective we can recognize many forms of social articulation, expressed by the varied ways slaves managed to obtain fractions of freedom and the manner in which they organized their lives with their owners. Negotiation involved issues such as whether workers lived in or outside a master's household, the amount of daily wages that had to be handed over to the master, and the management of slave children. Neither owners nor the Roman Catholic church were in a position to impose arbitrary rules without the validation of widespread cultural and social mores. In other words, this chapter also broaches a discussion of the legitimacy of power.

This discussion continues in the fourth chapter, where I explore the degree to which slaves were involved in white culture—or better yet—to what extent slaves' use of moral contradictions was self-defeating or created new traps. The lens of slaves' marital conflict lets us identify the limits slavery set on the formulation of alternative mechanisms of social cohesion. Both slaves' resistance and their family unit, which they fiercely defended, dissolve before our eyes when we see how inequality and conflict became social expressions that served to separate couples, dissolve marriages, or perhaps cause a female slave to wish to return to the protection of her master. The inevitable distortion of marriage and family relations transformed marital conflict into an arena open to the intervention of owners and in many senses turned these dimensions of social life into more subtle mechanisms that reproduced the slave system. In the fifth and final chapter I assess the more encompassing relations between slaves and masters as well as their implications on Lima's slave system as a whole.

The various axes of thought and historical analysis in this book are components of several current debates. Thus, extrapolating from the findings for Lima—while not losing sight of the particularities of Lima's slavery—I propose some comparisons with other slave systems. To a great extent, I echo Sidney Mintz's (1969, 27–28) contention that slavery is slavery but that not all slave systems are equal, economically or culturally.

Several reasons underlie my decision to study the region of Peru during the period of abolition. The first is the existence of an already classic study of Peruvian slavery during the sixteenth and seventeenth centuries, written by Frederick Bowser (1977). Bowser uses documents similar to my own to identify the type of slave system that developed in Peru, a generally peripheral area but one where urban slavery was particularly salient. Second, Peru represents an interesting case because its ethnic composition was so diverse: the interaction between Indians, blacks, and whites provides a uniquely challenging environment in which to explore colonial socioeconomic structures (1977, 12). Bowser's research traces Peruvian slavery from the arrival of the Spaniards to the middle of the seventeenth century when the Westphalia Treaty, which clearly interrupted Spain's commercial monopoly (and thus its slave trade), was signed. Bowser believes that the basic model of Peruvian slavery developed during this initial stage; subsequent changes would just be smaller adjustments. In a general sense he is correct; yet the validity of such an assertion always depends on how and from whose perspective changes are being assessed. I hope that someday we will have an account of Peruvian slavery for the intermediate period (i.e., between the mid-seventeenth century and the beginning of the nineteenth century, where my analysis starts). For the time being, my general sense is that substantial transformations took place between both periods, especially if we consider the changing attitudes of slaveholders and examine the acceleration and increasing fulfillment of slaves' demands. And a final reason for the choice of Peru—one that Bowser also mentions—is my belief that the broad debate on slave systems should incorporate the peculiarities of Lima and, more generally, of Hispanic American *urban* slavery.

Chapter One

Major Events
and Everyday Life

In 1800 the slave family Lasmanuelos lived on the Pando hacienda in the parish of Magdalena, ten kilometers from the Plaza de Armas, Lima's central square. The proximity of hacienda to urban center illustrated the city's rural character at the beginning of the nineteenth century. A decade earlier the urban nucleus held 3,641 houses along 355 streets, 4 districts with 35 barrios, and 6 parishes with a total of 13,483 slaves (Haenke [1808] 1901, 55–68). By 1876 the province that formed Lima counted 198 localities, within 16 districts divided into 2 towns, 9 villages, 18 hamlets, and 169 haciendas. Even in 1884 the city spread over 608,500 square meters but existed in the middle of a rural hinterland fifteen times larger (Clavero 1885).

Despite the intensification of the slave trade between 1790 and 1802 (Rout 1977, 97, 217) that brought *bozales*—slaves from Africa, knowing nothing of the Spanish language, religion, or customs—into the heart of the black population, the number of slaves kept decreasing in the following decades. In 1812 the viceroyalty contained 89,241 slaves, 40 percent of them living in the province of Lima. In 1818 the number of slaves in the city of Lima had fallen to 8,589; in 1836 it stood at only 5,791, and in 1845 it was calculated to be 4,500 (Jacobsen 1974; Aguirre 1990, tb. 1). The final years of the eighteenth century and the first decades of the nineteenth were marked by political turbulence followed by a long cycle of economic decline. Instability was symptomatic of this period. Problems such as food scarcities, fluctuating prices (Ramos 1967; Febres Villaroel 1964), labor unrest, and rapid presidential changes were all part of a hectic daily life.[1]

Added to the economic ups and downs were institutional uncertainties and their repercussions, which directly affected the black population: the publication in 1789 of the Cédula Real on the treatment of slaves,[2] the abolition of the Atlantic slave trade in 1808, the liberal constitutions of 1810 and 1820, the struggles for independence and subsequent civil conflicts. The respective contenders for power sought, on more than one occasion, the support of slaves to settle their disputes and battles, often broadening the vision that slaves had of their world. This public or "historic time," of increasing general awareness and of military participation, blended with and reproduced itself on a smaller scale in "family time" (Hareven 1977). The walls of houses were thin, streets were full of ears, and rumors flew everywhere: even individuals who did not participate directly in the events of the period felt and assessed the changes.

In 1800 the heads of the Lasmanuelos family, Manuel and Manuela, were single. Manuel was a *bozal* slave from Angola, purchased by the owner of the Pando hacienda from one of the last tradesmen to bring slaves through the Panamanian route.[3] Manuela had been born on the hacienda, and she was the daughter of a *mulata* slave (of African and Spanish descent) and a black slave ironsmith. By 1800 both her parents had passed away. In 1813 the Pando hacienda housed forty-five slaves, approximating the average holdings of the sixteen haciendas in the region.[4] Manuela was one of thirteen women under the control of the wife of the *mayordomo* (overseer) who were housed apart from the hacienda's twenty-one male slaves in a *barracón* (slaves' living quarters). In 1800 Manuela had a three-year-old daughter and a seven-month-old son, the only offspring who had survived her several pregnancies. The baby was sold to a priest of the Buena Muerte hacienda and monastery, a decision guided by the reasoning that child-rearing costs were too high and that male slaves, upon maturing, usually established connections with slaves on other haciendas and, more important, with the nonslave (including indigenous) population in neighboring towns. High infant mortality also lent credence to the idea that even if the amount was insignificant, at least something could be obtained for a young slave.[5] Another reason for selling a child might be that there were other "disgraces" to hide, such as the master's consanguinity.

The remaining child, Manuelita, was considered a *quarterona*—a person of one-fourth African blood—and her skin color revealed her descent from the administrator's *mestizo compadre* (his godfather, of European and Indian descent). Still quite young, Manuelita could play with ten other girls and share with them the small chores of production on the hacienda. An elderly female slave was in charge of caring for the children so that their mothers could work. The owner of the Pando hacienda was a member of the nobility, a marqués who lived in

Lima; a *zambo* (of African, indigenous, and European descent) oversaw the slaves and the production. Manuela, considered part of the hacienda's inventory, had been one of the contributions included in the marquesa's dowry.

To obtain a plot of land on the hacienda for cultivating corn, squash, sweet potatoes, and beans and for raising pigs was easier for slaves if they were married.[6] Partly for this reason, Manuel and Manuela decided to marry. The allocation of small subsistence plots was a way for owners to give slaves incentives for reproduction, to lower the costs of food, and also to strengthen the slaves' links to the hacienda. The ceremony took place in the hacienda parish church at the same time as the marriages of two other slave couples, one from the same hacienda, the other from the Mirones hacienda, which was smaller (it had only six male and two female slaves) and did not possess its own church. Naturally, the priest who traveled from the village of Magdalena to perform this social and religious ceremony did not wish to duplicate his efforts. And the arrangements for this wedding were simple: both the *mayordomo* of Pando and the *chino* (of undefined African blood) owner of Mirones had houses in the village of Magdalena.[7] After complying with the divine precepts and assigning land plots to the newlyweds, the *mayordomo* sent a letter to the *hacendado*, informing the owner of the ceremony's consummation.

In this fashion Manuel and Manuela participated in the Catholic ritual. After the wedding came a big party in the *barracones*; the *mayordomo* furnished special endowments of meat, salt, *cañazo* (an alcoholic beverage prepared with sugarcane), and bundles of new coarse cotton rope purchased from Magdalena's artisans. From then on, both slaves dedicated Sunday and their spare time to cultivating their plot and raising pigs, relying on the hacienda's tools for their work. Thanks to preexisting customs and links, they could later sell these products in Magdalena's market or exchange them for other products in or outside the hacienda. Occasionally even the *mayordomo* bought fresh vegetables from them. Each pig was worth twelve pesos. Manuela's price, according to her *conque* (the legal document detailing the conditions of a slave's sale or purchase), was 350 pesos, Manuel's was 500, and Manuelita's 80. Thus the sale of 6.4 pigs would have allowed Manuel and Manuela to purchase their daughter's freedom. The agent for the sale of animals and crops in Magdalena was a *mulata* midwife who had assisted Manuela and the administrator's wife during their childbirths.

On the Pando hacienda, slaves worked from dawn until four in the afternoon. The schedule followed the requirements of production and in seasons of sowing and harvest easily reached sixteen hours a day. Plot cultivation was subordinated to the demands of the hacienda, and fulfillment of these demands was one of the conditions necessary to maintain access to, or receive more land for, cultivation. At times the *hacendado*'s promise to grant his slaves plots of land was the only incentive effective enough to induce them to intensify their working day on the hacienda's commercial crops during key seasons.

When Manuelita reached seven years of age, the administrator's wife took her to the big house on the hacienda so the child could learn domestic chores and keep her two sons company. Moreover, in accordance with the tradition of "womb assignment," even before Manuelita's birth she had become the property of Doña Baltasara, the daughter of the owner of the Pando hacienda. Doña Baltasara wanted to take Manuelita to Lima where she would be trained in urbane propriety and household service. Manuelita was sent to the city in 1809 when she reached twelve years of age. According to an appraisal carried out to notarize Doña Baltasara's dowry to her husband, Manuelita's value had increased to 200 pesos. Because Manuelita observed modest and subservient behavior under Doña Baltasara's employ, and because Manuelita's mother (Manuela) had already been born into the marquesa's control and had further endowed her owner with two more living slaves (Manolo and Manolito), when the marquesa made out her will in 1812 she lowered Manuela's price to 180 pesos and declared that—provided Manuela could pay this price—she should be granted freedom. The marquesa's daughter, Doña Baltasara, was more generous. In her own will, she later stipulated that when Manuelita reached twenty-five years of age she should be liberated and should receive an inheritance of 200 pesos. Furthermore, she recommended that her husband and son make sure that Manuelita was "happily married," by the time of Doña Baltasara's death, to a man capable of giving her a comparable standard of life. In the meantime, this special consideration translated into teaching Manuelita not only to clean and take care of the house but also to sew, the central (and sometimes the only permitted) activity of white women and of *mestizas* who wanted to be white but whose economic status did not correspond with such racial aspirations.

Manuel and Manuela remained on the hacienda for some time longer. In 1812 their sons (Manolito and Manolo) were seven and eleven years of age, respectively, and the parents knew that time was against them. The older the children, the greater difficulty their parents would have buying their freedom. As they became a valuable labor force for the hacienda, their price would increase and *mayordomos* and *hacendados* would be much more reluctant to accept a slave's self-purchase money from slaves or from their parents.[8] As long as they remained slaves, the costs of maintenance and health were the owner's responsibility, even though—as we will see—the subject of who should assume these costs often generated considerable debate.

The year of 1812 had special significance. Regarding slaves, the liberal constitution of Cádiz reiterated many of the postulates of the Cédula Real issued in Aranjuez in 1789. The Caroline code stated that the central objective for slaves, "according to the principles and laws that dictate religion, humanity and the good of the state [that are] compatible with slavery and public tranquillity" (Clementi 1974, appendix), was to make good use of them. It granted freedom to slaves if they denounced a slave conspiracy or remained in loyal service to their master for a period of at least thirty years. This code represented full protection of the slave system, recommending fair treatment of slaves and installation of a fining system for excesses committed by masters and *mayordomos*; it demanded that masters make lists of slaves under their mandate.[9] There was nothing new about such recommendations. Their reiteration makes an observer suspect that they were often dismissed, not instituted.

Despite its liberal aura, the Cádiz constitution did not radically change this panorama. Few advances disturbed the general trend of the Caroline code (see King 1953), but several special situations reflected the social changes that had been taking place over the previous thirty years and marked contemporary burgeoning notions of liberalism. In general, an important fraction of American representatives at the Cádiz courts agreed that persons of color were "the source of all our good and happiness. They provide hands to cultivate the earth . . . to dig from its bowels . . . the river that activates commerce. . . . From them come our artisans and they lend themselves to any work, private or public. They order armed service in those countries . . . and at present they are the robust column of our defense . . . on whom fall the formidable blows of the rebellion of some of our brothers."[10]

On 17 August 1811 the Cádiz courts converted all vassals, except slaves, into citizens. On 29 January 1812 residents of black descent were declared eligible to enroll in universities, study at seminaries, and wear habits. On 17 August 1813 corporal punishment was forbidden in secondary schools, correctional facilities, and jails for being "contrary to the decency, the dignity of those who exist, and are born and educated, to be free men."[11] The *gracias al sacar*, a certificate that could be bought certifying lighter skin, and thus higher status, was abolished even in the military corps (Lanning 1985, 175–200).

The enmity of slave owners and the logic intrinsic to colonial domination based on ethnic segregation and distinct civil and fiscal treatment ensured that restrictions to these general and well-intentioned decrees were quickly implemented and adapted by the separate legislatures of colonial institutions. What was decided upon by the liberals of Cádiz, thus, would only be implemented provided that "blacks satisfy the rest of the requisites and conditions of [Catholic] canons, the laws of the kingdom and of the specific constitutions of the different corporations in which they wish to be admitted because according to the present decree, only specific laws or statutes opposed to the sanctions herein ceded to slaves are understood as repealed."[12]

Here, in short, was a way to vent and circumvent liberal and humanitarian aims in a society whose slaves and black population were a labor source that neither liberals nor conservatives were willing to relinquish.

Even so, there was a feeling of change in the air. Throughout the viceroyalty, amid two uprisings by indigenous groups and *criollos* (Spaniards born in Latin America), the authorities were drawing up lists of citizens capable of commissioning the delegates who would represent American interests at the newly founded Cortes de Cádiz after King Ferdinand VII had been dethroned. The public climate had changed considerably since the mid-sixteenth century, a time in which a Spaniard walked the streets of Lima surrounded by fifteen or more slave lackeys who either defended him from his neighborhood rivals or advertised his social position (Bowser 1977, 143–146); at the end of the eighteenth century blacks in Lima could congregate in city squares to stage parodies of the mayor's parade, dressing up like urban officials and toting a banner that depicted a black man with a chain around his neck (Burkholder 1972, 2, 33, 152n.). Some of the liberal mood infected even the slaves.

An atmosphere of anticipation was generated and contemporary ideology was polarized by several lawyers who defended slaves and owners before Lima's Audiencia Real (the highest court of justice and governing body under the viceroy). As in other urban settings, the free professionals here were the ones most persuaded by the liberal discourse, and they were willing to carry it to its furthest limit: they proposed the abolition of the slave system. Even the most liberal, however, did not believe in overnight changes and believed even less that their own slaves should become free unless the slaves paid the costs of their manumission or the state assumed its costs.[13] Certainly, there were also those who echoed the clamors of *hacendados* about the shortage of workers and the deterioration of the haciendas. They often hid these interests behind arguments about slaves' lack of education and the social disasters that would come about if slavery were abolished, even using comparative historical experiences to substantiate their positions.[14] The *juzgado de menores*, the court for litigation of cases involving legal minors (slaves included), was one of the entities to which slaves brought their complaints—to such an extent that many *hacendados* saw it as one of the main factors contributing to the downfall of agriculture. Many suits filed in the name of slaves reflected a conflict within the dominant sectors of society that would not abate until after abolition.

Directly, through her will that lowered Manuela's price and guaranteed the slave an inheritance, the marquesa of the Pando hacienda transformed Manuela's future. Lima's nobles sensed that control was escaping from their grasp, both within their landed estates and in the colony. From a greater distance, Manuel and Manuela heard rumors about the Cádiz constitution and the indigenous-*criollo* uprisings, which brought thousands of refugees to Lima, setting off a crisis of subsistence and driving up the prices of foodstuffs (Haitin 1986, 148).

Two circuits of production functioned on the hacienda: the basic foodstuffs produced by the slaves for their own subsistence and occasional sale at the nearest marketplaces; and the products cultivated on the grounds of the hacienda destined for larger markets and, to a limited extent, the international market. The relation between these spheres of production was determined by the quantities of available land and slave labor. Little by little—as will be detailed later on—the smallest haciendas in Lima's environs redirected their production toward the domestic urban market. To compensate for the lowering of prices over the long term they began to produce what was most in demand, thus approaching—and competing with—slave production. A rational response on the part of *hacendados* would have been to reduce or even eliminate the plots granted to slaves. It would have forced slaves to dedicate more hours to the hacienda grounds and would have restricted the competition between hacienda and small-scale plot production.[15] This response apparently did not occur, however, because the reduction of slave plots would have induced slaves to abandon the hacienda, for refuge either in the city of Lima or within one of the many groups of highwaymen in the valleys surrounding the city. Thus, from a microeconomic standpoint, this scenario not only demonstrates the difficulties of controlling slave labor, expressed in the outcries of *hacendados* over the "indolence" and the "impertinence" of their subordinates, but also explains why increases on the supply side tended to depress agricultural prices.

In the years that had elapsed between their marriage and 1812, Manuel and Manuela had managed to amass only enough money to free either Manuela or the two sons. Manuela, with the assistance of Manuel and her two sons, could take care of the cultivation of the plot and the breeding of the pigs; it was she who sold vegetables in the Magdalena market once a month. Buying the two children's freedom made no sense. The costs of maintenance outside the hacienda would only rise, adding new expenses such as paying a relative or friend in Lima to watch over the children. While the sons were still young and both parents on the hacienda, the most reasonable option was to pass the maintenance costs on to the owner or, in this case, to the unit of production. A rise in the slaves' price as they became adults would always be less than the cost of the children's upkeep. Following this logic and taking into account Manuela's lower price, the couple dedicated themselves to negotiating Manuela's departure from the hacienda. Manuela would have more opportunities to find an occupation and earn daily wages in the city. She could raise her two children, rent a truck garden from a widow or single woman in exchange for a monthly sum, sell bread dough in the streets, prepare food for transients, or look for a position as a domestic. In the worst case, she could find an urban owner willing to purchase her. Her low level of specialization and her knowledge of typically female tasks were a combination that promised more success to her than to a male slave with the same lack of specialization or with a specialization of little use in the urban realm (and who could not cook or be a wet nurse).

At the end of the eighteenth century, even though the archdiocese of Lima collected 37 percent of the tithes in the viceroyalty and though this revenue rose between 1775 and 1815, Lima was a city with few occupational alternatives beyond occasional jobs in craftsmanship, domestic service, or construction tied to investments in infrastructure. A handful of mills producing flour and chocolate, several textile mills, an active manufacture of ceramics and woolen alpaca hats, and a small soap factory made up the entire spectrum of the city's manufacturing. The only large-scale factory was the gunpowder factory; in 1791 the state-owned tobacco factory had closed (Haitin 1986, 117). According to the 1790 census, 76.9 percent of the economically active population was part of the tertiary or service sector and of the 16.9 percent located in the secondary sector, nearly all were artisans. Slaves were not considered part of the economically active population (Haitin 1986, 108–109, 122). Even if we must guess at the numbers of slave artisans who worked in the city, the wide divisions between economic sectors give us an idea of job prospects for slaves as well as nonslaves.

Manuela obtained her *carta de libertad* after two years of negotiation with her owners in which she struggled with the marquesa's heirs to get a copy of the will that showed her price reduction. One inheritor had asked for a new appraisal of the slave's value because the liquidation of the real estate had left the executrix indebted to several creditors. At last Manuela managed to leave the hacienda but without her sons, despite her claim that she and Manuel had been responsible for providing food for their children and that the owner should either return the couple's investment or renounce his ownership rights to their children. The court lawyer defending the marqués, however, managed to impose his opinion: the slave children had until this time lived on the hacienda and what the slaves had invested in their upbringing stemmed from the *hacendado*'s "gratuitous" donation of land plots. Thus children born of a slave womb were the property of the hacienda. The defender of the *hacendado*'s interests meticulously detailed the costs incurred by his client and other *hacendados* who elected to raise the children of slaves. He stated that, based on these costs, a realistic calculation of a slave's price meant that a slave of working age (fourteen years) should be worth approximately 1,500 pesos, a price that no one would pay and that greatly exceeded the average price (450 pesos) of slaves in Lima. Backed by this argument, the *hacendado* won the legal battle and Manuela's children remained on the hacienda. Pando's administrator tried to prevent Manuela from returning too frequently to see her family and conditioned the concession of her *carta de libertad* on the agreement that she would not visit her family more than once a month.

Walking barefoot, Manuela reached the parish church of San Lázaro, where a majority of Lima's black population lived. She was detained at the doorway by a sergeant from the company of dragoons. Accused of being a maroon, a fugitive black slave, she showed the soldier her *carta de libertad*. Because *cartas de libertad* had no standardized format and the soldier—a *pardo* (of mixed descent, two-thirds European and one-third African)—did not know how to read, he did not understand. Deposited in a *panadería* (a bakery and place of punishment where slaves and others were kept), Manuela was recognized by Antonio, a fugitive slave who had taken refuge on the Pando hacienda in 1807 to escape the viceregal forces. After capturing him the soldiers put him in the *panadería*.

Antonio was a slave with a profession and for a long time had worked with his brother, a free *mulato* (of African and indigenous descent), in a shoe repair shop near the *panadería*. One night the *mulato* brother heard screams coming from the *panadería*. Recognizing his brother's voice, he went to find the neighborhood mayor. When they reached the commotion, the manager of the *panadería* accused Antonio of inciting a riot and of offenses of "word and deed." Those present, including Manuela, later testified before a magistrate about the manager's mistreatment of Antonio; they complained about the *panadería*'s unsanitary conditions and bad food and indicated that the ruckus had been a consequence of inebriety. The inhabitants had been celebrating the manager's birthday. The judge ruled that the manager should moderate his behavior and further ordered an inspection of the approximately forty *panaderías* in Lima. A short time after this incident Antonio escaped and, with the intervention of his cobbler brother, tracked down Manuela's former owner, the marqués, begging him to intercede on her behalf and liberate her from the *panadería*. The marqués assisted Manuela, and she was freed.

Manuela had a few friends in the city. One, a *mulata*, was a maid in the marqués's house and had for a long time kept an eye on

Manuelita; another, a *bozal*, had worked on a neighboring hacienda and had then been sold to a *mestizo* widow, who relied entirely on the earnings she garnered from a small plot in Lima's outskirts. A third woman had a meat stall in the San Francisco plaza and a relationship with a slave from the Bocanegra hacienda. Mounted on a horse he owned, this slave would regularly take off from the hacienda to visit his girlfriend, a practice that caused the *mayordomo* of Bocanegra to nickname him the "regular runaway" (*cimarrón consuetudinario*). With the help of her friends, Manuela invented her own strategy of survival; her aim was to gather together enough capital to free her husband and sons on the hacienda. The "regular runaway" introduced Manuela to a small group of maroons on the outskirts of Lima who occupied themselves with cutting firewood.[16] They supplied Manuela with wood, which she then sold alongside her friend's stall in the plaza. Even though her family's land endowment had been trimmed when she left the hacienda, Manuela still received produce from the plot each month when she visited her family. Manuela's market basket now included an additional commodity: firewood, which stood for something more than just a salable product. It was the mechanism that allowed Manuela to establish new social relations with a wide range of members of the black population: slaves, freed slaves, maroons, *mulatos*, blacks, *zambos*—men and women linked by their shared occupation.

On one visit to the hacienda, Manuela found out that her husband had been cruelly abused by the manager, a free *mulato*, because Manuel had gone into town to buy tobacco—as slaves often did. In 1818, with allegations of the sustained abuse, Manuela presented a request before the criminal judge pleading that her husband's owner be changed. Once the abuse was corroborated, Manuela experienced difficulties finding a new owner because the *mayordomo* of the Pando hacienda insisted that the new owner purchase Manuel and the couple's two children at the same time. On the one hand, the *mayordomo* wanted to rid himself of the entire family in order to avoid the external interferences of having half the family outside the hacienda and half inside. On the other hand, he knew it would be difficult to find a new owner willing to pay 400 pesos for Manuel and the 300 and 350 pesos that he intended to receive for each of the children, given that they were now thirteen and seventeen years old and were thus old enough to start doing an adult's work on the hacienda.

Raising the total cost increased the likelihood of keeping the three men on the hacienda.

With the mediation of a slave realtor Manuela filed a suit, initially requesting an appraisal of her sons and protesting the arbitrariness of the *mayordomo*'s announced price. Manuela alleged that her younger son was physically weak and almost useless for labor. Neither son had a *conque* and had therefore never before been assigned a price. Two appraisers were chosen, one by the *hacendado* and the other by Manuela, the slave realtor, and the interested buyer. For ten months the appraisers could not reach an agreement, but finally in 1819 they decided on figures that partially vindicated the *hacendado*: the final agreement stated that he would receive 250 pesos for Manolito and 300 for Manolo. Through an arrangement of the realtor, separate owners residing in Lima bought Manuel and each of the children (now fourteen and eighteen). Manuel went to the Casa de la Moneda (the mint) in the parish of Santa Ana; Manolo, the older son, was placed by his owner with an artisan to learn the trade of chocolate making; and Manolito was bought by Doña Agreda, a spinster who already had an older slave whom she detailed to earn day wages as a water carrier. The realtor received 5 percent on top of the final transaction amount. The new owners were charged the legal fees, meaning that these did not translate into higher prices for slaves. One last desperate attempt by the *mayordomo* to retain his slaves was to accuse the realtor, a *moreno* (person whose appearance vaguely suggested African ancestry), of complicity with the slaves for "being of their same rank." In the end the administrator realized that his objection was pointless and opted to replace the slaves with free black laborers.

The Lasmanuelos family had taken the first steps toward the city, each at a different time and in a distinct circumstance. Now the family members were closer and could see one another more often. But one family member vanished: Manuela's older son, who had been given to the priests of the Buena Muerte monastery in 1812. Perhaps he died, as many others did, or ended up as just another slave on one of the various properties owned by the Buena Muerte congregation. Manuela had managed to accumulate 200 pesos through her market sales and thought that she would be able to purchase her sons' freedom when they and her husband relocated to Lima. Given the *hacendado*'s pressure, however, and the enormous increase of the requested price, this money was not enough to free even one of them, least of all her husband.

When in 1814 Manuelita, residing with the marqués, reached seventeen years of age, she was moved to the home of the marqués's daughter, Doña Baltasara, who was now married to a *criollo* merchant of Lima's consulate.[17] In this way, Manuelita was complying with her destined womb assignment. She had been there barely a few months when Doña Baltasara's husband, seizing the opportunity of his wife's excursion to mass, raped Manuelita. With the aid of her mother's friend who lived in the marqués's home and who had become Manuelita's godmother, and with the marqués's knowledge, Manuelita filed a report in the ecclesiastical court supplicating that her owner free her on account of "corrupted virginity." She added that in any case she had been promised freedom at the age of twenty-five but that—to avoid the advances of her owner's husband and to respect moral and religious precepts—it was necessary to adjudicate her freedom sooner.

Don Baltasar, Doña Baltasara's husband, contended that it was common for female slaves in Lima to accuse their masters of rape in order to obtain liberty, and that if everyone took notice of these allegations then the ties that bound slave to master would soon fall apart. The owner won the suit and Manuelita continued "under the authority of the master," subject to his sexual appetite. Doña Baltasara was aware of the situation and her anger fell on Manuelita's shoulders. This resulted in more work, worse treatment, and the retraction of all the small privileges Manuelita had enjoyed in the marqués's home. Manuelita ultimately became pregnant; Doña Baltasara knew that her husband had fathered the child born shortly thereafter. The young slave tried to prove her daughter's paternity, appealing to the Protomedicato, whose job it was to speculate on possible fathers based on skin color (then the best proof available). If Manuelita was *quarterona*, her daughter would be *quinterona*. The master, however, was an influential person. Therefore, the Protomedicato abstained from judging the obvious. Manuelita denounced the owner's immorality and claimed that he had abused his authority. Speaking before the judges with candor she declared it was strange that the child of a Spaniard could be a slave.

The life of the Lasmanuelos family went on quietly, far from all abstractions or debates between liberals and conservatives. Its daily life and interactions kept to their own rhythm. More than the liberal measures of the Cádiz constitution, it was the wars of independence (1820–1825) that influenced the lives of slaves during the conflict and its aftermath. Because of the repercussions and length of the wars of independence as well as the constant shifting of the battlefronts (which brought with them pledges of freedom), the slaves eagerly followed the struggles for independence. Many of the legal arguments later used by slaves (or in their names) were based on measures announced by the leaders of the rebellion between 1821 and 1828. Partly because these patriots needed the black population's support during these years, they generated a discourse about the possibility of freedom that the black population clearly understood.

In a more immediate sense, what the wars did was intensify the importance of urban labor. The ethnic-occupational rigidity began to crack. Before the wars of independence the position of officer or soldier in the regular viceregal forces could be a royal privilege or a duty for *pardos* and *morenos* and even for slaves who replaced their masters.[18] Later, experience in handling a rifle and in military maneuvers would give soldiers means to confront a growing state of anarchy as well as to gain social status.

In opposition to a long-term drop in overall prices, agricultural prices made amazing gains in the midst of the severe political crisis of the first half of the 1820s. War certainly affects prices, but it also affects the conditions and potential of production. There is much evidence of the participation of blacks in the struggles for independence and also cases in which masters and slaves abandoned the hacienda to flee closely occupying battalions or troops.[19] As an immediate consequence, areas of cultivation were reduced and haciendas lost workers. It is also clear that the open military conflict tended to break down the bonds of social domination; more than one *hacendado* (especially if he was a Spaniard) had to abandon a place where the ratio of whites to blacks (as on the Pando hacienda) was one to thirty-four. We probably cannot know the circumstances of each case, but we can assume that the slaves who managed to keep up their production and marketing of food had a good chance of accumulating some money during these years. Similar changes took place in artisanal activity. Begun so that slaves would provide their owners with a greater amount of daily earnings, artisanal activity later became indispensable for the outfitting of the army. This kind of occupational redesign could be observed in all the arenas of daily activity: marketplaces, transportation (muleteers and water carriers), and the farming of essential foodstuff on the outskirts of Lima. The war increased demand yet simultaneously took men and land out of commission and destroyed the centers of production. The wars of independence and the ensuing internal conflicts they engendered did not come to an end (at least temporarily) until the same year that slavery did.

In the decades before independence, the notarial registry of *cartas de libertad* tells us that the rate of self-manumission within Lima's rural and urban slave population remained constant (Table 1). The rate in turn reveals that many slaves were permanently bargaining with their owners and among themselves to lower their prices, save money, and free their children and themselves. How well they fared depended on the individual achievement or misfortune of each slave and on various overall socioeconomic and political conditions. In spite of the slaveholders' counterattack that began in the 1830s (Blanchard 1992) after decades of increased leniency toward slaves, slaves were able to maintain and even increase their pace of self-manumission. How much suffering this effort could involve emerges from the sketch of the lives of all the Lasmanuelos family members.

According to the newspapers of the era, on 28 July 1821 people went out into the streets to listen to General San Martín's proclamation of independence. Surely the Lasmanuelos family was there to hear that everyone born from that date on—including all slaves with Spanish masters who had abandoned the country, and all slaves who had enlisted in the ranks of the patriots—would now be free. But promise and reality frequently clashed. Shortly before the arrival of San Martín, when the Casa de la Moneda shut its doors, Manuel had been incorporated into the royalist army, under the command of Viceroy Pezuela. Manuela continued to sell firewood in the San Francisco market throughout the war; Manuelita remained with the marqués's daughter and lost a protector and mediator when the marqués returned to Spain. Manolo had to leave his profession as a chocolate maker. Before independence he had given to his master the daily sum of seven *reales*, a wage that placed him in the top third of slave workers. Alongside the daily wages contributed to his master, nonetheless, Manolo had managed to accumulate half of his purchase price; in other words, he had earned more than what he was obliged to give to his owner. In the middle of the war that continued until 1825, his owner demanded that he continue to pay him his usual daily wages. When Manolo did not comply with this demand, the owner ordered him interned in a *panadería*, charging him with being a maroon and a thief. Manolo escaped from the *panadería*, located his mother, and

TABLE 1. *Methods of Manumission in Lima: 1830, 1840, 1850*

Method	1830		1840		1850	
	Men (%)	Women (%)	Men (%)	Women (%)	Men (%)	Women (%)
slave pays	19 (32.7)	39 (67.3)	22 (35.5)	40 (64.5)	14 (31.1)	31 (68.9)
relative pays	7 (29.1)	17 (70.9)	6 (40.0)	9 (60.0)	8 (47.1)	9 (52.9)
owner grants	14 (35.0)	26 (65.0)	17 (33.4)	34 (66.6)	12 (37.5)	20 (62.5)
third party pays	1 (12.5)	7 (87.5)	6 (54.5)	5 (45.5)	3 (25.0)	9 (75.0)
Total	130		139		106	
(%)	31.5	68.5	36.7	63.3	34.9	65.1

Source. AGN, Protocolos Notariales.

became a member of the gang of maroons that had long been supplying her with firewood. During the war years he survived on the fringes of the conflict, raiding haciendas, *tambos* (roadside inns where travelers could sleep and buy various items), and villages.

Even during the war, firewood and water (sold by Manuela and her son) represented two key necessities, not only for civilians but for soldiers as well. As a water carrier, Manolito helped Doña Agreda and her aging slave survive. Doña Agreda did not demand a fixed daily wage from her slaves. She was interested only in having enough to eat; she let her slaves figure out how that could be accomplished. Her dependence on slave income was so great that in her will she requested that in exchange for their freedom, the two slaves take on paying her burial costs. She died in 1824. Manolito received his *carta de libertad* and in compensation for looking after the elderly slave, Esteban, was able to keep the water-carrying tools, pipes, and two mules.

Shortly after 1821 stirrings of dissatisfaction with the patriot forces emerged in protests and marches through the streets of Lima. These demonstrations were headed by Lima's artisans, the majority of whom were *castas* (persons of European and African ancestry without clearly indigenous or European traits).[20] The patriot army was not paying for what it consumed, they said; for artisans, the *patria*, or fatherland, had become a "thieving fatherland." Disenchantment with the promises of the patriots had begun. Little by little, the offers initially made to slaves and Indians had been pruned back. Black participation in the patriot, as well as the royalist, army was significant.[21] Each contending side offered freedom to slaves who enrolled in its ranks. To this background of the conquest of the black population must be added the options that the context of war made available to slaves. For many, enrollment in the army represented a way of loosening ties to their masters. Once enlisted in the army, slaves often deserted and turned to thievery or perhaps became a part of guerrilla groups, many of which rapidly switched their loyalties. This dispersal had its roots in the freedom previously granted to some hacienda slaves (Vargas Ugarte 1984, 6:172). Even before the wars of independence began—so masters believed—the bonds of subjugation were already coming undone. A similar image occurred to General Miller when he stated that Lima was from time to time infested with bandits, generally "mulattoes and mestizos of other colored races, an evil that has existed since time immemorial" (Miller 1829, 1:266 ff.). And, certainly, shortly after the struggles for independence, this line of reasoning and the fear it invoked became part of a broader justification about the advantages of keeping the slave system intact.

Over the five-year period starting in 1820, when the patriot incursions into the south of the country took place, until the war's close in 1825, much changed in the rural sphere, particularly in the vicinity of Lima. After all, the capital had been the center of victory marches, countermarches, and conspiracies. Rumors ran rampant: from Riva Agüero's plan in 1817 to greet San Martín in Ica by granting freedom to between seventy and eighty able slaves so that they would spread reports about the proximity of patriot forces and San Martín's intentions of liberty, to rumors that the royalist General Canterac wanted to liberate the slaves, make them proprietors of the haciendas, leave them all the women, and decapitate the most important patriot leaders.[22] These rumors increased the anxieties and uneasiness of everyone. In a relatively small city, where close black-white interaction was part of daily life, these events, attitudes, and propositions were unlikely to escape the notice of the slave population. For all slaves, these were years of expectation and also of the hands-on experience of freedom and death on the battlefield. Yet few slaves became citizens of the republic. Between liberal desires and the perpetuation of slavery appeared several conciliatory forms: patronage, the figure of the *liberto* (a freed slave who was required to stay with his owner for a specified time), and a sometimes imposed term of apprenticeship. No slave was freed by the decrees passed under San Martín. At very best a slave might achieve the status of *liberto*, which in the majority of the cases was synonymous with slave conditions of life until a certain age, yet might mean the payment of a minimal wage.[23] If during the wars of independence an owner had had to leave the country—an absence that according to the San Martín decree cost the owner his or her slave property—that same owner in 1830 could argue that the departure had not been caused by "hatred of the system" but by business obligations. In this fashion an owner could recover slaves.[24] If the authorities had carried out the declaration freeing slaves belonging to Spaniards, the slave labor force on some haciendas might simply have disappeared altogether.

After the war many soldiers (some who had even ascended the military hierarchy) found that offers of freedom often led to a *panadería*, into prison, or back to the hacienda. There was no dearth of cases in which the reconversion into a slave occurred through the violent retraction of a decree of manumission written by owners shortly before they died on the battlefield.[25] Surely the statement by one of these soldiers is true: "Considering this, will blacks lend their services, be ready to defend Peru? This, sir, would be deceiving oneself voluntarily."[26] The disillusionment that his words indicate coincides with more general assertions: "Since 1825, the war terminated, the demands made on blacks by their freedom statute seem in practice to equal the massive nullification of previous manumissions" (Sales 1974, 129).

As early as September 1822 one session of the legislature produced the rule that slaves should not be assigned to public works, and that only in situations of dire urgency and "considering first and foremost the good of owners and the promotion of agriculture," could the authorities call on their labor power.[27] Here the freedom of slaves was not even under discussion, rather the state itself was renouncing the use of their labor power to benefit owners. And this meant that slave owners were trying to firmly reimpose slavery. Political turmoil after independence and the state's dependency on their goodwill helped to push legislation toward this end.

In the first decades of the nineteenth century, slaves for their own part underwent experiences that would affect their attitudes and decisions, but by now they had to face owners willing to defend slavery with the traditional argument that coastal agriculture lacked laborers. In the decades following independence *hacendados* attempted to refinance their enterprises; they achieved skewed results as they applied a wide array of schemes to reverse the measures declared between 1821 and 1825. Opposing the interests of the *hacendados*—and continuing the liberal ideology that had rescued many slaves from misery—functionaries from the government and occasionally from the Church echoed the slaves' demands, as did several lawyers and defenders. A few scattered haciendas prospered, but inventories of several haciendas between 1836 and 1845 show that the number of slaves on the haciendas near Lima decreased an average of 60 percent. Working conditions on the haciendas, political and military turbulence, and unmet expectations all had their part in the decrease, which also reflected the new circumstances of the black and slave populations. The number of runaway slaves increased and banditry rose (Aguirre 1990, 145, 180), but many slaves also found their way to the city and to freedom.

Behind all these public experiences that affected the slaves' relations to the system, and alongside the conflict between master and slave, an analysis of everyday events in the heart of the black population reveals a multiplicity of individual strategies to obtain freedom. This battle was a daily one and went on unchecked during the earlier struggles for independence and the subsequent aspirations of *hacendados*. Its continuation relates less to official proclamations than to the specific characteristics of Peruvian slavery and to the delicate links between countryside and city.

Manolo was wounded in 1823 in an altercation with a patriot company on the outskirts of Yauyos. Taken in by this company, whose commander was the indigenous leader Ninavilca, he participated in the patriot army until 1825, convinced that his participation would lead to his freedom. Ninavilca's followers split; some remained guerrillas or became bandits in the following years.[28] Others, encouraged by the declarations of the discontinuation of recruitment, went back to their previous activities. The return to civilian life was qualitatively different. Slaves carried with them what they had learned along the road, and their horizons had broadened beyond the narrow confines of the household, the centers of production, and the universe that had until then constituted their social and mercantile relations. Manolo knew that during the struggles he had fought on the side opposing his father's, he had learned of the existence of patriots and royalists, he had heard from members in Ninavilca's company that royalists lopped the ears off their deserters, he learned how to handle weapons, and he could survive outside the law.

Manolo returned to Lima with these new experiences. Don Baltasar ran into him walking on the street; he called the barrio's *serenos* (night watchmen) and ordered them to throw the young man into prison. Don Baltasar thus reclaimed his slave property, while Manolo claimed that he should be free because of his involvement in the patriot struggles. Don Baltasar questioned Manolo's patriotism, accusing him of being a maroon and a bandit. Manolo would remain a slave for some time. The *criollo* merchants of the consulate and the *hacendados* had not lost their power; they still dictated the rules of the game.

To keep the slave was not Don Baltasar's idea, however. As a merchant holding a small bit of land inherited from his mother, he had little use for Manolo and knew that he had a problematic and rebellious slave on his hands. Given this, he requested that Manolo be transferred to one of his nephew's haciendas. When this request was carried out, and when Manolo reached the age of twenty-five, he asked Don Baltasar's consent to marry Manola, a free *zamba*, who worked in a store in Lima's central plaza.[29] Before independence, Manola had been the queen of a black *cofradía* (a mutual-aid society, established by the Church, dedicated to the cult of a specific saint). Don Baltasar refused. Manolo immediately presented himself before the Church's vicar-general, who wrote to the owner accusing him of not complying with divine precepts and of perpetuating the immoral cohabitation of his parishioners. Manola and Manolo were married in 1829. As a married man, Manolo was able not only to avoid relocation on another hacienda but also to negotiate the future terms of his existence. He offered to pay his daily wages in exchange for permission to live outside the master's household. For the entire year, Manolo religiously handed over the agreed-upon daily wages, and after a year passed he paid Don Baltasar his purchase price of 650 pesos. Manolo's value had doubled between 1812 and 1829 for two reasons: he was now an adult slave, and he had a job. A slave with a trade had better chances of accumulating capital but would have to pay more in the case of self-manumission. Manolo's price was an approximate average for artisan slaves. It is possible that Manolo picked up a portion of the 650 pesos during the war. Another portion came from his wife's savings.

Because of the marital conflicts between Manolo and Manola that soon followed, we know that Manola earned most of this money. After a brawl in the streets with his cronies over a game of dice during which accusations were exchanged about which player was the blackest, Manolo returned to his home in San Lázaro where he lived with Manola, who was now pregnant. He found her washing clothes for a soldier in the *pardo* battalion—as she often did—in exchange for money. Incensed with jealousy and blinded by liquor he attacked Manola, kicking her in the stomach. She lost the child. In her complaint before the Church's vicar-general, she stated that this was not the first time she had been left "completely black and blue" by blows inflicted by her husband. A medical report indicated that in addition to the beatings she had also contracted a venereal disease. Manola, therefore, filed marital litigation requesting that the vicar-general make her husband listen to reason. In addition to the beating, Manolo took all of the money and left her very little to eke out a living, aware the whole time that it was she who had helped him obtain his freedom. During the litigation, Manolo's entire past came to light; now it was Manola's turn to describe her husband's violence during his years among the maroons. He had even threatened her with sharp weapons. Manolo was summoned by the vicar-general, in the hopes of a marital reconciliation. But a similar incident occurred a few months later. This time, in 1832, Manola demanded permission to leave their matrimonial house in order to avoid worse harm. She asked for a divorce, which in the nineteenth century amounted to a temporary separation.

Manolo's father managed to return to Lima in 1827, at the age of forty-seven. His destiny with the royalists had taken him as far as Upper Peru (now Bolivia). No *carta de libertad* mentioned his participation in the war. The marqués—his master—was no longer around. Weak and recovering from a sword wound, he knocked on the door of Don Baltasar, who quickly recognized that this slave could neither do much useful work around the hacienda nor bring a high price at auction. Manuel was also aware of this; it was the reason he had returned to the protection of his former master. Don Baltasar, hoping not to forfeit everything and to be able to sell Manuel, lowered his price to 200 pesos. But Manuel's wife did not have enough money to purchase his freedom. She herself had fallen ill and, as a masterless person, had paid for her own treatment at the San Bartolomé hospital. Their son Manolo had lost a great deal of money gambling, and the funds furnished by his wife had dried up after the separation. Manuelita had married an expert silversmith, and neither she nor her husband wished to be reminded of her birth as a slave. After all she was a *quarterona*, three-fourths white, and following her former owner's wishes had married a white artisan. Manolito was in love with María, a black slave who worked in one of the houses in the parish of Santa Ana where he distributed water. He was determined to liberate her and convert his Sunday visits to her master's house into a union that existed outside the caprices and control of a master. The experiences of his half sister Manuela had warned him of the hazards María faced as a female household slave.

Manuel, not being able to turn to his family members who were scattered around the city, went out in the streets to look for a buyer. He found a *mestiza*, Doña Estefa, who specialized in the commerce of tinware and shoes between Lima and Ica. In exchange for his commitment to work for her, the *mestiza* lent Manuel the money to manumit himself. He received a wage for his labor, which he handed over, bit by bit, to Doña Estefa, assuming that with this he was paying off "the principal" of the loan. However, she would later claim (after Manuel had been in her service for seven years) that the slave had only paid the interest on the borrowed money. In other words, he remained a slave. Manuel died in 1837 on one of the trips to Ica when a small group of bandits attacked the pack train he was leading. Manuela died in San Lázaro three years later at the age of fifty-seven without ever finding out what became of her husband. Manolito paid for his mother's burial costs; he did not want her to be buried in a pauper's grave. The funeral cost 147 pesos, a sum that represented half of the price that would free his betrothed, María. María was thirty-five years old in 1853 when Manolito finally purchased her freedom and paid for the marriage. In the same year Manolito, still a water carrier, reached forty-eight years of age. Everything he had managed to save had been invested in María's manumission and his mother's burial. There was no capital left over to replace his tools, much less to expand his business. Fortunately for him, Lima was still a city with an undeveloped sewage system; his services were always needed and his trade did not encounter competition from members of other social groups. María and Manolito never had children. This state of affairs came about because of her long and continued residence at the master's house, their older ages at matrimony, and surely also their reluctance to bring more slaves into the world.

Manolo's destiny as an artisan was distinct from his brother's. The marriage dissolved, he continued as a chocolate maker. Market conditions, however, had changed. The start of guano exportation had altered patterns of consumption. Imported European chocolates began to appear; their few consumers were among the select group of colored persons who could purchase this luxury item. Thus, if indeed Manolo worked formally as an artisan, an important complement to his earnings came from a whole set of activities on the border of the law and through his affairs with various women. Economic shortage and instability followed him his entire life, including a judgment ordering him to supply his illegitimate children with food. For him the abolition of slavery also meant the loss of the final protective check against competition, from his cohorts as well as from new European immigrants who rapidly infiltrated the most sophisticated artisanal spheres.[30]

The economic growth sparked by guano production left Manolo behind. Probably the most important reasons for his state were his dark skin and a shortage of funds that came from his choice of self-purchase over the purchase of tools or the acquisition of new techniques. Closely following these explanations of lack of success in the labor market came what we might describe as the failure to transfer survival strategies from the family setting to society as a whole. The joint attempts and tactics that a couple might use within the family setting found no outlet in particular or original alternatives to shape the individuals' work or destiny in the larger world. Just as the bandit leader could personify "a sui generis seignorial actor" (Vivanco 1990, 41)—keeping both virtues and faults—slaves reproduced within the family forms of survival and expressions of conflict very like those of other groups.

Thinking Out Loud

The factors both large and small that shaped the life of the Lasmanuelos family would sooner or later affect the experiences of Lima's entire black and slave populations. Leaving aside several questions that unique or isolated cases bring up (for analysis in the following chapters), I attempt here to create a history close to the reality of the era. Its message is complex. On the one hand, slaves found imaginative ways to circumvent their masters' schemes and force their owners to confront their liberal hypocrisy. But on the other, a great deal of suffering took place, from beatings and lashes to unfilled promises and separated families.

Some hacienda slaves (above all, ones on haciendas bordering Lima) were able, through funds accumulated by individuals and by families, to buy freedom and take part in a heterogeneous range of urban activities. The most effective means of accumulation was the sale of goods either on or outside the hacienda, an activity that involved a constant exchange of ideas and products from one hacienda to another, and to villages, and to the city. The individuals who were the most successful and the first to leave the hacienda, often following a family decision, were women. Women were the ones who possessed, through mercantile activity, a certain level of urban experience. In addition, the mother-child bond could withstand long separations, female labor was always useful in the urban market, and the price of slave women was the lowest in absolute terms. When the hacienda slave managed to move to the city, be it through manumission or various rounds of negotiations with administrators or *hacendados* (for example, a slave born into the owner's possession could more easily arrange a lower price) or simply by a search beyond the hacienda for a buyer, he or she had preexisting connections with other members of black society. Some connections were established through runaways' experiences as they sought refuge in hacienda *barracones* (as in Antonio's case); others were part of the links established by masters and cases of selective relocation to the urban context (Manuelita, for example); still others were the result of commercial activity (Manuel and the midwife).

If male slaves were relocated to the city, masters usually sought to have them apprenticed in a trade. Women were basically destined to domestic service, hence to a common female position. This whole universe brought about the formation and consolidation of relations in the slave populace and among slaves and descendants of the black urban population. There was a clear tendency toward mutual support, according to an individual's closeness to other members of the group under consideration. The persons who assisted Manuela in her first contacts with the city were all women, black and slave, of varying levels of independence relative to their respective masters. Men (often maroons) were incorporated into this support network as the most distant node and through the relationships established by female friends or, for Manuela, through a maroon's temporary stay on a hacienda. And, even more important, the support Manuela received came from the least differentiated component of slave society: the women. This support reflected an attitude—which men shared—about the advantages of liberating women from the hacienda first. The gamut of mechanisms of social and spatial articulation also elucidates the fluidity of the links between countryside and city.

Different levels of experience in the urban context, influenced by the relative place in the ranking of jobs, along with skin color, determined the internal hierarchies of black society. Strategies of support and of domination existed among black, as among *mayordomos* on the hacienda (*mayordomos* versus *caporales*) and members of the military corps (the soldier in the company of dragoons); they found expression in the estrangement of family members (as was the case with Manuelita) and in brawls and street insults. These fissures manifested themselves in an even more subtle manner between married couples. It was the black Manolo who married a free *zamba* and later tried, with the approval of society, to impose his male authority. As we can see, the gender relation was used as a means of subjugation when others, such as ethnicity (more whiteness) or legal subordination (slave or nonslave), were missing.

The varying strategies also resulted from the imposition of cultural mores that ranged from the supposed modesty of women and Catholic marriages on the haciendas to denunciations of the immorality of masters. Thus, to a certain degree, divisions and conflicts within black society reflected the actions of masters. They assigned slaves to certain tasks and geographic areas, split up slave families, and often fathered not-so-black children (masters such as the merchant Don Baltasar, or the friend of the Pando hacienda's administrator). Along with the creation of an economic and racial hierarchy came the expansion of varying avenues of social mobility that the black population absorbed and used to procure freedom.

On the journey toward freedom over the course of the fifty years examined, we observe a progression that represents slaves' capacity to exercise freedom of choice. Mothers were the first to move toward freedom. Second came the children, and finally new wives or husbands. This final option (we could also call it preference) depended more than anything on the logic behind matrimonial alliances. Slave men sought free women: in this way their children were born free. And the likelihood of obtaining their own freedom would be greater, both because marriage allowed slaves to control what they earned and because it gave them a reason to leave an owner's home. The farther slaves were from the master, the better able they were to accumulate capital. Slave women who were whiter, however, preferred free and white men (Manuela married an expert silversmith). Only rarely did a free black man (like Manolito) choose a black slave woman; yet this choice offered a stabler marriage. Only with a wife of lower social status was it possible for a man to maintain control in the new household and submit the woman to his will; in marriages into an equal or higher social group, matrimonial conflict tended to be more intense, as it was in Manolo's case. But in his marriage—for which the ecclesiastical court records indicated no conflict—Manolito fought against his master to prevent him from sexually abusing his companion, not against his wife. And insofar as he was free and she a slave, the subordination of the woman was inevitable from the start. In these ways matrimonial choices, through gender lines, illustrated more sophisticated levels of internal conflict as well.

Perhaps the most dramatic image of divisions within black society was the very composition of the family I have described. In other words, the faction is visible in the family history. At no time in its family history did the Lasmanuelos family have only one racial or sexual actor. Different members always coexisted: slaves and freed persons, *zambos*, blacks, *quarteronas*, members in the city, members on the hacienda.

Despite the complex and manifold universe of internal conflict and faction, the priority of the slave population remained clear: freedom. All efforts aimed at obtaining it, and the most important methods were negotiation and the daily wage. Negotiation occurred in two ways. The first was a gradually lowering of a slave's purchase price; the second was the accumulation of money. In the end, a reduced purchase price and savings would come together in the acquisition of freedom. Many times this goal involved the intervention of relatives, *cofradía*, Church, and state. Clearly the possibility for negotiation was greater when the owner was a woman. As the weakest elements of the society—and many *limeñas* compared their own life to that of slaves—women relied more heavily on slave labor and perhaps had other sympathies. The two methods might combine. The vast realm of negotiation included a variety of factors: a slave's good behavior, a master's declared will, the number of children a couple had, whether a slave had been born into the master's possession. Negotiations reflected conditions that ranged from those in which slaves had little part (generally ones predetermined by masters and their views) to those that slaves could actively manipulate and that varied from case to case. They all, however, had a common characteristic: the slaves' skillful use of the system's own contradictions to their advantage.

Probably the number of slaves who could choose their profession was low, despite the fact that one could feign inability in a wide assortment of professions in the hopes of finally obtaining the one desired (obviously within certain limits). This choice, however—which occurs as frequently today as yesterday—determined the outcome and the slave's relative success in life. Manolo and Manolito well exemplify the use of artisanal possibilities. The most sophisticated artisanal jobs were off limits to the black population, and probably the construction of sewage systems at the end of the nineteenth century also put laborers with jobs like Manolito's out of work.

What this family history shows is an initial process of success. Savings accumulate, and family strategies allow their members to survive; nonetheless, misfortune and layoffs follow. In the background of this process are the particularities of Lima's urban slave system. Not even the overwhelming diversity of personal conditions and the high degree of internal conflict and differentiation could keep the black population from a common destiny: exclusion. In Lima the slave system fell apart because the slaves caused its downfall and the owners permitted it to collapse. All this took place at an economic and political crossroads where the liberal ideology absorbed by the slave population was gaining ground, where the movement of prices and internal productive rearrangements on the hacienda started to revalue slave relations, and where the state was losing its ability to rule.

In synthesis, we cannot understand the events in the sphere of Lima's rural hinterland without examining the connections between the rural and urban realms. And to perceive these connections, we must look at the relationships established by the slaves themselves and must chart the direction and the success of changes in the slave system. Slaves' acts and deliberate attempts to exploit moral and social gaps in the Peruvian urban fabric explain not only the increased numbers of slaves in Lima's workplaces but also the absolute decrease in the number of slaves. In the case of Lima, therefore, the transformation of the slave system, based on urban articulation, fueled the system's collapse and promoted the specialization of urban work to satisfy growing demands. The paths slaves took to this end were many and myriad. Artisanal activity was often key to their success. Misfortune reflected changing patterns of consumption and the reduction of import duties; and artisans could not get organized to protest against cheap imports because non-black artisans had superseded them and because the black population was economically and ethnically divided.

In the follow chapters we attempt to look more analytically at the experiences of the Lasmanuelos family in order to document the processes examined here and to compare the experiences of Lima's slaves with other slave realities. And, as we have seen, part of the history of urban slavery starts on the haciendas.

Chapter Two

From Rural to Urban Life

Slaves living in Lima did not always come from the countryside and many never underwent a rural experience. Disembarked in the port of Callao, they were purchased by *limeños* anxious to enjoy their services. Urban life without them would have been unthinkable, and slaves with urban experience tenaciously resisted relocation to haciendas or rural labor. Whatever they knew of rural life, slaves devised an endless number of mechanisms to resist transfer to the countryside—they worked, multiplied, and died in the city. In order to understand why the slave population in Lima remained high throughout the colonial period and what took place in the urban sphere, we need to examine the rural sphere and the links that the slaves established between the two, allowing them to move from the countryside to the city. These forms of rural-urban communication are a theme of particular relevance, but little studied, for places such as Mexico City, Lima, Buenos Aires, Rio de Janeiro, and São Paulo, which all received large numbers of rural migrants and saw slow increases in their black slave and free populations.[1]

A drop in agricultural productivity marked the beginning of the nineteenth century and caused many slave owners on the haciendas bordering the city of Lima to relocate their slaves to the urban nucleus (Romero 1980). If a hacienda slave did not have skills that were useful in the new urban environment, with a little money an owner who had chosen to move the slave to the city could apprentice him or her to an expert artisan. In this way the slave's daily, monthly, or annual wages (depending on the contract agreed upon at the end of the apprenticeship) increased, and so did the slave's sale value. Such transfers of hacienda slaves can explain the growth of the urban black population and the decrease in rural slaves despite the intensification of the slave trade at the end of the eighteenth and beginning of the nineteenth century. They also shed light on the rise of the rate of manumission. Training in crafts expanded slaves' potential for accumulation, lessened their owners' control, and generated closer and more fluid connections within the black population.

Owners had many production-related incentives to transfer their slaves to Lima. And slaves had their own reasons to accomplish the same end. This chapter examines the process of relocation to the urban sphere from the perspective of the slaves themselves. My chief hypothesis is that moving to the city was a goal slaves desired and attempted because they knew—even given the impositions of the slaveholding system—that heading toward the city was a way to accelerate their attainment of freedom. The conditions on the hacienda and the character of the slave-master relationship shaped and often facilitated migration to the city. However, it was the relationships within the slave family and its links to the urban world that first and foremost determined the success (or failure) of slaves' relocation.

Statistics demonstrate that the number of slaves on haciendas decreased (as we will see, above all, on haciendas of small and medium size), and that the city's *casta* population grew. An analysis of rural conditions and of life inside the production units makes it clear that the reduction of the slave population on some haciendas was a result of the slaves' transfer to the city. The growth of the free *casta* population and the parallel decline of the slaves in the city was the result of self-manumission. But first, slaves from Lima's hinterlands had to reach the city.

Parishes and Haciendas: Geography and Statistics

According to a treasury census of 1829, the city of Lima had retained its colonial characteristics.[2] It housed 58,326 inhabitants, of whom 4,602 were slaves living on estates and haciendas of various sizes on the outskirts of the city. The rural realm represented roughly the actual area of the province of Lima or the so-called valley of Lima.[3] In this area approximately 200 production units classified as haciendas competed for the available cultivable space, a situation that would not change very much between 1780 and 1910.[4] In this relatively small rural sphere I intend to correlate the size of the productive unit to its slave laborers, the slaves' opportunities for accumulation, and the links these *haciendas* had with the city.

There is no information about slave numbers or conditions of slave labor for all the haciendas on the outskirts of Lima. Nonetheless, the

TABLE 2. *Population of San Lázaro (Guia and Amancaes): 1813*

	Urban Barrio[a]				Rural Estate
	VII	VIII	IX	X	
male citizens[b]	266	1,105	419	395	29
female citizens	276	626	482	570	22
male Spaniards[b]	32	535	365	132	27
female Spaniards	48	508	660	253	23
priests and nuns	—	52	—	59	—
male slaves	178	420	219	186	496
female slaves	141	349	190	191	454
Total	941	3,595	2,335	1,786	1,051

Source. Adapted from AA, Sección Estadística, L 6, Año 1813.
[a]Barrios VII–X correspond to the first *cuartel;* estates are lands outside the urban area.
[b]"Citizens" included individuals who owned some property—Indians, *castas,* and *mestizos*—but not those who were of European ancestry, which the census termed "Spaniards."

1813 census provides some clues, and for Surco and Chorrillos, two rural areas located about ten miles from the city's main square, a second census allows us to compare the evolution of slave distribution between 1790 and 1813. Supplementary information from notarial registries for subsequent years has been elaborated by Aguirre (1990, 17 ff.; 1993, 51–52).

The rural environment was not uniform. Each parish had its most proximate rural region. And a little farther off was the area occupied by the haciendas, small conglomerate villages, and towns. One of Lima's six parishes, San Lázaro, may illustrate the rural environment's diversity. San Lázaro housed the largest black free and slave population. After independence this parish—like all others—was divided into *cuarteles* (districts) and the *cuarteles* into barrios. The small plots, farms, and estates were spread out behind the barrios. In *cuartel* one, formed by four barrios and several small plots of land scattered in the two areas of Guia and Amancaes, an examination of the distribution of people called citizens or slaves allows us to decipher the rural component of the environs of the urban centers (Table 2). If, based on these figures, we contrast the distribution of the Spanish and the slave populations in the rural and urban spheres, we obtain some interesting indicators. The average ratio of slaves to Spaniards in the four barrios amounted to 1.3:1, while the same calculation for each barrio denotes a high degree of disparity (4.0:1, 0.7:1, 0.4:1, 1.0:1 respectively). Thus, we can see that the proportion of slaves to Spaniards was much higher in barrio VII than in the other three barrios. The dividing line between the rural and urban spheres was imprecise. This inequality probably reflects the more or less rural character of the barrios and their greater or lesser proximity to the estates or the city center. In the rural area of this parish (i.e., on the estates) the ratio of slave to Spaniard was even higher: 19.0:1.[5] If we exclude the persons listed as female Spaniards on the estates, the result is a ratio of thirty-five slaves to each owner. The ratio would be only slightly higher if we included the fifty-nine priests and nuns in barrio X; they were probably also Spaniards. This is a low density per unit of production if we compare it to similar figures from the plantation zones of the northern and southern coast.[6] Similar calculations suggest an equivalent density (as we shall see) for nearby areas of San Lázaro parish such as Surco, Chorrillos, Magdalena, and Miraflores. On the level of laborers per productive unit this figure indicates the existence of relatively small haciendas in Lima's hinterland. In a rural register of 1837 that took in the province of Lima—that is, all of Lima's hinterland—were 152 haciendas with 2,004 slaves (Aguirre 1993, 52). In a broader area encompassing the coastal valleys we see a similar distribution of the slave population (Figure 1). Seemingly, despite the great disparity among these haciendas, between 1813 and 1837 the average number of slaves per hacienda had dropped from 35.0 to 13.2. Only two years later, in 1839, the register listed 189 haciendas with an average number of 16.6 slaves (Córdova y Urrutia 1839, also quoted in Aguirre 1993, 52).

In San Lázaro's rural area there were 950 slaves, and in its urban center 1,874 (that is, rural slaves lived in the heart of the urban parishes). However, the urban presence alone was by far more important. According to the important 1792 census, Lima relied on 13,482 slaves. In 1818, the date of the next census after that of 1813, there were 8,589 slaves in Lima (Jacobsen 1974). If we assume that the two censuses covered the same geographical regions (though the later census did not refer to this matter), we notice that 32.9 percent of Lima's slave population lived in the parish of San Lázaro and that this slave population was concentrated in the urban zone of the parish, in the barrios. Thus, approximately one-third of the population within the parish of San Lázaro had occupations in the rural sector.[7] The

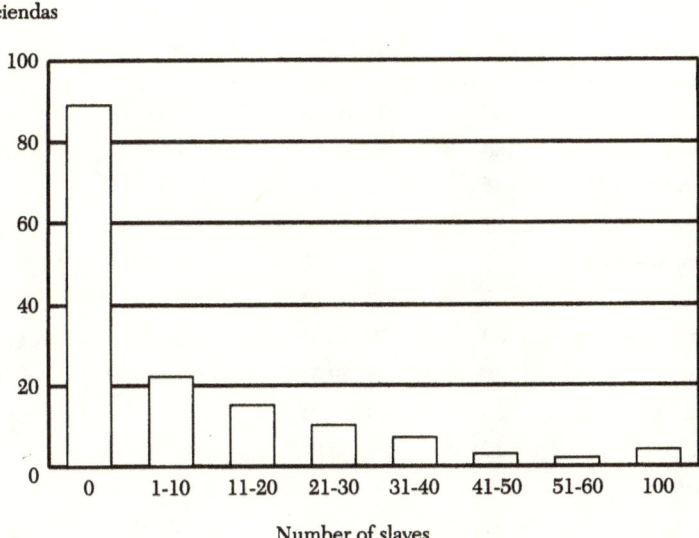

Figure 1. Distribution of Slave ownership in five Lima valleys: 1837.
Source: Aguirre (1993,52).

parish's hinterland, in accordance with the boundaries established by decree in 1626 and apparently still valid in 1884 (Clavero 1885, 32 ff.), embraced a vast area whose borders were the present zones of Lurin, Hauchipa, Naña, Carabayllo, Surco, Pachacamac, and Magdalena. The rural space and the urban zone were extremely interconnected. San Lázaro was a parish located outside the city walls and a parish where—as we will see—a critical component of the daily life of the black and slave population evolved.

For Surco, Chorrillos, and Magdalena, three minor locations next to San Lázaro, we rely on separate figures that allow us to look more closely at the situation of slaves on some of the haciendas, the estates named in the next three tables. The essentially rural physiognomy of these sites farther removed from the urban center is evidenced by the much lower proportion of inhabitants than in the barrios of San Lázaro.[8]

The distribution of the slave population on the haciendas, as well as the ratio among men, women, and children in the productive unit was quite unequal. In Magdalena the average number of slaves per pro-

TABLE 3. *Slave Population in Magdalena: 1813*

Hacienda	All Slaves	Men (%)	Women (%)	Children[a] (%)
San Cayetano	40	34 (85.0)	6 (15.0)	— —
Maranga	125	47 (37.6)	53 (42.4)	25 (20.0)
Matalechuzas	46	31 (67.4)	11 (23.9)	4 (8.6)
Palomino	11	7 (63.6)	— —	4 (36.4)
Desamparados	7	6 (85.7)	1 (14.3)	— —
Mirones	8	6 (75.0)	2 (25.0)	— —
Cueva	60	29 (48.3)	13 (21.7)	18 (30.0)
Oyague	42	25 (59.5)	11 (26.2)	6 (14.3)
Borda[b]	20	10 (50.0)	8 (40.0)	2 (10.0)
Orbea	37	21 (56.8)	10 (27.0)	6 (16.2)
Aramburú	27	19 (70.4)	6 (22.2)	2 (7.4)
Concha	56	36 (64.3)	11 (19.6)	3 (5.4)
Pando	45	21 (46.7)	13 (28.9)	11 (24.5)
Ríos	37	30 (81.1)	6 (16.2)	1 (2.7)
Buena Muerte[b]	26	13 (50.0)	10 (38.5)	3 (11.5)
Ascona	23	22 (95.7)	1 (4.3)	— —
Total	610	357 (64.8)	169 (22.8)	84 (11.6)

Source. AA, Sección Estadística, L 5, 1813, Padrón de la Doctrina de Magdalena [signed by Lic. Domingo Anzures and Gregorio Dávalos Maraco].

[a] Children are slaves under the age of 16.
[b] The census recorded property as *chacra* (small estate farm) rather than hacienda.

duction unit amounted to 38.1, which closely corresponds to the average (35.0) found for the rural setting in the parish of San Lázaro. If we leave aside the population of children, we obtain a figure of 32.9 (Table 3). Before hazarding what these figures mean, we should look at the equivalent data for the parishes of Surco and Chorrillos (Table 4, which also permits us to verify the variations between 1790 and 1813) and for the site of Miraflores (Table 5).

In Surco and Chorrillos the average number of slaves per productive unit was 88.8 in 1790, and 102.0 in 1813. We can attribute this rise to the existence of the Villa hacienda, the largest in either area.[9] If we exclude it from the calculation, the average drops to 35.4 in 1790 (approaching the average of San Lázaro and of Magdalena in 1813) and to 56.3 in 1813 (still a high average given the enormous expansion of

TABLE 4. *Slave Population in Surco and Chorrillos: 1790 and 1813*

Hacienda	All Slaves		Men		Women		Children	
	1790	1813	1790	1813	1790	1813	1790	1813[a]
Valverde	12	9	12	9	—	—	—	—
Chacarilla	3	23	3	10	—	13	—	—
Villa	356	376	132	168	145	208	79	—
San Borja	82	89	33	47	25	42	24	—
San Juan	68	191	17	114	27	77	24	—
Porras[b]	14	4	7	4	5	—	2	—
La Merced[b]	—	22	—	12	—	10	—	—
Total	535	714	204	364	202	350	129	—
(%)	(100)	(100)	(38.1)	(50.9)	(37.7)	(49.0)	(24.2)	—

Source. AA, Sección Estadística, L 2, 1790, Estado actual de los Havitantes de los Pueblos de Santhiago de Surco y Chorrillos, inclusas Haciendas y Chacras con expresión de Castas y Hedades, con arreglo a los Padrones respectivos a él hehos por mi, Santhiago de Surco, noviembre 16 de 1790; and AA, Sección Estadística, L 5, 1813, Censo de Población del Pueblo de Santiago de Surco, su Anexo San Pedro del Chorrillo, y Haciendas circunvecinas, pertenecientes a dicho Curato [both censuses are signed by Dr. Carlos de Excilbengoa].
[a]The 1813 census did not separate the slave population into children and adults.
[b]Porras became La Palma and La Merced was probably an abbreviation for La Calera de la Merced.

the San Juan hacienda between 1790 and 1813). For Miraflores the average number of slaves per productive unit was 53.7 (excluding the case of Brabón), and 45.5 (omitting children). From these rough averages we can perhaps infer that the further from the urban nucleus, the greater tended to be a hacienda's ratio of slaves to productive unit and the ratio of slaves to Spaniards, if we consider Spaniard to be equivalent to owner. Here is the very small difference between the estates of Amancaes and the haciendas of parishes that bordered the urban center (Miraflores, Magdalena, Surco, and Chorrillos). Also reflecting this concentric gradation from the urban center is the size of the haciendas (which is not necessarily the same as the number of slaves). The closer to the city, the more dispersed the land-tenure pattern, and the greater the number of small-size productive units. The pattern held true for a later period as well. If we examine what was called the *Lima-región* between 1825 and 1840, we find that 53.4 percent of all production units in five valleys were garden plots. The Rí-

TABLE 5. *Slave Population of Miraflores: 1813*

Hacienda	All Slaves	Men (%)	Women (%)	Children (%)
Surquillo^a	43	33 (76.7)	7 (16.3)	3 (7.0)
Sta. Cruz	69	46 (66.7)	20 (28.9)	3 (4.4)
Brabón	—	(+3)^b —	— —	— —
Villar Lucro^a	65	42 (64.6)	23 (35.4)	— —
Orrantia^a	52	29 (55.7)	21 (40.4)	2 (3.9)
Lobatón^a	26(+5)	11(+4) (48.4)	15(+1) (51.6)	— —
Limatambo	91	44 (48.4)	29 (31.8)	18 (19.8)
Sta. Beatriz	98	61 (62.2)	35 (35.7)	2 (2.1)
Lince^a	20	11 (55.0)	6 (30.0)	3 (15.0)
La Calera	14	14 (100.0)	— —	— —
Total	486	298 (61.3)	157 (32.2)	31 (6.4)

Source. AA, Sección Estadística, L 5, 1813.
^aThe census identified property as *chacra*.
^bThe laborers in parentheses are not slaves.

mac valley, the valley closest to the urban nucleus, in the parish of San Lázaro, contained by far the greatest number of small landed properties: 172 garden plots, 79 larger plots, 23 farms, and only 9 large estates (Table 6). Of the total of 183 garden plots, thus 172 (94 percent) were in the Rímac valley.

The size of a hacienda had a great deal to do with the degree of relative freedom slaves had within the hacienda, the mechanisms of control, and also the types of production that would eventually allow slaves to sell basic foodstuffs in the urban markets. Lima's haciendas were definitely much smaller than other coastal properties.

Pando (the hacienda where I placed the Lasmanuelos family), located in the district of Magdalena, was a typical hinterland hacienda with its forty-five slaves. Since I contend that family bonds were one important ingredient of manumission, let us analyze the gender composition of the slaves on haciendas. Here our central objective is to clarify how the distribution of men, women, and children inside the hacienda shaped families' and individuals' strategies of accumulation and the way in which slaves linked themselves to urban life and to other social groups. What determined the ratio of men to women in

TABLE 6. *Distribution of Land in the Lima Region: 1825–1840*
(*in* fanegadas)[a]

Valley	Garden Plot	Plot	Farm	Estate
	1–20	21–50	51–125	126–350
Chancay	6	6	3	3
Carabayllo/Chillón	—	6	6	8
Rímac	172	79	23	9
Lurín/Pachacamac	5	2	5	1
Cañete	—	—	—	8
Total	183	93	37	29
(%)	(53.5)	(27.2)	(10.8)	(8.5)

Source. Readapted from calculations by Engelsen (1981, 282) of haciendas with water rights set after independence, from a list compiled by Francisco García Calderón (1879, 73–84).

[a] A *fanegada* (or *fanega*) is a Spanish measure of area, about 1.59 acres.

the haciendas is unclear. The type of crop might have influenced the ratio and conversely, changes in the gender composition might have altered cultivation. Otherwise gender ratios may have been either completely arbitrary, as women also performed typically male tasks, or a conscious strategy in order to encourage slave reproduction. There is no evidence for either of these arguments. It is surprising, nonetheless, that in both Surco and Chorrillos the increase of the slave population between 1790 and 1813 exhibited an almost perfect balance between the female and male populations, even if on the level of each unit of production this balance was quite skewed. Despite the fact that marriage was not proof of a couple's union—much less in the world of the hacienda—in Surco and Chorrillos a significant portion of the women who lived on haciendas were married to slaves working on the same hacienda. On the Villa hacienda in 1790, 180 of the male and female slaves (out of a total of 277 male and female slaves) were married couples (65.0 percent); in the case of San Juan, of 44 slaves, 26 were married (59.1 percent); on San Borja there were 32 married slaves out of a total of 58 (55.2 percent). On the smaller haciendas, Valverde and Chacarilla, only three married men appeared in each case, and on the estate of Porras out of twelve slaves, six slaves were married (50.0 percent). These figures indicate that an average of 60 percent of slaves were married to other slaves on the same hacienda. These percentages were slightly higher on the larger units of production.

The 1813 census of Magdalena gives us a good idea of some of the gender ratios on its haciendas.[10] Above all, the largest haciendas tended to maintain a balance between the female and male populations. This makes sense as these percentages corresponded to those slaves who were actually married. Perhaps many more just lived together. This assertion echoes the findings of Cushner (1972, 193) for the Jesuit haciendas in Peruvian territory at the end of the eighteenth century. Among Magdalena, Miraflores, Surco, and Chorrillos, Magdalena and Miraflores exhibited quite similar total percentages of men and women, with about 30 percent more slave men; in Surco and Chorrillos the total number of male slaves almost equaled that of female slaves.[11] Insofar as we believe that both family life and a strategy for freedom were important to slaves, the landed properties that contained the greatest conflict and instability must also be those in which the greatest gender imbalance prevailed. When slaves on one hacienda could not foster family ties there, they often moved from place to place and established contact with neighboring haciendas and towns. Marriages among slaves from different haciendas and transfers through purchase from one hacienda to another explained such mobility. Higher mobility in turn reflected (at least in slave owners' eyes) weakening control over slaves; for the latter it certainly meant broader experience. Mobility made them aware of what was happening on other haciendas and allowed them to adjust or strengthen their arguments before owners or administrators. Thus, although slave marriages were a desired goal for masters who wished to augment an increasingly scarce labor force, when marriage or sexual contact meant higher mobility it also widened slaves' perceptions, anxieties, and possibilities.

There is no evidence that any hacienda except Palomino in Magdalena lacked female slaves. To compensate disparities or imbalances in the distribution of men and women throughout a broader geographical area without the purchase of new slaves, possibilities and opportunities for movement beyond the edges of the hacienda were needed, to give the slave population a certain amount of emotional satisfaction. Contemporaries were quick to interpret the slaves' greater circulation as idleness and even arrogance and boldness or worse, when slaves ran away. It diminished the slave owners' control over their labor force, in spite of the fact that on occasions—as was the case with Manuel—slaves were severely punished because they left the hacienda. Such punishment was arbitrary and depended on specific slave-owner relationships; contemporaries usually interpreted punishment as an act that contravened established customs.

Marriage was a serious matter, even on the haciendas. Owners and slaves alike took into account and honored the matrimonial rules valid for the rest of society. Beyond respect for marriage itself, and for ecclesiastical rituals, we find that in slave society it was possible to annul a marriage on the grounds of a "second degree of illicit copulation," or opposition from parents or newlyweds.[12] Even slaves had to declare that they were voluntarily consenting to marriage. These factors further weakened masters' ability to make marital decisions on behalf of their slaves and demonstrated the extent to which the sacrament of matrimony could interfere with notions of private property.

In terms of the characteristics of economic development at the end of the colonial period and the significance of the Bourbon reforms, what is salient in this microscopic examination is that Lima's haciendas experienced an overall increase in the slave population. Only two haciendas, Valverde and Porras, reported a reduction in slave population; in 1790 each had twelve slaves. We might infer that the slave population on smaller haciendas decreased, even if Chacarilla, which between 1790 and 1813 augmented its slave labor force from three to twenty-three, contradicts this fact. Perhaps an additional argument that substantiates the decrease of slaves on small haciendas is that many of these recorded the presence of a non-slave labor force at the beginning of the nineteenth century. Such was the case with Brabón and Lobatón (in Miraflores).[13]

The objectives and the organizational logic of the labor force are less clear if we include in our analysis slaves who were minors. We simply assume—but have no way to determine the reality—that all the under-age children were born of slaves living on the hacienda. The documentation available does not differentiate them from minors purchased outside the hacienda.

To evaluate the extent to which attempts to reproduce slaves within the hacienda were successful, we will construct two indicators. One records the average number of children per married couple and the other, of children per woman over sixteen years of age. Once again the only censuses that include these figures are the 1790 census of Surco and Chorrillos and the 1813 census of Miraflores and Magdalena (Table 7).

TABLE 7. *Slave Children on Haciendas in 1790 and in 1813*

Hacienda	Children per Couple	Children per Woman
Surco and Chorrillos: 1790		
Valverde	—	—
Chacarilla	—	—
Villa	0.9	0.5
San Borja	1.5	1.0
San Juan	1.5	0.9
Porras	0.6	0.4
Average	1.1	0.7
Magdalena: 1813		
San Cayetano	—	—
Maranga	0.9	0.5
Matalechuzas	0.4	0.4
Palomino	—	—
Desamparados	—	—
Mirones	—	—
Cueva	1.4	1.4
Oyague	0.5	0.5
Borda	0.3	0.3
Orbea	0.6	0.6
Aramburú	—	0.3
Concha	0.3	0.2
Pando	5.5	0.8
Ríos	0.2	0.2
Buena Muerte	0.4	0.3
Ascona	—	—
Average	1.1	0.5
Miraflores: 1813		
Surquillo	—	0.4
Sta. Cruz	0.1	0.1

TABLE 7 (continued)

Hacienda	Children per Couple	Children per Woman
Brabón	—	—
Villar Lucro	—	—
Orrantia	0.1	0.1
Lobatón	—	—
Limatambo	0.9	0.6
Sta. Beatriz	0.7	0.6
Lince	0.5	0.5
La Calera	—	—
Average	0.2	0.2

Source. Elaborated from AA, Sección Estadística, L 2, 5, and 6, 1813.

The five factors that researchers at various sites use to explain the low numbers of slave children are: (1) rates of low fertility and high infant mortality; (2) suspected (but not proven) choice of slave women to abort in order not to bear slave children; (3) matrimonial age and composition by age of the entire female slave population in each unit of production; (4) sale of children by an owner outside the unit of production; or (5) simple lack of concern among owners, a reason that could underlie all the others. Other researchers argue, on biological grounds, that a woman's procreative capacity might diminish as a result of excessive work or mistreatment. Some evidence suggests even more dramatic explanations for the cases in which masters, family members, or *compadres* were the parents of slave children. There were masters who, wishing—for a multitude of moral reasons—to erase traces of paternity, subjected pregnant slaves to harsh treatment and beatings. Their objective was to provoke an abortion or secure a confession that would blame the pregnancy on another man. In the case of Josefa Aparicio, for example, who in 1842 worked on the Retes hacienda, the owner had her locked in the pillory to be "subjected to a beating session every 24 hours ... compelling her with these punishments to ascribe paternity to Don Manuel Andrade."[14]

It is true also, however, that the thesis of a low fertility rate is hardly surprising in a context where the fertility rate in general was extremely low.[15] Although the proof is yet far from convincing, we observe a decrease in the number of children per slave woman in Lima, to the point that the number of children dropped below the already very low birth rates on eighteenth-century Jesuit-owned haciendas (Cushner 1975, 190n.). Other factors beyond those we noted help explain why children were absent from haciendas. The closer to Lima proper, the more frequent the physical absence of owners; sometimes we might infer that slave children were taken into the city as house servants, were inherited by family members, or were sold. Combining the theses of an extremely low fertility rate, geographic proximity, and the particular characteristics of a hacienda's operation, we can infer a sixth reason for the low numbers of slave children: parents managed—even in the arduous context of the hacienda—to liberate their children and thus children appeared only randomly in inventories or censuses. Confirming this hypothesis are several different cases and some evidence that depicts slaves' capacity to accumulate on the haciendas, in order to pay or negotiate their children's purchase price. This is exactly what Manuel and Manuela did on behalf of their two sons, Manolo and Manolito.

Thus, even though a high degree of differentiation existed among haciendas in Lima's hinterland, on average these productive units were much smaller than the sugar and winery haciendas on the northern and southern coasts, where concentrations of six hundred or more slaves were common. The size of the property often determined a slave's success at procuring freedom. The smaller the property, the closer the connections between slaves could be; in a parallel manner the greater the chances of negotiation with owners, *mayordomos*, and *caporales*. Surely the capacity of these latter individuals to control the lives of their slaves was also greater, but greater control did not automatically bring harsher treatment. It is not necessarily true that larger productive units offered greater levels of liberty or provided slaves with any more anonymity. The slave's potential for negotiation—where channels of negotiation existed—increased when proximity between individuals was higher, that is to say, on the small and medium-sized units of production.[16]

Production Units and Labor Relations

The relations between countryside and city were dynamic and fluid—for masters as for slaves. Lima's rural panorama consisted of estates

TABLE 8. *Methods of Manumission in Rural Areas: 1830, 1840, 1850*

	1830			1840			1850		
	Man	Woman	(%)	Man	Woman	(%)	Man	Woman	(%)
slave pays	3	4	(41.2)	2	—	(33.3)	5	6	(50.0)
relative pays			(47.0)			(33.3)			(40.9)
mother	1	2		—	1		1	4	
father	1	—		1	—		1	—	
sister	1	1		—	—		—	1	
other relative	1	—		—	—		1	1	
spouse	—	1		—	—		1	—	
owner grants	1	1	(11.8)	1	1	(33.4)	1	1	(9.1)
Total	8	9		4	2		10	12	
% of all *cartas de libertad*			(13.1)			(4.3)			(21.0)

Source. AGN, Protocolos Notariales.

(eventually large truck gardens) and haciendas, divided principally by size, administration, and labor relations. With the work of Febres as a base, Haitin (1983, 140) estimates that of the approximately two hundred units of production in Lima in the 1820s, at least 47 percent did not exceed 145 hectares, and at least 16 percent had even fewer than 73 hectares. In spite of the difficulties of demarcating which properties belonged to which category because over the course of time names remained but the conditions of production changed, *chacras* (small estate farms) generally appeared to be the smaller units, and on those, obviously, the relation between owner (or in his or her absence the *caporal* or *mayordomo*) and slave was more direct. Many of these estates were farmed by slaves, in conditions quite different from those in force on the haciendas, which were larger entities where organization and control were in several hands and the depersonalization of relations was greater.[17]

The Working Life of Hacienda Slaves

Life on the farm—on the outskirts of the cities—was part of the first African experiences on the new continent (Bowser 1977, 128). A male or female slave was often put in charge of a rural estate while the property owner, male or female, awaited the profits of cultivation in some corner in Lima. Thus a key element of country-city relations involved handing the administration of rural duties over to slaves, who—in their terms at least—exhibited excellent management skills. What was true in the sixteenth and seventeenth centuries still held true in the nineteenth century, when what had once been a necessity of survival transformed itself into tradition.

In this respect the experience of Doña Elena Maldonado, the owner of a slave named Romualda, is exemplary. Doña Elena purchased a female slave in 1790 for 250 pesos. As soon as she verified that the slave had been born into the possession of her former master and was convinced of her "honest management," she entrusted the slave with an estate called Compuertas. To facilitate the running of the estate, Doña Elena Maldonado "kept the slave for a long time, granting her all discretion with regard to money and other things necessary for the upkeep and construction of the lands and crops. As a consequence she ended up losing a considerable amount of money." The owner had invested in the estate, hoping to garner profits through the slave. But in the meantime the slave hired a black woman named Juana, the slave of Doña María Garses, as a sharecropper for the course of two years; during this period Romualda (and Juana too) "forgot" about the owner.

The owners of small estates or truck gardens, especially if they were single women or widows such as Doña Elena and Doña María, had little choice but to hire slave labor, in part because of their racial and social status: for individuals with white skins (or who considered themselves white), the only proper and decent work option was sewing. And there were more than enough tailors and seamstresses in Lima. Single women and white widows could furnish the work tools and the means of production in exchange for the slave's daily wages or a percentage of the proceeds from landed property. However, all intermediate decisions that led to the acquisition of the daily wage or the marketing of produce were in the hands of the slave. Thus, it can be understood why Romualda hired another black woman, and furthermore, given the relative distance from Doña Elena's control, why she did not remit earnings and the daily wages to both owners. Doña Elena was able to recover her losses and Romualda was deposited in a *panadería*, from which she later fled—protected by a prospective buyer in Lima. Given the unpaid amount she owed Doña Elena, the judge increased Romualda's purchase price from 250 to 400 pesos. Even though this case had a negative outcome, it shows what slaves might do, and the dependence of certain urban sectors on slave labor.[18]

Even though the mechanisms of subjugation were stronger on the larger haciendas located along Peru's coastal valleys, there is evidence even these slaves had margins for maneuver. The traveler William Bennet Stevenson transmitted an image of the Huaito hacienda, property of Doña Josefa Salazar de Monteblanco during the second decade of the nineteenth century.[19] According to the visitor—who had seen many haciendas—it was one of the best organized estates. It was located north of Lima, in Barranca, and housed 672 slaves (thus surpassing Villa, the largest hacienda recorded for Lima's hinterland). It produced primarily sugarcane, but a portion of the land was dedicated to the cultivation of basic foodstuffs (corn, beans, sweet potatoes, squash) and it had pastures for livestock. The visitor wrote that the annual value of its produced goods amounted to 55,870 dollars and its expenses, including payment of clothes, food, and recompense to slaves, to 6,320 dollars.[20] The slaves were sustained by the hacienda's products and often a surplus remained after goods had been sold in the local market.

Whatever space—even on large haciendas—slaves had to maneuver, whippings and other harsh treatment were part of slaves' lives and of strategies used to discipline an increasingly disobedient slave labor force. But whippings never proceeded without the explicit consent of an owner, who based the number of lashes the slave would receive on the complaint from the hacienda manager or *caporal*. The slave's allegation was usually ignored in order to avoid questioning the manager or *caporal*'s authority. The beatings were public so that all other slaves on the hacienda would be informed of the reasons for the punishment. If a slave was captured while attempting to escape from the hacienda, he or she would have to carry irons on his or her legs for the number of weeks equal to the days he or she had been absent. Captured after a second attempt to escape, the slave was condemned to the harshest labor in the sugar mills. If the slave tried once again to escape, he or she was sold. At least the attempt gave a slave the chance for sale to another, better, owner.

In order to encourage marriage between slaves, all children born out of wedlock were sold while they were young. Another objective of this sale was to prevent male slaves from establishing relations with the inhabitants of surrounding villages.[21] On the haciendas black girls of eleven to twelve years of age lived apart from the men under the surveillance of the female owner until they married; the oldest female slave cared for them. The marital policy was also expressed by the particular attention given to married women who had children: they worked less, ate better, and had separate quarters with beds. If a slave bore six children who lived at least until they were old enough to walk, the mother obtained her freedom or a reduced workweek of three days. If she remained on the hacienda during these days off she was paid for her labor.[22] Furthermore, married and widowed slaves annually received a pig that was fed with leftover sugarcane and squash, and a plot that could be cultivated with the hacienda's oxen and plows. The traveler Stevenson estimated that each year an average of two hundred pigs were sold in Huaito, and that each pig yielded the amount of twelve dollars. The workday started at seven in the morning and ended for some at four in the afternoon, for others at six; slaves had a two-hour break at midday. The remaining time was used to cultivate one's own plot. Giving credence to a benign interpretation of Peruvian slavery, Stevenson commented that "a laborer in England worked more in a day than any slave in three days . . . in the Spanish colonies." Portions of tobacco, two changes of work clothes each year, and the use of the remaining sugar mill and sugarcane equipment to prepare *guarapo* (an alcoholic beverage made from sugarcane) completed the picture.

Situated between the large sugar plantation and the tiny garden plot was a large sector of intermediate units that exhibited some characteristics quite distinct from those of the units already illustrated. These properties combined traits of the small estates and the big haciendas: the freedom of activity common to the small estates, a certain amount of control by *mayordomos* or masters, as well as collective responses from slaves to the daily conditions on the hacienda. Here communication among the slaves was effective and would occasionally manifest itself—as we will see—in requests to the authorities in Lima or even in protest marches to the city. These middle-sized haciendas supported twenty to fifty slaves, an average number of slaves per productive unit recorded for some of Lima's haciendas.

In July 1816 José Chala lodged a complaint against Don Manuel Menacho, the new owner of an estate in San Lázaro's rural hinterland.[23] On his own behalf and that "of my companions," he claimed:

Ever since the said owner purchased us he has not let us rest for a moment, and where it has happened, *Señor Excelentisímo*, that he makes us work on holidays, even the Indians observe this day of obligation and we, for being slaves, have to suffer. This is impossible and for this reason God has sent Your Excellency to be a father to the poor in order that my master be summoned and in order that he let us seek another owner since we already have someone who will purchase us and give us our papers. When we have said to him that we wanted a new master, our owner has forced us to work until two or three in the afternoon, and forced us to return to the hacienda at six in the afternoon just to be locked up, without being able to leave even to buy a few cigarettes. This causes us pain because not even criminals of the worst kind undergo the hardships we undergo.

What José Chala described here does not reflect the work conditions on the Huaito hacienda recorded by Stevenson. In San Lázaro the workday usually ended before two in the afternoon and afterward slaves could leave the hacienda to buy tobacco. They did not remain locked in the hacienda's usual slaves' quarters or *barracones*. The new owner felt the slaves' claim was exorbitant:

The clauses of the claim are enough to manifest the inconstancy and credulity of the proceedings. These slaves are used to extraordinary freedom that produces the most deplorable effects in the environs of Guía [in the parish of San Lázaro], where the estate that, along with the slaves I have just purchased, is located. The slaves have found it strange that owners should contribute to controlling their laborers, especially those on rural estates, so that surrounding estates do not experience robbery and looseness, to which these owners are subject when there is no master willing to tighten the limits on slaves' behavior; and just as they consider all that does not flatter this permissive attitude to be oppression, cruelty, or irreligion: hence it is that they fabricate stories of their feigned hardships, that they demand with no limit what their whims dictate.

When the new owner acquired the estate and saw how these slaves worked, he gave them the option to leave in exchange for their appraised price. None of the slaves accepted. And now, "when they see that the work necessary on a rural estate is more urgent because we are in the months of the greatest difficulty, that is when they complain and when the integrity of Your Honor cannot accede to their demands: if everyone involved in this conspiracy were to leave, the estate would be ruined with no other cause than caprice."

Slaves knew well how to choose the moment of their protest, and the new owner could do little. The harvest was in jeopardy while the slaves advanced their desires for a new owner and asked for a month's extension to carry out the transfer. The master interpreted their request as a pretext to stretch the protection of justice. He argued, additionally, that even before he had brought an old black man to the hacienda to teach the slaves how to prune, break up the soil, and clean the irrigation ditches, the only thing they did was "go out onto the road and assault and intimidate unwary travelers." The judge called for a summons and listened to both sides. He decided that the sale of the slaves should be realized slave by slave as the respective replacement for each was sought; in this manner the estate's operations would not be harmed: "so a door detrimental to other haciendas and estates of this class would not be opened." As would happen over and over again in later years, courts mediated between slaves and slave owners, giving precedence to ownership and thus supporting landed interests. But at the same time slaves found an audience and vindication for their basic desire to switch masters.

Here was an example of what owners perceived and feared as possible contagion. Furthermore, in the same summons the property owner declared—and this the slaves confirmed—that he sometimes appealed to day laborers. Apparently, in the described context more could be exacted of a day laborer than of a slave—one of the reasons, as I suggest, that slavery collapsed first on small agricultural enterprises. Disobedience, pressure on owners, and lax supervision were making slavery a less satisfactory system for haciendas. Added to these factors were slaveholders' fears of possible revolts and their spread to other haciendas, and owners' preference to sell unruly slaves in the best possible condition.[24] In several contexts, slaves' protests increased, leading to the killing of *hacendados*, *mayordomos*, and administrators. Although these actions never spread into a slave uprising, the threat convinced many proprietors that it was dangerous to restrict or modify the privileges gained by slaves and to deny further claims.

The acquiescence of slaveholders to the demands of rural slaves seems more plausible given that those slaves often included ones who had been accused of several crimes, escape, or nonfulfillment of their obligations (after a judicial ruling) and who had been sold to haciendas outside the city as a form of punishment. Following this logic, the "most vicious" slaves often ended up on haciendas. But rebellious and disobedient slaves, thieves, and clever maroons had an advantage: from the point of view of owners eager to buy slaves, they were cheaper. These slaves' urban and criminal experience, however, could easily "contaminate" other slaves on a hacienda, estate, or farm, especially if the number of slaves was relatively small and the communication among them effective.

In the first decades of the nineteenth century the valleys surrounding Lima had become dangerous places. Don Juan Evangelista Theves, a colonel of the regiment of trained dragoons in the valleys of Palpa and Nazca, was accused of causing the death of one of Pedro José Mejía's slaves. In his defense the colonel exhibited a letter describing "the repeated homicides, perpetrated by the slaves of the said Pedro José Mejía, as he buys nothing else but villainous blacks for ridiculously low prices. These slaves have scandalized the valley of Palpa and all its borders with their insults, robberies, and murders." In one of the frequent and dreaded skirmishes the *mayordomo* of a hacienda had died.[25] Many times maroon incursions and slave revolts did not correspond to the mission and goals of the slave population but grew rather from incidents only marginally connected to the slave population or were of little concern to the slave or black world (Blanchard 1991). The possibility of local riots was perennially present in the minds of those who dared to alter relationships and ways of daily life that had become a part of tradition and established custom.

Beyond the size of the productive unit and its proximity to the city, the characteristics of internal control on the hacienda played a key role in determining slaves' behavior and the alliances realizable with other social groups. A more diversified spectrum of working conditions (i.e., the presence of racially mixed laborers, and variations in payments), as well as the coexistence of "good" and "troublesome" slaves in the labor force accounted for the difficulties administrators and *hacendados* encountered. These difficulties also explain the complaints *hacendados* voiced about insubordination and irreverence. We also gain the impression that the degree of control over the labor force was linked to the ethnic features of the owner or *mayordomo* as well as his or her physical presence or absence. Oftentimes those who were in direct control of hacienda business were not the white owners, but rather hired nonwhite administrators. Seemingly slaves showed more resistance to nonwhite governance.

Hacendados *and* Mayordomos:
Absence, Presence, and Ethnicity

An element that influenced the form of labor in the productive units was the type of control owners exercised. Some *hacendados* had no control over the labor force and others rigorously established varying relationships with their slaves, according to marital status, years of residence, their perceived loyalty, and their abilities and familiarity with the work. Masters varied from those who barred or at least limited slaves' contact with the outside to those who were concerned only with receiving daily wages: in short, from the situation documented in the words of Stevenson about Huaito to that on the smaller estates in the parish of San Lázaro. Apart from the owner's level of leniency and his or her ethnic group, the slave's readiness to receive and comply with orders also depended on the owner's gender. There were distinctions between a male white owner—or in his absence—of a *mayordomo*, an indigenous man or woman, or a *casta*. Even if frequently the larger properties were in the hands of whites, and the small and medium-sized properties in not-so-white hands, it was another issue altogether who effectively managed the reins of production. In the eyes of the slaves, perhaps the combination that merited the least respect was that of female and indigenous.[26] In order to gain an idea of the relative looseness that contemporaries carped about so much, perhaps it is worth the trouble to examine the figures we have for the owners, *mayordomos,* and *caporales* of the haciendas of Magdalena and Miraflores.

In Miraflores, all the property owners lived within the gates of Lima and had entrusted their properties to third persons; two haciendas had been leased to Spaniards. For Magdalena, six of the fifteen owners lived in Lima, whereas the remaining nine managed their own properties and six of these employed neither *mayordomos* nor *caporales*. Regarding the composition of *mayordomos* and *caporales* we see that of the fifteen *caporales* two were *mestizo*, three were *casta*, and one was black. In the ten noted properties of Miraflores, five were in the hands of Spanish *caporales*, one in the hands of two *mestizas*, and two in the hands of *zambos*. There was a relatively high percentage of absentee owners on the larger properties. The average number of slaves for all Magdalena's haciendas with absentee proprietors was 57.6, whereas the same average for those with owners present was 26.4. For Miraflores where, as we have indicated, all the owners were absent, the mean number of slaves per productive unit was 53.1 (close to Magdalena's average). In Miraflores the average number of slaves per unit of production not controlled by Spaniards, whether owners or *mayordomos*, came out to 59, and of those controlled by Spaniards, 49.8. This number suggests a slight imbalance toward non-Spanish *mayordomos* or administrators on the bigger haciendas, even if the numeric relation weighed in favor of the white administrators. The participation of *castas* and *mestizos* is surprising and seems to have been stronger on the properties of Magdalena.[27] If it is true that there existed a correlation between absentee owners, nonwhite administrators, and greater disorder on the haciendas, then ethnic relations could serve as clues to explain the complaints and fears of those who observed the conduct of slaves in Lima's rural zones. What turns out to be more difficult to explain, without recourse to subjective racial evaluations, is the owners' choice of nonwhite *mayordomos* and administrators. Disinterest, falling agricultural profits, and even fear could be plausible explanations.

Less open to subjective evaluations is the analysis, in more general terms, of what occurred on a medium-sized hacienda when the legitimacy of control was under question. We have an extreme case: the events on the estate of Buena Muerte, administrated by the religious order of the same name, where the property and management were in different hands. This estate in 1809 housed some twenty slaves. Apparently the religious order's chaotic condition (which the hacienda only prolonged) had been fermenting for several years.[28] In March 1809 twenty black slaves, nine women and eleven men, decided to march to Lima. They came from Cañete, from the Quebrada hacienda, and wished to speak with the Buena Muerte priests since the hacienda belonged to the order. On their way—the hacienda's *mayordomo* reported—"Yesterday afternoon the people from Quebrada arrived, so haughty and insolent that from Cantagallo they started to throw flares: and when they arrived, even the church bells rang." The slaves brought to Lima a request for a change of *caporal* because of excessive abuse. They reached the church and were immediately surrounded by the city's militia. The slaves defended themselves with dried adobe and bricks from the convent's tower, but they were caught and taken to a *panadería*. They left the *panadería* each day from two to three in the afternoon to take food to all those in the monastery. Soon they were transferred back to the convent, from where—now that they were pacified—it was decreed that "persons not acquainted with these occurrences made them disappear from the place, without others ever seeing the action."[29] Authorities tried to prevent such occurrences: people in Lima could easily be thrown into a panic.

After the convent episode the slaves were sent back to the hacienda, and soon afterward another priest came to speak to them. A riot broke out; the slaves reiterated that they did not want the *mayordomo* they had been assigned; the *caporales* they had were enough. They did not complain of excessive work but rather of a state of permanent punishment and said that even though they possessed papers giving them permission to leave their hacienda, the *mayordomos* still considered that to go beyond the hacienda's gates was a misdemeanor. Finally, the rioters among the slaves were removed from the hacienda, and the priest in charge of the hacienda and considered responsible for the happenings was recalled to the monastery.[30]

Slaves from the Quebrada hacienda had managed to procure some sort of papers that granted them the privilege to venture outside the hacienda. The papers enabled them to leave Cañete and go as far as Lima, confront the militia, and alert all the *hacendados* in the region.

This episode worked to intensify the fears of *hacendados* and *limeños* that if this stray gang were not contained—as one of the *mayordomos* explained—"all the haciendas would be up in arms, they have assured me that with news of the revolt, those in Gualcará were stirred up, and also those on the Guaca hacienda, and the slaves said that if those of la Quebrada being so well attended to and cared for, more so than on other haciendas, committed such excesses and fared well, they themselves had an even greater reason to protest." The dissemination of news of insurgency and defiance was not to be allowed. The desire to hush up such acts explains the swift judicial decision that ruled against the priest who had run the Quebrada hacienda and also sentenced the slaves to imprisonment.

The Quebrada case was an extreme one. Not all slaves marched to Lima to complain about mistreatment. Yet this case illustrates the mobility of slaves, as much in the context of relations established with the hacienda (they could live outside it and move about relatively freely), as in relations between countryside and city (march to Lima) or in the countryside (slaves on other haciendas perceived how much better or worse they were treated). Cañete was a few days' walk from Lima, and opposition had recently been encountered there. The slaves knew where to look for their owners to complain; they went straight to the Buena Muerte convent. If we listen to the tone of the *mayordomo*'s comments, we can add that apparently the slaves were taken aback by the lack of immediate reprisals and that they and many others interpreted the officials' response as an invitation to act as the Quebrada slaves had and with even more reason because on other contiguous haciendas slaves were more harshly treated.

And in fact, despite the precautions, there was an uprising on the Gualcará hacienda, which belonged to the marqués de Fuente Hermosa, and on the Guaca hacienda (owned by the count of Vista Florida), over the course of which nine male slaves, one female slave, and seven "vagrants and suspected thieves" were caught and sent to Lima with a company of soldiers consigned by the viceroy. Four more slaves were later sent to Lima by the subdelegate of Cañete, among which figured the leaders of the riot. The slaves from Guaca (more than twenty) returned to the hacienda after having tracked down a *padrino*; the royal forces were unable to capture those from Gualcará.[31]

A higher incidence of banditry or an increasing number of maroons often accompanies situations of economic crisis. Following this line of reasoning, Vivanco (1990, 42, 50) suggests that until the end of the eighteenth century the gangs that crowded the outskirts of Lima were primarily drawn from household slaves escaped from their masters. Between 1796 and 1810 agrarian slaves and hacienda day laborers dominated these groups of outlaws. To explain their increased presence, we must look beyond economic cycles to differing levels of internal control within the haciendas. A higher number of rural slaves in bands may reflect the loosening of social control on haciendas, which in turn reveals a decreasing interest from owners of small- and medium-sized estates. It is no coincidence that cases such as that of Gualcará or that of the priests of Buena Muerte involved the specific racial conditions of their respective owners and *mayordomos*, an intermediate property size and number of slaves, and the absenteeism of proprietors. Diversity of control, as well as access to maroon gangs, marked the slave population's options and opportunities for mobility and therefore influenced its avenues to freedom. Although slaveholders still exerted control and power, they saw this same power fade right before their eyes, as more and more slaves secured their small new prerogatives. The changes were tenuous but real and we can appreciate them if we turn our attention to slaves' deeds and actions within the hacienda. Recounting the episodes and lives of slaves helps us document the heterogeneity of conditions within, and the probability of leaving, the hacienda.

Accumulation on the Haciendas

Though the journey from the hacienda to Lima and eventually to freedom could be long and dangerous, it was often possible. The roads to emancipation were many and limited only by the ingenuity of the slaves themselves. Testamentary bequests, family relations, and complex strategies of accumulation all helped pave the way to freedom, which stretched forth even in the difficult context of the rural hacienda environment. In the following pages we will retrace the vicissitudes and the paths slaves devised as they accumulated money and decided which family member would be the first to leave and how the links with those still remaining on the hacienda would be maintained until their freedom was obtained. A whole array of mechanisms existed, mechanisms subtler than dramatic marches to Lima demanding an audience with a hacienda owner. Our portrayal of negotiations within the hacienda will help reveal the dynamics and perceptions of slave families as well as give us insight into the relations between the free and slave populations. In this context, we will again be reminded of the lives of Manuel, Manuela, Manuelita, Manolo, and Manolito.

Mobility and Accumulation

In order to understand how slaves were able to leave the hacienda and use legal mechanisms to achieve increasing degrees of freedom, it is necessary to begin where the cycle of liberation began—within the world of the hacienda. Because the connections between the countryside and city were relatively fluid, as soon as an urban link was forged, the likelihood of relocation and freedom increased. Relocation did not automatically imply the accession of freedom: reaching the city might simply mean changing ownership and duties. But slaves knew that there were greater prospects for accumulation in the city; thus, a first step to freedom could be relocation to the city.

As if imitating the slaves on the Buena Muerte hacienda who one day marched to Lima, more than a handful of slaves staged similar actions, either on their own or collectively, with or without the permission of the *mayordomo* or owner. Generally, these slaves, dissatisfied with their situation, left the hacienda in search of a new owner; their owner or *mayordomo* had abused them or perhaps he or she had not provided the slaves with their accustomed provisions or treatment. In the city slaves would find someone who might take pity on them or see profit in them, and assign them to day labor. Many slaves took this first step from the hacienda to the city; *hacendados* did not protest, and no one stopped them as possible bandits or runaways. The move was too common to rouse suspicions. All might proceed smoothly if the *hacendado* was satisfied with the new owner's payment, the new owner was content with his slave, and the slave paid the agreed-upon daily wages. Nonetheless, conflict was almost inevitable. As in many transactions, and even more so when so many conflicting interests existed, some link in the chain of agreements could give way. The courts were full of the complaints of sellers, buyers, and slaves. For some slaves, the daily wage arrangement did not signify profits; the seller rarely received the slave's appraised price or agreed to the appraisal price. Furthermore, buyers would always find defects in the slave. One urban owner, a free *moreno*, who had acquiesced to the requests of a slave couple originating from a *limeño* hacienda, described the conflicts that could arise:

> I have as my slaves the couple of José and Mariana Saldonado . . . the same slaves I purchased for 400 pesos each six or seven years ago from Don Ramón Saldonado to spare them the terrible punishment he was intending to give them. I assigned them to daily wage labor in order to make them more profitable, this assignment by virtue of the tasks for which they have the disposition and for which they have been effectively apprenticed, they certainly have not religiously paid me the moderate sum that I designated because, abusing my goodness and as I was of their same class, they have paid their daily earnings when they have so desired, leaving me to incur the greatest debts while they have profited from their diverse occupations.[32]

The slave couple had not become a free man and woman, they had simply changed their owner and environment. Once in Lima and under the roof of a new owner, they agreed to the daily wage as a possible arrangement. Not much time passed, however, before the *moreno* owner claimed that the slaves had not complied with payment of the daily wages.[33] To settle this complaint the Defensor de Menores (the judge or defender who represented legal minors) intervened in favor of the slaves and began a process of negotiation through rounds in which the slaves increasingly neared freedom. The Defensor alleged that the slaves had not complied with the payment of daily wages because they had fallen ill and that the owner had not fulfilled his duty of administering them medicine. Moreover, the owner had demanded advance payment of the daily wages in order to acquire more slaves.[34]

The daily wage was not a novelty in the experience of slaves in nineteenth-century Lima. It existed in slaveholding environments as rigid as those of the southern United States (Hart [1906] 1968, 130 ff.), and in Lima during a much earlier era than the one under analysis (Bowser 1977, 172 ff.). What is distinct in this case was its significance and value for slaves on their path to freedom. The argument of the Defensor de Menores illustrates that a new owner would not necessarily satisfy his proprietary obligations. The owner attempted to pass on to his slaves not only the costs of their maintenance but their medical expenses as well. Slaves could be subjected to demands for money from an owner who might place his or her slaves in the city and turn them into his or her most important source of capital accumulation, using the daily wage system in order to purchase more slaves. Such were the contentions heard over and over again in the judicial courts, and they elucidate—despite the uncertainty underlying most decisions to abandon the hacienda—the gradual attempts by the slave population to expand mobility and gain ground on the road to freedom.

In spite of owners' exigencies and urban vicissitudes, it was not unusual for a slave to abandon a hacienda on his or her own in order to leave behind rural slavery. The complaints of hacienda owners and Lima's citizens about the looseness and disobedience of slaves outlined in earlier paragraphs shows that this was not an isolated occurrence. As long as these complaints were part of a widespread rhetoric, officials such as the Defensor de Menores (in the case of José and Mariana), became the protectors of slaves and opposed the interests of owners. For some officials the defense of slaves became a lucrative profession, as slaves paid them to assume this task. As we can see, legal arguments were useful not only to masters but also to slaves and eventually to a new kind of professional. In the words of Don Manuel Arsola, the *hacendado* of the Bocanegra hacienda:

It is correct to say, Your Honor, that the Defensor de Menores is agriculture's greatest enemy and most terrible obstacle. The smallest detail that any slave reports to him is enough to support notoriously unjust judgments against his owner, and enough to spark rural disorder between owners, slaves, *libertos*— this being so true that there is not one *hacendado*, who if asked, would not answer affirmatively.

Other slaves did not need or desire the intervention of the Defensor de Menores. Sometimes hacienda slaves did not even try to settle in the city. For these persons, escape from the hacienda and residence in Lima for given periods of time was a routine pattern. Generally, these slaves knew where to go in the city upon arrival. Tiburcio María, a slave on the Palpa hacienda (which in 1802 belonged to Don Vicente Salinas) located in Ica, south of Lima and much more remote than the *chacras* of Amancaes, provoked the ire of his master more than once. Each time the threat of punishment hung over his head Tiburcio fled and took refuge in Lima. He ran off three times between 1798 and 1802, each time hiding for five or six months in Malambo (San Lázaro), where he maintained relations "in no way honorable" with "certain half-breeds and *mestizas* . . . sleeping in their houses or lodges where he stored his clothes and saddle."[35] Tiburcio's owner could not control the slave's behavior; Tiburcio left and entered the hacienda with ease. To avoid a beating he would take himself off and return when a half-breed in San Lázaro began to demand a longer stay or perhaps even a wedding ring. Ownership of a horse and saddle facilitated Tiburcio's movement, and perhaps for him the horse was an intermediate investment option until he gained freedom. His chosen solution was not a permanent escape from the system but rather an eloquent demonstration of how a slave could maneuver on the fringes of a slave system. Nonetheless, the repetition of such acts created the impression that slaves moved everywhere in search of work, day labor, change of ownership, or simply diversion. Some contemporaries interpreted these ventures as typical instances of maroonage, in part because they wished to elicit some response from those officials who were entrusted with the control and maintenance of public order and who—when faced with such slave behavior—exhibited a great deal of inertia and incapacity (or fear). Meanwhile, physical movement and contact with the city allowed the slaves to forge relationships (even matrimonial) and to have a destination. Slaves gradually grew familiar with the urban territory and their unsettled behavior and relative geographic mobility can explain why news traveled so quickly, not only in Lima, but also from one hacienda to another. Even if this freedom of movement did not exist on all haciendas or estates, it had wide recognition and was a key argument owners used to seek state support.

As we have seen, many owners were absentee; they controlled neither production nor the labor force. Nonetheless, they occasionally visited their properties. During arrival and departure they were usually accompanied by one or several slaves, who thus moved with regularity between the rural and urban spheres.[36] And when *hacendados* or *mayordomos* had to leave the hacienda, for example, to buy or sell products, they were accompanied by one or several slaves who had privileged positions within the rural environment. Several episodes of rather peculiar negotiations have been recorded for slaves in this position. Given the frequency of arrivals and departures, slaves often had a relative or friend in the urban realm to ease their relocation from countryside to city. The mobility of owners as well, and conflict within an owner's family, created connections for slaves and perpetuated existing ones. Comings and goings were opportunities for family reunions—for example, allowing one grandmother to find her granddaughter who was living as a slave on a hacienda. When a slave was unable to negotiate his or her purchase price or simply did not have sufficient capital for manumission, the slave could use such intervals to attempt an escape to Lima, even if the fear of being sent back to a hacienda provoked scenes as dramatic as flight over a flat roof, fall and injury, and stay in the hospital.[37]

How disagreements within the families of owners could favor slaves and become part of the field of negotiations for freedom is illustrated by the case of a son who disobeyed the orders of his family, the Ocharán family, which owned a hacienda in Ica.

The destiny of the young slave was the subject of judicial debate from 1811 to 1815. The slave's mother, Tiburcia, lived in Lima. She stated that according to the orders of the owner, Doña Teresa de Arroserena, Doña Teresa's son had put Tiburcia's son up for sale in the city of Lima. Tiburcia had purchased him for 150 pesos because the owner's orders included "the condition that [the slave] could not be sold for a greater amount, nor leave this city, and that when and where he provided the money, to be free or slave, freedom be granted to him." One fine day when Tiburcia was walking with her son through the streets of Lima, a poor Spaniard, an agent of Doña Teresa, intercepted them and alleged that the slave had been sold for a sum below his true value. He seized the young slave and sent him to the Serrano *panadería*. The agent stated that the slave's stepfather and mother took advantage of the presence of the owner's son in Lima, the son's pressing need for money, and his defiance of his mother, in order to encourage the young Ocharán to sell the slave for the stated price. Furthermore, it appears that there was a romantic liaison between Tiburcia and the owner's son. By 1813 the slave had again changed owners. The owner this year, Doña Juana Lezpus, stated that she had paid 300 pesos for the slave but that the stepfather had appeared and made off with the slave for eight months, until he was captured by the patrol of dragoons. In his declaration the stepfather admitted that he had removed the slave and stated that he was disposed to pay the slave's guarantee of person and daily wages. But, the stepfather contended, the slave was a victim of cruelty: given the inflicted abuse, it would befit the slave's parents at this time to initiate litigation in the court of Ica.[38]

Thus other members of an owner's family could become mediators of freedom as long as they received the money from the slaves themselves. The combination of Tiburcia's position (mother of the slave and lover of the owner's son), the stepfather's intervention, and the speedy sale in Lima (eased by discord within the owner's family), made it possible for the slave to remain in Lima for an extended time. Furthermore, the confluence of these factors also allowed a devalued price, even if the owner later managed to offset her loss through successive sales. This case exemplifies—in spite of its scant success—the existence of well-honed strategies slaves could use to reach the final goal: lower price and manumission.

Undoubtedly, contact with the city was part of daily life and essential to explaining the transfer of slaves from the countryside to the city. But each journey started from the hacienda and within the conditions of a master-slave relationship there. It required a complex range of maneuvers and strategies in discrete and diverse patterns of accumulation.

A slave's first step toward freedom involved the capacity to procure money. One viable tactic on haciendas of all sizes (from Huaito to Guia and Amancaes) was the sale of goods in urban and village markets; this process was especially successful in those cases where owners supplied their slaves land in usufruct and allowed them to sell the crops they raised, keeping their earnings as peasants did (a "peasantization of slaves," observed in Brazil [Cardoso 1979]). The level of control exercised by masters varied, as did the rate at which slaves could amass their purchase price and place it in the hands of their respective owners. We view one side of the process in an image of Lima's marketplaces transmitted by the English traveler Proctor.[39] According to him, in Lima's two big markets at the beginning of the 1820s in the main squares of San Francisco and San Agustín all the wares were very expensive. In the plazas of the other churches many smaller markets existed, and they were the filthiest part of the city, crowded with people cooking and selling food in the open air.

> Those who sell fruit and vegetables spread them on the ground beneath a huge umbrella of canvas: these commodities are conveyed by slaves from the farms and orchards in the vicinity of Lima: they are paid by their masters according to the price they can procure, and in general, everything of the kind is extremely dear.[40]

Indigenous women from Chorrillos also sold fish in these same vivid marketplaces. Commercial activity offered wide margins for social interaction and also capital accumulation. An owner could not easily sit down beside his or her slave in the marketplace in order to control the slave's profits—from farm or market vegetables if from the outskirts of Lima or from pigs if from Huaito. The slave could also claim that sales had been bad that day; inevitably the difference would go into the slave's pockets. Whatever the level of sales, in contexts such as these owners preferred to ask slaves for a fixed weekly, monthly, or even annual sum. This arrangement transferred the risks of a bad harvest and an unprosperous day of sales to slaves but also gave them more responsibility and independence. Buying and selling directly correlated to slaves' mobility, just as leaving the hacienda of their own volition did. The greater the capacity for movement, the greater the chance to shun the master's control.

It is reasonable to assume that not all slaves had an opportunity to leave the estate or hacienda. Where slaves were more tied to the hacienda, the forms of negotiation became more sophisticated and were less visible at first glance. The small prerogatives granted to slaves for good service or for "abundant childbirths" (for example, for a woman on the Huaito hacienda who had borne six children) generated opportunities for accumulation. These privileges were the consequence of a slave's good service or level of specialization, at times simply of old age, and at others of pity. The slaves utilized all these bargaining tools to redefine their position on the hacienda. Slaves who had obtained perquisites usually remained on the hacienda. However, they generally spent fewer hours on hacienda labor than their slave status implied. As a consequence, these slaves had more time to cultivate their truck gardens and sell their goods in the small markets near the hacienda or eventually in larger city markets.

However, slaves also had at their disposal a reserve of work time that they could sell either on the hacienda where they worked or on other haciendas. In principle, they sold their labor to the highest bidder, and demand depended on the type and level of individual specialization and on the hacienda's requirements and rules. By staying on the hacienda and carrying out the same or different duties, slaves could receive a wage. The existence of this possibility indicates that the organization of the labor force on the haciendas was changing. We have scattered figures for several haciendas in the district of Miraflores (which registered the emergence of salaried blacks) and information systematized through the *cartas de libertad* in notarial record books. Given the informality of these arrangements, they are difficult to measure. Nevertheless, some cases illustrate the varying ways in which this process of transition to wage labor took place.

In 1807 Francisca Suazo was a free *morena* day laborer on the Chancay hacienda; her slave daughter lived with her. This same year the hacienda owner passed away, and Jacinta, Francisca's daughter, was included in the appraisal of the hacienda's assets. In opposition to one of the heirs who had requested a new appraisal of the slave girl (valued at 350 pesos), Francisca petitioned to buy her daughter. The heir's request was denied, and Francisca paid her daughter's purchase price.[41] In order not to abandon her slave daughter (from the sought price we infer that the girl was at least sixteen years old), Francisca probably remained on the hacienda. The price exacted of Francisca was equivalent to the price of her own manumission. The question that arises in this case concerns the source of the money Francisca used to purchase her daughter. We do not know if others contributed, but lacking evidence of assistance we must assume that Francisca, still on the hacienda's borders, was able to amass a sum of money that was quite an expenditure in that era, approximately equal to the annual salary of a state functionary or thirty-five years of an Indian's tribute.

Obviously, the fewer free hours dedicated to the slave's plot on the hacienda, the slower the process of accumulation. After all, an exemption of labor time or, as in Francisca's case, release from all type of obligatory labor, did not mean that the individual could abandon the hacienda. Thus, the potential for accumulation also depended on the regulation of work within the hacienda and hence on the master's control.

However, alongside opportunities to reduce the hours of required work on the hacienda were other levels of negotiation that could approximate the purchase price and the needed amount of remunerated free labor. Slaves used a two-sided strategy; on one hand, their objective was to acquire their own labor time, and on the other, to reduce their price. The closer slaves could come to both goals, the greater the amount of free labor remunerated on the hacienda, and the faster the reduction of their own price, the better the chances for freedom.

Conditional freedom granted in a will can be seen as a form of internal accumulation on the hacienda, to the extent that it represented a daily wage (i.e., for the number of years of service under the testator) that masters would repay at the end of the contract with the liberation of the slave. Many slaves were aware of this trade-off, and they were not convinced by promises of freedom that an owner would devise and bequeath, an option that masters cherished as warrant for the trumpets of the Last Judgment. For many slave owners such divine redemption meant an expensive trade-off and they preferred to settle their matters in more mundane fashion.

According to the testamentary wishes of Don Dámaso Jáuregui, his *mulata* slave, Bernardina León, was to be manumitted at the age of twenty-five. Until that time, the will redacted in 1795 placed Bernardina in the service of Doña Nicolasa Lobatón who was entrusted to find a husband for Bernardina before she started on the road toward freedom. When she had barely reached twenty-five years, Bernardina presented herself before the Cabildo and requested that the promise of freedom be expedited immediately:

I will not address the inexplicable desires that I had of this moment's arrival because I have undergone misfortunes that have disturbed me, having been victim of the work and demands that in this period have been exacted of me; without hyperbole I can affirm that I did not receive liberty by the grace of my master, but rather, by justice in force of the work with which I purchased it.[42]

Bernardina affirmed "without hyperbole" what she knew very well: her labor generously repaid her purchase price. She feared her owner's retaliation because of the legal proceedings Bernardina had initiated. But without incident she was declared free that same year. For Bernardina, having access to Lima's judicial court was critical, and apparently she managed to use the legal system without any problems, even though she had resided in the town of Supe on the northern coast her entire life.

Many years could elapse between the promise of freedom and actual emancipation. While the master was still alive, until the slave reached a certain age, until the details of the testamentary bequests were settled, the slave had to remain under the tutelage, property, or control of the master or those who had taken on the responsibility of executing a testator's wishes. In the end, sometimes the wait revealed that a testator's debts were greater than his legacy.[43] Furthermore, all slaves knew that what brought them closer to freedom was not their labor alone; each and every condition imposed on their freedom was vulnerable to legal judgments beyond their control. For this reason, slaves needed to accelerate the promise of freedom, make recourse to legal courts, and seize and make effective any initiative expressed by the masters that indicated their desire to free them. Freedom was the coveted goal at the end of this chain of possible situations of negotiation, perhaps more than simple relocation to Lima.

Testamentary pledges had another side. From the masters' perspective, conditional freedom was a way to assure the submission and permanence of a slave, even if cases existed in which a slave—the promise of freedom or price reduction already existing—wished for the quick death of his or her owner. In May of 1854 the female slave Candelaria Mora, a native of the town of Chincha, who classified herself as a *liberta*, signed a petition before the judge of Lima's court of appeals. This petition stated that her owner, Doña María del Rosario Velásquez, had requested in her will that Candelaria remain in the service of her daughter and one of the inheritors, Doña Irene Mora, until the latter died. Many years passed, but one fine day Doña Irene's husband decided to sell Candelaria "for the exorbitant amount of 350 pesos," to a *señora* who lived in Lima and, Candelaria alleged, "no doubt making no mention to the buyer of the testamentary clause that declared me free in an earlier epoch. As a result of that illegal sale, I have been transferred to this capital from Chincha, which is my birthplace." After a few months in Lima, Candelaria had located a relative of the Mora family, a presbyter, in whose house she found shelter while she wrote her petition. Candelaria's new owners would claim that she had been transferred for only four years, and that this did not contradict the testamentary wishes of her first owner. Nonetheless, it was decreed in 1855 (i.e., one year after President Ramón Castilla declared the abolition of slavery) that the money be refunded and the slave returned to the Mora family.[44]

It is not clear if the slave wished to go to Lima or if, for reasons not mentioned in the document, the presbyter was interested in keeping the slave. Candelaria stressed the fact that Chincha was her birthplace, and given the connection of last names (the female slave, the presbyter in Lima, and the will's beneficiary all have the surname Mora), a common ancestor is possible. At the very least, the slave acquired her surname through birth into her master's control. Even if circumstances suggest that the slave wished to return to the hacienda, what this case demonstrates is that when a fixed temporal horizon for freedom existed, an interim change of ownership became more difficult. Moreover, this transfer proceeded by the masters' initiative and included a high price for the slave (or perhaps, in Candelaria's case, set the slave's price for the first time in her life). The apparent philanthropy of conditional liberty was but a way to entrap a slave on the road to freedom. When the promise of freedom depended on someone else's death, permanence on the hacienda was almost assured; conditional freedom was a way to perpetuate the slave's loyalty. We should not forget that cases such as Candelaria's took place in an environment in which the slaves were becoming aware of the centrality of their work and claiming monetary compensation.

The manifold strategies of accumulation and of negotiation that slaves gradually secured from wills always revolved around the slave's price. Once the channels of negotiation were open, the purchase price was the bridge between slavery and freedom. At the beginning of the nineteenth century the average price for a male slave was 465 pesos, and 494 for a female slave (Haitin 1983, 166). Because of these elevated prices, it is not surprising that many manumissions and sales were transacted on credit. The ways varied. One form of credit was the successive reduction of a slave's value owing to good service, extraordinary service, or simply to aging; another was the payment of small installments to the master over many years, which a slave usually amassed by appealing to an entire network of family and urban connections. The most complex form of credit involved a third person who lent the money to the slave in exchange for services until the debt was settled (the arrangement between Manuel and Doña Agreda noted in chapter 1). This last way gave the slave freedom but kept him or her subject to slavery. It is possible that these various forms of credit help explain the depreciation of the average price for a slave, for slaves whose value was fixed by the market as well as those whose mean value can be deduced from an analysis of the *cartas de libertad*. Between 1840 and 1854 the average price of male slaves on the market was 289.4 pesos, of female slaves, 267.3. Of those slaves whose names appeared in the *cartas de libertad* in these same years, the mean price of men was 229.4 pesos and that of women, 207.3 (Aguirre 1991, 122).[45] The average for slaves who obtained a *carta de libertad* was lower: their owners were apparently willing to accept the gradual reduction of their slaves' value and the slaves' emancipation as well; perhaps the masters had no other alternative. It is also significant, despite the biases of averages, that female slaves at the beginning of the nineteenth century cost more than male slaves. The preference for female slave labor on Lima's big haciendas (such as Villa and San Juan) surely was part of this situation. A greater demand resulted in a higher price.[46] However, it is also true—as we will see later—that the lower price of female slaves had to do with their particular skills (see chapter 3).

Arrangements even less transparent appeared in the lives of Lima's slaves. These fell somewhere between wage labor arrangements (with varying amounts of free time on or off the hacienda) and price reduction. Often, instead of paying a slave a daily wage in exchange for the market value of additional labor power, an owner calculated the daily wage according to the price stated on the slave's *conque*—in which case there was no promise of a grant of freedom or a sum of money to go into the hands of slaves; the slaves would make incremental payments that slowly reduced their price. Manumission was a calculable arrangement; masters and slaves carried debit notes. The manner in which this payment and its related negotiations could vary suggests that this arrangement allowed owners to assure the slave labor force's immobility and faithfulness, especially if both sides kept its terms. In a more sophisticated version of this process, the reduction of the slave's purchase price appeared to be a concession by the owner who had sold a slave below his *conque* value. What seems to be a benefit resulting from the owner's initiative might mask a sum owed to the slave's first owner, which the slave continued to pay after the official sale.[47] The male or female slave labored for two masters, the work intensified, yet the slave's price decreased.

Among the most common explanations for the depreciation of a slave's price was old age, when the slave became useless for the work on the hacienda. The only way to sell him or her was to reduce the slave's price, adjusting it to the changes in the "quality of merchandise." Price reduction within an urban labor market permitted rural masters to minimize their losses and urban owners to exploit slave wage labor—a way to stretch the profitability of the system to its final limits, although slaves still found and benefited from some opportunities beyond the control of masters.[48] Sometimes the master's final choice was emancipation of aging slaves, in order to avoid the medical costs and care.

Francisco Calderón and his wife had been slaves on the Monterrico hacienda, owned by the entailed estate of Quintanilla. In 1826 the hacienda was leased to a priest who had been granted the right to buy and sell slaves, provided that he replace them. Appraised, the slave couple received a document stating that they could freely circulate in search of a new owner. (Here the impetus to seek a new owner came from the priest, whereas in other cases slaves fled the hacienda to do the same.) On their journey, Francisco was caught by the police; he was not offered an opportunity to show his document and was deposited in the Tigre *panadería*. Soon thereafter, the military captors were reprimanded for this blunder, and under the protection of a bondsman Francisco was liberated.[49] In this case it was the proprietor or the *mayordomo* who guaranteed the slave's departure and was willing to lower the slave's price and even endorsed the slave couple's quest to find a new owner. From another point of view, sadly, aging was also an aspect of credit that gradually eroded the slave's value but allowed greater and greater spaces of freedom. Freedom became a double-edged sword, especially for slaves with little or no urban experience if kinship and wider social networks could not subsidize their old age.

Time and time again, price is the reason behind negotiations. Price was a crucial issue for owners because business depended on it and for slaves because access to freedom rested on it. Price increases benefited owners who wanted to sell their slaves, and price reductions advanced slaves and those wishing to purchase slaves. Thus, the issue of price split owners into buyers and sellers, and buyers often invented strategies, working in unison with slaves, in order to obtain cheaper slaves. In chapter 5 we will look at this phenomenon as it affects the lives of masters and slaves in the urban context. Contemporaries frowned on the practice of increasing a slave's price. Occasionally, the infringement of a *conque*'s stipulations would invalidate the new owner's contract of sale. For the slave, this annulment could even mean return to the hacienda or relocation to Lima after several years. In a case in which the price of a female slave had been raised from 100 to 250 pesos, the slave's defender asked:

"What authority did these owners have to alter the price of the original *conque*? Never [the Defensor made clear] has it been permitted to increase the value by even one real, and when owners have desired to do so, they have had to turn to the court and file a suit, in order to prove the fairness of the reasons they have alleged for such pretensions."⁵⁰

Beyond fluctuations in value and negotiations between countryside and city were small sums of money that many slaves gradually amassed while in the service of their owners. They handed these amounts over to owners as collateral for the freedom they would earn when they had gathered together the entire purchase price or as repayment of sums they borrowed for self-manumission. This type of arrangement was ever-present in the minds of the slaves who put stock in the November 1821 decree on patronage, which stated that work should be remunerated.⁵¹ But slaves' wages were not the same as those of a free person, and the difference (along with its legal implications) never figured in coherent legislation. What value did the labor of a slave halfway between slavery and freedom have—especially within monetary arrangements so complex that slaves were paid? A rather unusual *mulato*, Patricio Negrón, related his experiences in 1840:

> Being a slave originally from the city of Ica, I was brought up in the manner appropriate to my condition and according to the talents that were discovered in me. Nature more actively inclined me to the work that should occupy women. I washed and took care of the linen with skill, cooked, and ran a house as the best housekeeper might do. Never did any aspect of my integrity, conduct, or social behavior give occasion for remark. However, displeased with my master, I came to this city, and he arrived soon after in search of me—he wished to take me away by force; however Doña Estefa Palacios, who understood well the importance of my services, lent me 200 pesos to free myself, in such a way that I managed to release myself from servitude. The owner received the money for my freedom—returned to his estates, and I remained in Doña Estefa's service.

But from this moment on, Patricio realized, none of his services were going to be effectively remunerated:

> My work earns more than 24 pesos monthly, however this *señora* did not give me anything. She planned a trip to Ica and took me with her. There I served her for the length of the four months that included the arrival, stay and return. There I gave her from the total amount of 200 pesos she lent me, 47 pesos and 7 reales, but she did not give me a penny in those four months. There I gave her 11 pesos on the one hand, and 8, on the other, according to her receipt, making her at the time a debtor of 133 pesos and 1 real; and the said *señora* owes me for all the time that I have served her without payment. Finally, she tells me that I have to give her the money or a guarantee.

When Patricio had offered to pay a guarantee, he was unexpectedly placed in the Pericotes *panadería* and cruelly whipped. Bed-ridden, he wrote his accusation against the owner and the *panadero* who had lashed him. He appealed to article three of the decree issued on 16 October 1821, which stated that owners who whipped their slaves were to be punished. He furthermore argued that even if this article had been later modified by the law of 1827, it still forbade an owner to flog a slave with more than six lashes (in the colonial era the maximum allowed was twelve) and required that the barrio commissary be present during any and all punishment. Owners who violated these laws were to be deprived of their slaves. Patricio managed to prove that this had not been the first time that Doña Estefa had advanced money and later abused the labor of her debtors.[52] Patricio had not been her first victim.

The slave knew that the value of his labor should have been gradually subtracted from his purchase price. Formally he was free, he possessed a *carta de libertad*. But since he was a servant of the person who lent him money to manumit himself, his work was considered to be an interest payment, and the money for his purchase price was assumed to come from outside the established relation of servitude. Thus in fact Patricio remained a slave with a limited margin of accumulation.[53] Persons such as Doña Estefa, who invested money in the manumission of slaves and later used slaves as retainers, were probably the last social agents who took advantage of a system in decline and of slaves' yearnings toward freedom as well. Not only did their actions change the patterns of slave ownership and the composition of slaveholders, they unbalanced the master-slave relationship.

When President Ramón Castilla decreed the abolition of slavery in 1854 many slaves were caught in the middle of paying for their freedom. Some had given money to their owners, were bargaining to lower their prices, or were fighting to obtain salaries their owners had left unpaid. Abolition also created tensions among owners eager to make their slaves pay and determined not to give back any part of the money that formed the slaves' price of freedom. None of the negotiations established clear dividing lines between salary, interest on invested capital, and self-purchase money.

Perhaps the events at the Molina hacienda best synthesize the crux of the issue in 1854. Ownership of the hacienda was contested, which meant that its slave population had no master or *mayordomo*. Absenteeism—as we have seen—was an impetus for slaves to mobilize, and for hacienda slaves to request transfers and price appraisals. But on the Molina hacienda these petitions coalesced into a collective effort toward freedom, whereas in the cases previously examined such negotiations had involved action only by individuals and by several couples. The slaves on the Molina hacienda sought the intervention of the courts. The complaints of the slaves had been building up over the previous years; many of the slaves from the Molina hacienda figured in the registers of the *cartas de libertad* in the 1850 notarial record books. One of the *cartas de libertad* referred to the free black Simón García, who in 1854 was pleading for the freedom of his sister, who was over forty years old: "the service rendered, her age, and because the many children she bore and raised have aged her." His sister's price was 400 pesos and Simón asked for a new appraisal, based on the argument of her age, "to try to grant her freedom so that she die free and in old age does not suffer what slaves must suffer." But on 18 August 1856, almost two years after Simón had filed his request, the case was ordered closed, "because the reasons for which this suit arose have disappeared since all slaves have been declared free."[54]

Thus what started as a personal negotiation grew into a strategy that attracted more and more slaves from the same hacienda. Not only did rumors about the Quebrada slaves who marched to Lima to protest work conditions spread throughout the rural region, but communication among slaves on haciendas—especially the smaller ones—was also quite effective. Slaves were using the arguments of old age, or of numerous children and the exhausting effects of rearing them, to legitimize their requests for freedom. These arguments were no longer the exclusive property of masters. Since more than one slave learned about the abolition decree through the sentences issued in a pending file, and often after some time had elapsed, the delay brought in new claims for retroactive payment of a free laborer's salary. And an owner might argue, as in the case of Simon García's sister, that the slave hardly deserved payment—hadn't her brother stated she was too old and tired to be of any use to the hacienda? In this final expression of resistance to abolition, owners neatly reversed the slaves' arguments and built up a case for compensation payments from the state.

In contrast to a city such as Rio de Janeiro (Karasch 1987, 356 ff.), Lima had no mediating institutions specifically concerned with the negotiation of freedom—lending banks or savings associations. In Lima, negotiations between masters and slaves were much more direct, although they often took place before civil and ecclesiastical tribunals. Perhaps this absence of bureaucratic or state mediation explains the enormous diversity of means slaves devised to survive or leave the haciendas, as well as the intricate patterns of accumulation that existed. And perhaps it links the universe of family and kin that was so important to slaves in Lima. The lack of more organized intervention probably underlies the preeminence of slave family relations and the "moral" arguments asserted by slaves in defense of their right to form families and live a home life.

Family Relations

On the hacienda at least 60 percent of the slaves lived as couples, and any negotiations regarding freedom were likely to involve two heads of household. Insofar as slaves could gradually reduce their value or that of any specific family member, the probability of purchasing freedom for the entire family increased. In the worst of cases it would at least be easier to find a new owner and eventually live in Lima.

The incentive that encouraged slaves to remain on the hacienda also encouraged them to leave: namely, their families. Leaving or remaining on the hacienda depended on trivial, everyday, and personal factors: children's ages, other work opportunities, and earning potential on the hacienda. As we have seen, free persons might stay on the hacienda to assure the freedom of their children or spouses.

An entire family only rarely amassed enough money to leave the hacienda, on which all its members may have been born, at the same time. The usual pattern was staggered migration: one family member would leave, then another. If behind this gradual abandonment of the hacienda there was any logic that determined who should leave first—based on who had the greatest capacity to earn money to free the remaining family members or who had the best chances to exert pressure on the *hacendado*—then it should emerge from the frequency of such occurrences. Which family members would stay, which would leave first? How was this departure to be accomplished?

A common figure during this time was a mother working in Lima whose slave children remained on the hacienda. The mother-child bond appeared to be the strongest, one that survived despite separation. When slavery was abolished in 1854 Magdalena Garcia, a free *morena*, was living in the city of Lima. Earlier she had worked on the Molina hacienda, where she had left a legitimate son under "exclusive patronage of the hacienda."[55] After having worked in Lima for some time Magdalena asked the court for a transfer of her son's patronage. In her petition she stated:

> I, Sir, have yearned to free my son, the mentioned child, but my present work conditions have not allowed me this wish. It is for this reason, and as is a natural maternal feeling, that I am suffering from this separation from my child. Beyond this, in one of the visits I made to see my son, I found him incapacitated by wounds inflicted upon him in a cruel whipping by the present leaseholder. I made this fact known to the Síndico del Concurso who, aghast at the harm done to my son, consented to the request that I made . . . that is, that my son's patronage be changed immediately.

As was usual in such cases, the slave was appraised, the former owner paid by the new owner, and the change of ownership ordered. Generally owners asked for a higher price—if only to keep the slave a bit longer. In Magdalena's case, given the maltreatment, this request was not heeded by the civil court; shortly thereafter the court determined that the sale of her son (in this case for 200 pesos) should proceed.[56]

The slave's mother had maintained continual contact with her son on the hacienda, visiting him regularly. Thus, the mother—already free—became an external agent of security for her son; her goal was to free him. With much skill, she sought—given the inflicted abuse—the intervention of an official (in this case the Síndico del Concurso, since the hacienda had gone bankrupt and a judgment regarding its division among the heirs was pending) and quickly managed, while not to free, at least to loosen, for a relatively low price, the ties that bound her son to the hacienda and to relocate him to Lima. She had taken the first step toward his freedom and now she had him closer.

The Santa Clara estate was less removed from Lima than the Molina hacienda. Francisco Mansilla worked here as a *liberto* among the many slaves. His patronage belonged to Don Cristóbal Armero, owner of the Santa Clara estate. Francisco had worked there for eight years. Although still a minor, he fell in love with a slave girl who worked on another estate belonging to Don Isidro Aramburú. One fine day he decided to elope with her. He immediately sought refuge with the Defensor de Menores in Lima, who, in a petition directed to the court judge, stated that Francisco had appeared in his office to accuse his master of maltreatment and noncompliance with the weekly payment of eight *reales* as decreed in November 1821. In addition, he pointed out that Francisco had found a new owner in Lima who was willing to purchase him for 250 pesos. Opposing the sale of his slave, Francisco's owner claimed:

Far from having acted with cruelty toward Francisco, I have always treated him with affection and generosity, and for that reason he remained with me, even after the emancipation of his mother and two sisters, which he took part in because of his prodigality and good behavior. Furthermore, Francisco Mansilla's mother, who should supervise and maintain guardianship of her son as he is still a minor, also opposes a transfer of ownership because under my patronage she has more facilities to free him, for which she has already amassed a certain amount of money.

While the slave was working on the Santa Clara estate, he had been able to free his mother and two sisters. The "prodigality" to which his owner refers can be interpreted in many ways, however; the most likely is that after many rounds of negotiations, Francisco was able to collect enough money to free the three women. The owner indicated that Francisco's mother had already accumulated a certain amount of money to purchase her son's freedom. And, effectively, the story ended when, three months after the Defensor's initial petition, Don Cristóbal Armero issued Francisco a *carta de libertad*. The mother paid his purchase price.[57] Probably the next step was to purchase the girlfriend's freedom.

Here was a visible chain of decisions regarding freedom, with priorities based on the capacity for accumulation: inside the hacienda were the male slaves, outside the hacienda were the women, often mothers.[58] Just behind them were collateral family members. And, once this process began—even if as in the previous case there were obstacles—the speed of accumulation increased as the number of family members multiplied. The owner's final allegation was probably correct:

Please permit me before concluding this petition, to make it known to the court as well, the pernicious example that has been set for the already corrupt slave population of this capital city, by favoring under false and frivolous pretexts the freedom of a slave who has committed a crime [in carrying off the slave girl from an adjoining estate], which has demoralized my own slaves, and which would demoralize them yet more, if this slave were to be granted the status he is requesting.

Perniciousness and corruption, however, often loitered on the road to freedom, and the slaves knew that the established facts made allegations of immorality mere rhetoric.

Part of the considerations of slaves to leave the hacienda was their family life cycle. It would be difficult for a mother with small children to leave for the city and quickly earn enough to free her husband and children. Neither could a parent easily abandon young children. Given such a situation there were three options, wait for a different phase in the family cycle, twist the master's arm, or struggle for permission to leave the hacienda. If, in addition, life on the hacienda offered no paid work, the only alternative was to find an owner in Lima interested in purchasing the slave and assigning him or her to day-labor. Some episodes on the Bocanegra hacienda illustrate the last two possibilities. A case of spectacular arm-twisting was perpetrated by Francisca and Josefa of the mentioned hacienda in 1840. The owner stated:

When the slave Francisca, wife of Joaquín, and Josefa, wife of Nicolás, managed to free themselves, each one was nursing a child, named Leandro and Evaristo, and had been ordered to leave the hacienda for being ungovernable. I mandated that each one be given four pesos a month to nurse their children.... A few months later they made several requests that I let them return to the hacienda, where the women, their husbands, and their children could be cared for.[59]

Shortly afterward the *hacendado* threw them off the hacienda again, but this time they took their children and husbands. Other slaves followed their example. The Defensor de Menores, entrusted with the slaves' defense, claimed that the owner had not supplied them with food and that therefore in accordance with the law they were free. While the ex-slave mothers were outside the hacienda they lived in Lima, on Malambo street (in the familiar parish of San Lázaro), where they had contact with black maroons who cut firewood that the women sold in Lima. This urban experience of survival offered them enough security to abandon the hacienda. The Bocanegra hacienda had long been considered a haven of thieves and maroons;[60] it was probably the place where the link with the maroons came about. The judgment in this case was in favor of the *libertos*. The *hacendado*, Don Manuel Arsola, attempted an appeal but the sentence was upheld. During the case the Defensor de Menores reappeared as a key player.

When in 1830 the same Don Manuel Arsola was Bocanegra's *hacendado*, one of his slaves, Udon, requested that he be sold, seeking protection in the decree on patronage of 1821. The *hacendado* stated that he would not consent to the sale because Udon had not been a victim of cruelty, and that in any case Udon should leave the hacienda with his wife and two children, one older, one recently born. Udon and his wife had both been born on Bocanegra. Apparently Udon's wife opted to stay on the hacienda, an understandable decision given the uncertainty of urban life and the minimum of security that the hacienda offered, especially for small children. This being the couple's choice, Don Arsola finally agreed to sell Udon, under the condition that he come to visit his wife and sons only on Saturdays and Sundays. Don Arsola received 300 pesos, and Udon went to work as a day laborer in Lima.[61]

The *hacendado* knew that Udon was going to maintain relations with his family and thus become an external agent, who would not only free his family but also bring outside news that would spread to the other slaves on the hacienda. Therefore, he first attempted to remove the entire slave family and then to restrict Udon's access to the hacienda; family relations intervening, however, he could not prevent the perpetuation of family ties. The more slaves acted as did those on Bocanegra, the more time masters spent in court.

As time passed, slave children would mature and thus their value would increase. Therefore, many slave parents negotiated possibilities for purchasing their children before they reached full working age. This meant obtaining a pledge from one's master that he or she would proceed with the sale of the children and also quickly raising the money needed for manumission. The exposure of very young children to the unpredictability of the city not only represented a burden but also increased the risks of their death. Nearly adult children were too expensive. The most logical option was to free children at an intermediate age, between eight and ten years old, when they could contribute to the family's expenses and were in good health. Circumstances did not always coincide, but for some these calculations worked out. Cases like that of the free *morena* Magdalena Garcia, who paid the appraised purchase price of 130 pesos to free her son on the Molina hacienda when he reached ten years of age,[62] were repeated not only on haciendas but in the urban context as well and explain—as stated earlier—the very low concentration of a slave infant population on the haciendas.

Throughout the cases we see two important processes. One indicates a cycle of decisions by the slave family unit geared to finding bridges to Lima. The women were the first to leave, even if they had young children on the hacienda. They were the ones who forged and stabilized the urban links. This dynamic probably had much to do with the competition in the labor market between the free black and slave populations. Above all, men were the individuals who competed in an increasingly narrower labor market. Yet women also worked (because slave women did compete in the masculine labor market), at tasks always needed on the margin of the labor market's cycles of expansion and contraction (e.g., as wet nurses, cooks and bakers, household servants). An additional reason why women left the hacienda first could have been the greater propensity of masters to let women depart, not because they worked less but because without them the costs of reproducing the slave labor force were lowered. Although *hacendados* sought desperately to augment their slave labor force, bringing the costs of reproduction down was a way to confront the short-term crises of agriculture. Even though the average price of slave women was higher, their average productivity was less because they bore children.

A second key process was the nature of the relations that were established and maintained after women had left the rural sphere. The strength of these bonds was illustrated by the frequency of visits and by the degree of control exercised by those outside the hacienda over the status of those who remained inside. Furthermore, almost as an expected consequence of this behavior was the fear felt by owners who faced situations in which a slave outside with family inside became an agent of external security. Not only did the slave's own family have external ties, but by extension the rest of the hacienda workers did too. The new urban experiences of slaves could be transmitted even to those who had always experienced their world on the hacienda as a microcosm of conditions equal to or perhaps better than those beyond the edges of the hacienda. Apprehensions about daily life existed among *hacendados* in Palpa, Nazca, and other areas discussed earlier.

Maroons, Bandits, and Militiamen: Darker Links between Countryside and City

Sporadically—yet persistently—maroons and brigands turned up in the life of the Lasmanuelos family, and one of its members even belonged to a band. Bands of guerrillas flourished before, during, and after the wars of independence. They appeared on the haciendas, cut firewood on the periphery of the city, and languished in jails and *panaderías*. They were the most mobile component of the slave population: an important link between countryside and city, a terror of the road for travelers and merchants as for the indigenous, *casta*, black, and slave populations.

At different times and in varying contexts, militiamen, soldiers, bandits, and maroons shared two fundamental experiences: segregation by ethnic group and use of weapons within or beyond the law. Slaves were members of all these groups and often found that participation broadened their horizons and increased their awareness of the weaknesses of the slaveholding system.

Companies of urban soldiers were formed during the seventeenth century, and blacks and their free descendants were found in their ranks. Their central function was ceremonial: to welcome and see off the viceroys. They occasionally achieved police duties. Around 1765 this situation began to change. Isolated signs of indigenous discontent in northern Peru (O'Phelan 1976), sporadic slave revolts on the coastal haciendas (Kapsoli 1975), as well as the Tupac Amaru uprising in 1780 in the southern Andes, convinced the colonial state that it was necessary to think about the permanent and conscientious organization of a military corps.

In 1776 Lima's infantry regiment of *pardos* included 947 men and the battalion of *morenos* had 474. The cavalry regiment of *pardos* numbered 104 horsemen and the cavalry battalion of *morenos*, 77. Similar companies began to emerge in the cities of the coastal region. They were commanded by whites; the colonial state preferred officers who were *peninsulares* (Spaniards) or *criollos* (Spaniards born in the New World) to an entirely *casta* corps with its risk of greater and greater autonomy. The presence of *castas* tarnished the image of military duties, and *morenos* and *pardos* themselves soon realized that serving in these armies was not a privilege but rather an obligation from which it was difficult to free oneself (Burkholder 1972, 142–143). Moreover, the salaries they received were so low that soldiers usually engaged in some artisanal trade on the side and had permission to marry only if they could prove that their future wife had adequate resources to maintain the family. Yet in 1816 blacks, *mulatos*, and *pardos* made up approximately 4 percent of the entire viceregal military, and 53 percent of Lima's contingents.[63]

Soldiers were part of the viceregal military structure under the ultimate authority of the viceroy. Before independence these corps had demonstrated the potential to rebel and revolt against the colonial state. In 1779 when Inspector Areche came to the colonial territory and wanted, among other things, to impose taxes on the *castas*, the soldiers of Lambayeque refused to pay what they called the "military tax." They wrote to the viceroy, who, faced with the threat of a *casta* riot, had to yield to the soldiers' petition. Armed and united, blacks, *mulatos*, and *pardos* negotiated an exemption from a payment they saw as denigrating because it relegated them to the same social rung as the Indians (Burkholder 1972, 124 ff.). Whatever the authorities' apprehensions and experiences, they had to trust the *castas* with some of the duties of defense and repression. Between 1779 and 1812 new military corps were created, but none in Lima.

We can assume, for lack of evidence, that a substantial part of these corps organized before the struggles for independence later enlarged the ranks of the royalist army. It is possible that many grew disaffected and deserted—as some in the patriot army did—since the wars of independence crystallized loyalties and perceptions but allowed margin for maneuver on the fringes of official acts.

Before the struggles for independence, the varying attempts to conscript slaves into the patriot ranks and the reactions by slaves illustrate an interesting gamut of alternatives and options. The choices slaves made reflect the diversity of labor conditions and life on the various rural production units. In fact, General San Martín sent commissioners to the haciendas of Lima's northern outskirts to read edicts to the slaves. They promised freedom and rewards for slaves who enlisted in the patriot armies: emancipation for slaves and capital punishment for owners who infringed the new proclamations (see chapter 1). Recitation of the edicts was to proceed in the absence of masters; it was believed they would inhibit the slaves' free choice. The responses documented by the commissioners varied. After visiting several units in the district of Sayán, the commissioner Juan Delgado reported the outcome of his trip to the secretary of war and the navy, Bernardo Monteagudo: "I installed myself in the Quispico hacienda . . . and ordered all the hacienda slaves to assemble without the presence of their master. And after making the proper reflections, eighteen slaves declared their willingness, stating that they would gladly serve in the army."

Matters proceeded otherwise among the slaves on the Andahuasi hacienda, many of them "having been deserters for some time, only one slave who desired to serve in the army voluntarily was produced." In the village of Sayán the commissioner ordered all the slave owners to present their slaves in the plaza, and when they were assembled "they were not only read the edict and communiqué on this matter but I also made known to them the prerogatives they would enjoy from their freedom by taking up arms; to which they replied that they could not forsake their owners."[64]

The possibilities of slaves reflected the range of limited choices during the wars of independence. Slaves could take up arms and have faith that they were fighting for a cause and their freedom. They could flee from an uncertain future at a time when the overall atmosphere was turbulent. Or they could, as in the village of Sayán, remain with their master, either as the result of threats or as the most secure alternative in the general disorder of the time. Despite slaves' active participation on the battlefield, promises of freedom and rewards were not usually kept. Given the circumstances and opportunities on the haciendas and estate farms, the choice of remaining at the side of one's owner was surely the most rational because it allowed slaves to continue on a slow but sure route to freedom. Not all slaves were ready or willing to become soldiers.

Far from one's master, with a rifle in hand, in contact with free blacks in the armies, and with permission to kill whites of the adversary's flag, a slave struggled with issues more complex than loyalty to patriots or royalists. The wartime experience undid old social ties and brought distinct ethnic groups, rich and poor, face to face (Bonilla and Spalding 1984, introduction). After five years of war, events such as that documented in the city of Callao in 1825 where the "slaves on the

Spaniards' haciendas revolted, . . . imprisoning all officials," were not unusual.[65]

In contrast to armies drawn from descendants of the black population and from soldiers captured by either side during the struggles for independence were the maroons, slaves who had escaped rural (and sometimes urban) slavery to band together and live by robbery and looting. Maroons did not emerge during the struggles for independence; they had existed since the establishment of slavery. Maroonage relates to slavery in the same manner that contraband does to monopoly, as a natural response to an arbitrary imposition. Throughout the colonial period the viceroys sporadically felt obligated to dispatch military expeditions to exterminate the havens of maroons each time that the complaints of those affected by the presence of the fugitives grew too loud. These complaints voiced not only property owners' fears of continual assaults, especially around the perimeter of the Lima valley, but also apprehensions of Lima's slave owners that the impunity of bandits and maroons would become a permanent incentive for their own slaves to escape.

It is not an easy task to uncover the essence of these groups of fugitives, vagrants, and social renegades. They had distinct strengths, leaders with divergent goals, and missions of varying objectives; and they were wary of one another. The strongest absorbed the weakest and kept the biggest part of the booty. In some respects their behavior was not unlike that of other sectors of society. Lima's wealthy residents paid certain gangs to protect their assets and properties against the urban incursions of their lesser cohorts. A contemporary noted dryly that "the practice of respecting persons of influence must to a great extent be attributed to the degree of impunity that these gentlemen of industry enjoy" (Miller 1829, 2:267). His statement indicates the propinquity of gangs to the urban area and explains the fluidity of relations between maroons and slaves, in Lima's hinterland as well as the city proper.

However, we can occasionally detect the more clear-cut and coherent objectives of these gangs in terms of a shared social aim. Army deserters, restless household slaves, and artisans displaced from their trades not only added members to these bands. The growth of their presence helped encourage attitudes that reflected incipient notions of social justice. It is no coincidence that their recorded beliefs were based more on social status than on ethnicity. Rather than bar certain ethnic groups, some gangs brought together the displaced of all colors and occupations.

In 1811 a gang was captured that consisted of nothing less than the Europeans Antonio and Juan, the Oriental native of Chincha, Blanco, the friend of el Segatón, Mariano Marchan, black Joaquín from the Biejo sugar mill, Francisco Negro from the Puente estate, José Salas, Antonio Barrionuevo, known as Antonaso, Agustín Lesama, an old mulato, the *zambo* known by the learned woodcutter of Bocanegra, Indian Lucas of the Monte de Santa Rosa, and the black Josef Carabali, an alfalfa muleteer.[66]

Assistance to the poor, downtrodden, and imprisoned could be seen as the concrete expression of social concerns.[67] A short history of what happened in the Chillón valley illustrates not only this new social dimension, but also the manner in which maroons, slaves, and other social groups organized their relations, conversed, and communicated. Not everything that highwaymen needed to survive was found in sufficient quantity and at the appropriate moment in the knapsacks of travelers. For this reason, they would negotiate for whatever else they could secure through owners of *tambos* in exchange for protection, a strategy similar to the one wealthy *limeños* used. It was through these contacts—with merchants and shopkeepers—that the neighboring population could communicate with these gangs. And this dialogue did indeed exist.

On one of their raids the bandits stole chickens from a *mestiza*. The *tambo*'s owner, a Spaniard, described the events:

Owing to the fact that I am in charge of the *tambo* called Chillón, a *mestiza* named María came to me and told me that the stated blacks had taken some hens and chickens from her, and that since the aforementioned blacks intended to go to the *tambo* to secure food, I should tell them to hand over the chickens. She was poor and in need and advised me to give the said blacks something so they would agree to hand over the stated chickens. As a result of the request made of me by the aforementioned person, I summoned the black Antonio, who was the first to arrive at the *tambo* after this miserable girl had given up the chickens, and he responded that he would send the fowl, but only under the condition that I give him four reales because he was in need, and that I give a peso to another black, his companion, the one who would bring the fowl later. Thus it was that considering the good of the *mestiza* and in virtue of her request, I gave him the four reales; soon afterward the other black arrived, with fourteen chickens and hens in all, ten live and four dead, and I gave him the peso.[68]

Although we have descriptive gauges to measure the composition and frequency of the actions of maroons and brigand groups (also see Flores Galindo 1990, Aguirre 1990), exact figures are elusive. Furthermore, to assess their numbers we must weigh accusations of banditry and maroonage that may owe more to fears than to objective and observational interest. In many of the cases examined we have seen how a slave's departure from the hacienda—even with a paper signed by the owner or *mayordomo*—could, in the hands of a soldier or urban owner, be taken for maroonage or banditry. In spite of this, there seems to be a consensus on two points. First, that maroonage and brigand bands (of mounted rebels, guerrillas, or maroons, the differences are not very clear) increased during the struggles for independence; and second, that brigandage in general (whatever its social connotations) seems, in the words of Flores Galindo, "to distance itself from the conscious history of the popular classes, reducing itself only to the expression of social malaise, a sign of the deterioration of the haciendas, the beginning of the commercial crisis and the political decomposition that preceded independence" (1990, 67).

The experiences of these groups during the independence period are pivotal to our general assertion that manumission through self-purchase accelerated. Bands of fugitives grew, in part because slaves did not want to join either army and there was no other option but to flee haciendas. Slaves felt increasing uncertainty, as from every direction came promises of freedom intended to gain their support. Occasionally, these gangs of maroons managed to ally or associate themselves with bands of bandits with more diverse ethnic composition and during the struggles for independence to become more cohesive, and dangerously autonomous, forces. Some of the leaders of the guerrillas and mounted rebels (such as General Miller in the south and Commander Francisco Paula Otero in the central highlands) incorporated these heterogeneous bands into their ranks. The most important bands were located in provinces nearby Lima and could block and stash in their headquarters supplies of food and munitions headed for Lima.

The English traveler Proctor described the extent of this situation:

This species of force [i.e., bands of guerrillas] was first encouraged by General San Martín and produced such an effect by its intrepidity that the men of which it was composed actually sometimes defeated large bodies of regular troops. They received no pay, but were allowed to plunder from the enemy wherever they could fall upon them. Nor were their depredations as may be supposed, confined to the Spaniards; for ere long they degenerated into bands of licensed and organized robbers, under the lax and defective police of the patriot governors: any wild idle fellow who had a little spirit and a great deal of disinclination to useful employment had nothing to do but to set up as a guerrilla official, or as he was termed, Capitán de Montoneros.[69]

These groups became the "terror of civilized society" and sporadically appeared, always acting beyond the control of the current governor or military commander.

On the whole, the experiences of soldiers, bandits, and fugitives cover the diversity of the black and slave population's military options. The distinctions between what lay within the law and what was outside it grew increasingly tenuous, even though the military tried to locate fugitive havens and combat the maroons. The haziest distinctions were those assembled and coordinated throughout the struggles for independence. The experiences of the black population during the struggles for independence—spread among patriots and royalists, brigands, guerrillas, and mounted rebels—generated greater fluidity in the relations of mutual aid and support. Slaves' experiences and insurrectionary desires were absorbed into a changing system. In 1851—three years before slavery was abolished—fewer people were frightened by rumors of slave uprisings, "rebellious slaves" were sentenced to minimal punishments, and soon warnings of slave insurrections were revealed as little more than rhetorical flourishes to disguise the interests of white political factions (Blanchard 1991).

Patterns of Manumission in Lima's Hinterland

Amid the enormous variety of connections between countryside and city that we have seen, two questions remain. The first relates to the frequency of slave manumission on the hacienda and in the city; and the second concerns the significance and the trajectory of the changes.

The notarial record books and the *cartas de libertad* illustrate the frequency and methods of manumission (Table 8).[70] If we take 1830 and 1850 as parameters, we observe an increase in the percentage of manumissions of slaves coming from haciendas: it went from 13.1 percent in 1830 to 21.0 percent in 1850 of all recorded manumissions in Lima. Rural manumissions were on the rise but urban manumissions predominated and explain slaves' desire to abandon the hacienda and their strategies to relocate. Around 1840, in the years in which slave owners tried to reverse the trend toward manumission, the relative percentage of manumissions dropped; only about 5 percent of total manumissions were recorded in the rural area.

Self-purchase was the most common method of manumission on the haciendas and increased over the decades (from 41.2 percent in 1830 to 50.0 percent in 1850), and other methods (a master's grant of freedom—often conditional—and the intervention of relatives) declined. Among these, the mother intervened more and more often, as we have seen in the cases examined.

In the twenty years before slavery was abolished, the number of *cartas de libertad* registered in the notarial record books dropped in absolute terms, from 130 in 1830 to 106 in 1850 (the change was even greater for 1840: only 77 appear). But the speed of manumission was almost the same in 1830 and 1850, rising from 2.2 to 2.3, as the number of slaves decreased.[71] The figures from the censuses of 1836 and 1845 show that Lima's slave population decreased from 10.4 percent to 6.9 percent of its total population. If we project the speed of manumissions over the percentage decrease of slaves, we see that the records of the *cartas de libertad* reflect the rhythm of decrease of the slave population in almost the same fashion. In other words, they not only verify the reliability of the figures but also show that slaves, through their own volition or ability to maneuver, were the agents central to this process. In 1850, acts by slaves—the total number of manumissions by self-purchase or purchase by a relative—account for 90.9 percent of all rural manumissions.[72]

Even if the figures for Lima are above the average, it is not surprising that in broader terms, the conditions in Lima coincide with tendencies recorded elsewhere in Latin America:

> A surprisingly high percentage of manumitted slaves were Africans in urban manumissions from Mexico City to Buenos Aires. . . . From 40 to 60% of the ex-slaves purchased their freedom, and one-third have been granted theirs free and unconditionally by their masters. The remaining 10 to 20% of the manumitted slaves had been granted conditional freedom, mostly having to do with continued demand for familial service. All recent studies have found that approximately 2/3 of the manumitted were women (from 60 to 67%) and few were found to be 45 years of age or older. (Klein 1986, 227)

Although maroonage and banditry were ways that some slaves used to free themselves from labor on the haciendas, day-to-day opportunities and attempts at permanent negotiation were the core responses of slaves on the road to freedom; these were the slave population's long-term options.

Maroonage and brigandage were considered crimes, subject to intermittent massive repression by governments—between 1760 and 1809 and between 1836 and 1839, coinciding toward the end of the colonial period with final attempts to strengthen ethnic segregation (Moerner 1969, 225) and in the 1830s to reinforce order on the haciendas—until slavery was abolished in 1854.[73] Yet many times what the authorities termed an escape was nothing more than a search for protection (by a godfather, for example), a change of jobs (from rural work to day labor), or a protest against excessive or unlawful punishment. Slaves were attempting to deal with the conditions of rural slavery in *legally* defensible ways that owed as much to their involvement in the independence struggles as to their awareness of marches and countermarches against laws that were always imprecise and vague enough to permit the extreme alternative of escape.

The likelihood that slaves would use the methods of day-to-day and permanent negotiation we have described depended on various factors: occupational situation in Lima, contacts with persons (free or slave) who had urban experience or were willing to help, and circumstances on the hacienda. The actions of the Defensor de Menores, who represented the slaves in several of the cases examined, and—even more important—their chances of arrival in the parish of San Lázaro, where both social and working contacts (even with maroons) were established, illustrate that slaves quickly grasped opportunities for moving from countryside to city life.

Like their counterparts elsewhere in Latin America, female slaves were the earliest and most fortunate travelers from the hacienda to freedom in the city. They owed their success to individual strengths and to a family strategy intended to benefit all its members. As we have noted, the bond between mother and children could survive the painful setbacks and obstacles of the journey; on the hacienda female slaves were judged less productive and more costly (Haitin 1983, 167). Less useful on the hacienda, women had better possibilities for work and friendship in the city.

On the whole, countryside-city connections indicate a blurry image of the rural-urban boundaries and may help explain those "tricky boundaries" in the census information. At the same time, this haziness perpetuated mechanisms of vertical ascent (the slave population's internal differentiation) and geographic-horizontal mobility. In slave patterns of mobility, agents appear (family members in Lima, relatives of masters, state officials, bandits and maroons, owners of *tambos*) who interceded or acted unwittingly in favor of slaves. Thus, given the vast array of conditions and actors, we cannot think of rural slavery as the defining factor of the prevailing slave relations. The rural sphere without the urban, particularly in the context we have seen, is a partial truth.[74]

Finally there is room for reflection on the significance of the success of slaves in arranging rural-urban relations and on what the overarching implications of this dynamic implied with respect to slave relations in *limeño* society.

We have seen that, given the resistance of individual slaves and couples and the support proffered by authorities upon satisfaction of the *conque*—as well as slaves' preference for the city—masters could not simply transfer their slaves from the urban to the rural realm. Only in cases judged as extreme could the punishment of relocation be ordered. Apart from the recorded opposition, an owner's greater or lesser control depended on the conditions on the hacienda (which as we have seen were varied) and on the relations slaves established with the city. All forces were not equal: what prevailed was movement from the countryside to the city.[75]

In the rural sphere we record a great variety of productive units, from units where relative control over the labor force existed, to cases of an owner's depravity or utter neglect (interpreted by the contemporaries as alarming). The margins of "rebellion" diminish if we evaluate the priorities of slaves in terms of their access to freedom. The contemporaries' rendition seems exaggerated. A related issue is to determine if the transfer of slaves to the urban realm could be considered part of this "chaos," which contemporaries spoke of so readily. If it was masters who assigned slaves to earn daily wages, they passed the costs of upkeep to the slaves themselves or to another master, by putting the slaves into a socioeconomic framework better suited to exploit (and control) their work. Along with Scott (1988, 31), I believe that the appearance of "chaos" did not necessarily coincide with the system's collapse. In the short term, at least, slaves' options could bring about new contradictions, which could even revive the slave system. In addition, from a logic of urban expansion—which occurred at a still relatively slow pace in Lima—change could generate an increasing demand for services (Algranti 1988, 23), especially if other ethnic groups sold more expensive services or pursued other circuits of consumption, and if the ethnic-occupational structure were very rigid. Consequently, slave owners had incentives to hire out slaves' labor.

All such expansion and change eventually involved a certain amount of chaos and entailed above all the rationalization of a system, with greater individual exploitation, and not its eradication. The question is, thus, if the transfer from a hacienda to earn daily wages in Lima was the result of a greater rationalization of the system. And it is at this point that we must restate an apparent paradox, between more daily wages and less control (rather than more slavery), which we can resolve if we evaluate the logic of the system *not* from the interests of the owners but from the viewpoint of the slaves.

We have no evidence to show that masters transferred their slaves to the urban area. More likely the slaves were the ones who took the initiative, although a slave's advancing years might make this alternative the most rational option from an owner's perspective. Our assertion challenges the hypothesis that a decline in productivity in Lima's rural zones caused a relocation of slaves to the city and that the transformations of the slave system reflected a greater rationalization by slaveholders to safeguard a threatened system. In actuality, what took place (at least in the first two decades of the nineteenth century) was an increase in the number of slaves on big haciendas. Furthermore, the generalization of rural stagnation in the Lima valley at the end of the eighteenth century and the beginning of the nineteenth—as Haitin (1983, 145) points out—is also questionable.[76] Another fact that contradicts the view that it was masters who initiated the hiring-out system is the gender composition inside the haciendas. The ratio of men to women documents a conscious policy of retention of the work force and of an aversion to its transfer to Lima. A complementary argument along the same lines is what has been termed in other regions as the "peasant gap," the cultivation of basic foodstuffs that simultaneously solved three problems for owners: it gave slaves food, secured the labor force, and served as a counterweight to the expansion of commercial crops for the international market (Cardoso 1988). We have seen that in Lima, and beyond Lima (in Huaito, for example), slaves used this peasant gap not only to solve problems for *hacendados* and to meet a rising urban demand but also converted it into a base of accumulation within the hacienda through the supply of local and regional markets.

What owners did in a marginal fashion (for example, by paying their slaves) and slaves did in a substantive manner (by filling the "subsistence gap," earning wages, buying freedom) was to introduce a component of monetary interdependence into the relations on the hacienda. This interdependence eroded the basis of the slaveholding authority, practically at the level of interpersonal relations. Perhaps the most dramatic expressions of this relation between money, slave price, and freedom were payments on credit and reductions of a slave's value, which were considered a posteriori payments of outstanding daily wages. All things considered, these are also very specific aspects of the lengthy processes of formation of both the rural and urban labor markets. In the following chapter we use the same perspective—that of the slaves—to observe how distinctly urban processes unfolded in both a similar and a contrasting manner.

Chapter Three

In the City

We have watched many members of the black population—free or slave—travel from the country to the city. For individuals and families alike success or failure depended on a multiplicity of strategies and links. The Lasmanuelos family gave us an example that many other slaves traced; now we turn to their experience in the city to compare their aims and strategies on the way toward freedom with those they used in Lima. For men and women the experiences of journey and arrival were distinct. Economic and racial heterogeneity, as well as the slaves' ties to the haciendas, the city, and their owners, underlie the differences. What circumstances awaited them and how did they live?

In 1792 the city of Lima had 56,627 inhabitants and 3,641 houses, of which 2,797 belonged to private individuals and the rest to religious entities, including hospitals and *cofradías* (mutual-aid societies or sodalities established by the Church and dedicated to the cult of specific saints). Life revolved around the small marketplaces and seven parishes (Bromley and Barbagelata 1945, 76 ff.). The census taken by Egaña in 1790 (cited in Romero 1980, 31), which considered only those living in the precinct of the city of Lima, found that of a total of 3,287 persons in monasteries and similar residences 1,060 were slaves.[1] In 1828 the reported number of houses was 3,380 and of entrances, 10,605 (Haitin 1983, 102).[2] An earthquake that occurred in 1828 probably caused the number of houses to decrease, even though the number of entrances increased. In 1857, two years after public gas lighting first illuminated Lima (Fuentes 1866, 506), the population had almost doubled, with a concomitant increase in demand for goods and services. Lima's black population represented 44.7 percent of the total inhabitants in 1792; by 1818 this number had decreased to 38 percent. And more than a century later, in the 1940 census, the number of blacks recorded on the national level would reach only the figure of 29,054—a statistic that equals less than 0.5 percent of the total population (Labarthe 1955, 15). Intermarriage and aspirations to whiter skin explain the long-term diminution of the black population. During our period, however, other factors account for the decrease in this population.

In 1792 slaves represented 25.6 percent of Lima's residents and only 15.8 percent in 1818, dropping to 10.5 percent in 1836, and to 6.9 percent in 1845. The gradual decline resembled that recorded for the viceroyalty and republic: in 1792 slaves were 3.7 percent of the total population, in 1854 only 1.1 percent (Jacobsen 1974, 82–84). Although the traffic in slaves began in the sixteenth century and increased throughout the colonial period, the slave population's natural growth did not compensate for the high mortality and low fertility rates or for self-manumission. The demographic shifts suggest that Peruvian slavery was a system highly accessible to social mobility. If we consider the reduction of the black population in Lima's rural sector after the wars of independence and also remember that a substantial part of this population relocated to the city of Lima, we recognize that the rate of manumission after 1821 continued to grow.

The Complexion of Black Society

Urban society offers more fertile ground for social conflict than the countryside ever can. Its internal divisions result equally from authorities' strategies of divide and conquer and from the beliefs of the varying actors involved in this process. The city offers more opportunities for internal differentiation than the countryside, both because of its complex social relations and because of its organization of labor.

A society is never homogeneous in a racial, cultural, social, or economic sense. As the criteria to determine and shape segregation develop, they define not only how persons will interact but also what form society will take. The black population found in segregation by skin color a means of conscious opposition to the dominant white sector and a mechanism of individual and collective survival. Slave and free black populations developed hierarchies and perceptions that differentiated darker-skinned blacks from lighter individuals, poorer from richer, and free blacks from slaves. In Lima, as in other places, ethnic diversity among blacks and differences in social status explain the absence of slave revolts (Karasch 1987, 325), or of revolts by all blacks against the domination of whites.

At the bottom of the black social pyramid were the *bozales*, newly arrived from Africa. They were the group least touched by the *criollo* experience; white owners preferred them for their docility. Even the *criollo* blacks who had lived in the colonial territory for some time described *bozales* as less refined. General Miller, who wrote his memoirs in 1829, noted that "the black *criollo* believes himself superior to his brother brought from Africa." At the apex of this pyramid were the *quarterones* or *quinterones*, who thought of themselves as white and had the greatest chances of obtaining freedom. Lighter-skinned women were the ones most likely to marry *mestizos* or whites.

The lot of *bozales* was not enviable. Those who survived the high mortality rate of the Atlantic trade to be unloaded at their port of destination were handed over to the representative of slave *asentistas* (who held long-term contracts from the Crown to buy or sell goods or services) or, barring their presence, to the boat's captain.[3] Eventually, slaves were transferred to the port's *barracones*, where the conditions were often more horrifying than those on the boat; many slaves took their last breath here. The survivors were taken from quarantine in the *barracones* to a central location where they were grouped according to size, physical condition, and gender. They underwent a medical examination so that a report about their health and skills could be written up; the objective was to appraise them and classify their respective duty payments. This process, referred to as *palmeo*—literally, measuring by hands—culminated with the sear of an iron brand that served as permanent proof that all slaves had been brought into the country legally. Sometimes this procedure was repeated with the *asentista*'s emblem in order to prevent the theft of slaves before they were sold. Once these formalities were concluded, blacks were ready for sale. Petty merchants from near and far came to the marketplace; slaves would accompany them on yet another journey to their final destination: house, hacienda, trade, mine, or textile mill (Rout 1977, 69 ff.).

This process fragmented the identity of black inhabitants. First, violent removal from the natal environment and subsequent encounters with men and women belonging to different African cultures weakened a slave's chance for communication with other human beings. Next, dispersal of the slaves to different units of production in the colonial territory brought them face to face with other Africans and with an additional network of laborers from distinct and equally disparate origins: indigenous and *casta*. The dual rupture required, as a response, the recreation of lost social spaces. The more fortunate *bozales* were those who remained in the urban environment. The city, more than the countryside, offered a realm where slaves might keep any social contacts established during the passage, and whatever they still held of their African identity and culture. A particular tribal group might predominate on the transatlantic journey; the preservation of these ties would ease the reordering of slaves' social space in the new setting. Reorganization along tribal lines could take a long time. During this process many slaves joined *cofradías*, where members could worship a particular saint within their cultural and ethnic traditions. The *cofradías* fulfilled a broader social function in helping blacks reconstruct their identity. But even within the refuge of family relations or *cofradías*, conflicts always beset the process, intrinsic conflicts that hampered collective endeavors. Through an examination of incidents within the *cofradías* and (in chapter 4) of matrimonial strife, we observe the different levels of conflict that simultaneously expressed notions of hierarchy—in class, ethnicity, and gender—within black society at large.

In 1615 there were fifteen *cofradías* in Lima, while in the rest of the viceregal territory, the black presence in cities and towns was so low that the creation of other *cofradías* was not warranted. Until approximately 1630, *cofradías* received any and all blacks; twenty years later we find that three groups existed, differentiated by skin color. The first rupture occurred between *criollo ladinos* and *bozales*. The former had learned Spanish and were familiar with Spanish customs. They insisted on breaking away from the black *bozales*. The second rupture arose between *mulatos* and *criollo ladinos* and resulted from the pressures of a third black generation that had established sexual and matrimonial alliances with women from the indigenous population. The monopolization of power within the *cofradías* by whiter *mulatos* paralleled their increasingly superior placement in other arenas of society. These ruptures slowly transformed the *cofradía* into an institution that housed a black elite (Bowser 1977, 307–311). Almost always the most visible manifestations of internal rupture were racial; racial tensions accompanied any competition over jobs within black society.[4]

The social and individual function of the *cofradías*, as well as the relations between owners and *cofradías*, are illustrated in the account of the traveler Stevenson:

In the suburbs of San Lázaro are *cofradías* or clubs belonging to the different castes or nations of the Africans, where they hold their meetings in a very orderly manner, generally on a Sunday afternoon; and if any of the royal family belonging to the respective nation is to be found in the city, he or she is called the King or Queen of the *cofradía*, and treated with every mark of respect. I was well acquainted with a family in Lima, in which there was an old female slave who had lived with them for upwards of fifty years, and who was the acknowledged Queen of the Mandingos, she being, according to their statement, a princess. On particular days she was conducted from the house of her master by a number of black people, to the *cofradía*, dressed as gaudily as possible; for this purpose her young mistresses would lend her jewels to a considerable amount, besides which the poor old woman was bedizened with a profusion of artificial flowers, feathers and other ornaments. Her master had provided her a silver sceptre, and this necessary appendage of royalty was on such occasions always carried by her. It has often gratified my best feelings, when *Mama Rosa* was seated on the porch of her master's house to see her subjects come and kneel before her, to ask her blessing and kiss her hand. I have followed them to the *cofradía* and have seen her majesty seated on her throne, and go through the ceremony of royalty without a *blush*. . . .

The walls of the *cofradías* are ornamented with likenesses in fresco of the different royal personages who have belonged to them. The purpose of the institution is to help those to good masters, who have been so unfortunate as to meet with bad ones; but as a master can object to selling his slave, unless he proves by law that he has been cruelly treated, which is very difficult or next to impossible, the *cofradías* raise a fund by contributions, and free the slave, to which the master cannot object; but this slave now becomes tacitly the slave of the *cofradía* and must return by installments the money paid for his manumission.[5]

Indoctrination and religion certainly did not cease to be the central objectives of the *cofradía*, but shortly after their diffusion into the New World *cofradías* also assumed a social role and were helping to liberate slaves from their owners, advancing money for manumission or mediating as the slaves searched for a new owner, extending credit for the most abused and discouraged members of the slave population, and serving as a temporary refuge. At the same time *cofradías* became a cultural emporium for the black population's most privileged sector and imitated the larger society's dominant layers, which in turn often supported these associations. This support often led owners to loan clothes and jewels and to attend the ceremonies as spectators. But many other slaves chose not to turn to the *cofradías*. An almost endless litigation filed by slaves in their quest for freedom did not mention the intermediation of *cofradías* or note the case of any *limeño* hacienda slave who knocked at the door of a *cofradía*.

Despite the attractions of their elite status within black society, *cofradías* also reproduced within their ranks the divisions of black society. In theory each *cofradía* corresponded to one African ethnic group and excluded the rest but in practice racial justification often meant that the whitest among the blacks occupied the highest posts in a *cofradía*'s internal hierarchy, or economic motive made the richest into creditors for its needier members. Above all, *cofradías* accommodated the master-slave relation. They came to function as a parallel judicial system; owners could turn to the associations not only to purchase new slaves but also to request that their slaves be punished for robbery, idleness, cursing, or running away (Bastide 1969, 90). For owners, an additional advantage of their intermediation was that owners could occasionally avoid the lengthy petitions and high costs of official court litigation.

Cofradías exist today and still have an essentially black complexion. We find *cofradías* described by travelers at the beginning of the nineteenth century, by which time racial splits seem to have subsided, perhaps because slaves had more possibilities of moving up the social ladder without becoming white. At this point different criteria began to determine the occupant of a *cofradía* post: the preoccupation with pigmentation gave way to a more intense interest in legal status. As these positions carried power—both in ecclesiastical and social realms—age and legal status, or rather, experience and seniority came to be perceived as central characteristics for the leaders of *cofradías*.

Even the *mulato* elite, which had the resources to manumit a slave so that he or she could escape from a bad owner or to finance the festivities that the *cofradía* life-style implied, also tried—albeit timidly—to secure positions of control. The hierarchies within the *cofradía* were expressed visually in the physical placement of the brothers and sisters in reunions (Fuentes 1866, 83). Members avidly maintained these internal hierarchies, even at the cost of having to resort to white judicial intermediation. A sequence of events that began in 1812 with the death of the queen of the Congos-Mondongos *cofradía* illustrates the shift from criteria based primarily on color or tribal affiliation to ones based on legal standing.

In accordance with the traditions and customs of the Congos-Mondongos *cofradía*, the successor to the queen should have already occupied the post of the queen's captain-assistant. Being the captain-assistant implied considerable expenditures, as it was this person's charge to finance the *cofradía*'s festivities and events. In fact, these payments had more weight than putative or bona fide descent from an African king or prince (which Stevenson suggests), and the privilege of becoming queen or king could be bought. However, in 1812 the Congos-Mondongos *cofradía* (consisting of twenty-nine persons), in opposition to this unwritten law, divided over the question of the throne's successor. The majority opted not to elect the present captain-assistant but another queen who had one decisive attribute: she was free. In response to this decision on the part of the *cofradía*'s members, María Santos Puente, the dethroned, presented an appeal before the civil court in order to protest what she perceived to be a divestiture of her authority:

On the grounds of being a member of the Congos-Mondongos *cofradía*, I declare that I have been the queen's captain and assistant for twenty-five years with the hope of being successor to her post, because the deceased queen promised me as much, in front of witnesses . . . and additionally I paid the funeral costs, without any other motive than anticipation of the promised recompense. In the meantime I supplicate that in the name of justice the post be given to me, or that the money I spent be returned to me.

A few days later, María requested that several of her witnesses be interrogated in accordance with a questionnaire she had presented. The witnesses, seven in all, responded affirmatively to the following question: "State if it is true that examples exist of others of the nation who being slaves just as I, have been elected queen; that due to an unjust mishap, the queenship was rashly taken from me and given to Manuela who is free."

María Santos was aware of the reason for her removal and was relying upon the *cofradía*'s traditions in order to reclaim the post of queen. At this point there was a long abeyance in the trial. The public prosecutor stated:

This silence, for the interested party as much as for the other individuals in the *cofradía* and group, who are inventing the farce of the election of a queen (which might perhaps be of importance to them) causes the responding minister to think that this is not a case of law and private interests but pertains rather to the public order and the preservation of the customs and practices that these blacks are permitted, and in whose possession they should remain provided the public peace not be offended.[6]

Since the minister no longer knew if what he had in his hands was a farce or a case concerning the public order, he appealed to the *cofradía*'s own traditions that had until now guaranteed the public peace. Nonetheless, the votes of the *cofradía*'s members went against tradition. The result of the elections, after this run-around in the official courts, was twenty-one votes for and seven against the free queen. No one returned the invested money to María, the deposed captain-assistant. The dream of becoming queen had left her penniless. Instead of purchasing freedom with her money, she had financed the *cofradía* and kept its hierarchy and structure intact. This defeat was not only a legal loss. Settling this controversy of succession cost the *cofradía* approximately half of the contributions that *María* claimed she had made over the past twenty-five years. According to her, her expenditures had reached ninety-two pesos—at a rate of four pesos a year—an amount that the elected queen was supposed to return to her, in addition to sixteen pesos "for taking to the streets the standard of the nation, with nine more pesos for the price and release of a barrow."

The breach of long-standing traditions at once reveals more intense yearnings and greater chances for freedom that existed. Substantial support for these desires was slaves' ability to earn daily wages and to save a portion of them. By 1859 the Congos-Mondongos *cofradía* had been abandoned, and the Merced convent, which had declared itself proprietor, was embroiled in a judicial dispute over the site. Moreover, there was no queen.[7] In 1866 sixteen *cofradías*, each affiliated with an African tribe, were still recorded (Fuentes 1866, 83), but over the course of time the *cofradías*—as the institution of slavery declined—lost their social function for slaves and their disciplinary usefulness for owners. Long before slavery was abolished, the black population's core institution had shifted its priorities.

Seen in this manner, the changing visions within the *cofradías* reflected one facet of the black population's perception of itself, a facet that escaped Stevenson: he depicted poor creatures with pretensions of royalty. In a context in which blacks could obtain freedom relatively easily, there was no reason to choose a slave queen. Consistent with broader political and social changes, Lima's blacks were willing to throw aside long-held customs. Perhaps the increasing presence of free blacks also made *cofradía* members feel more represented by a free queen. Times had changed and everyone had observed the events in the Congo-Mondongos *cofradía*. More concretely, the value that participants in the election put on the status of freedom undoubtedly influenced slaves' decisions to accumulate and to try out their own variants on the association's message.

Similar antagonisms would express themselves in another type of organization: the guild, in which the black and *casta* populations predominated. Some guilds were formed exclusively by people of color. When the mayoral guild election of carriage-makers and handbarrow-carriers took place in Lima in 1774, the *bozales* made it known that they did not wish to be controlled by an "enemy," which was their label for the *criollo* who was its leader. In retribution, the *criollos* accused the *bozales* of "a callous spirit and lack of obedience." Additionally, the *criollos* portrayed the *bozales* as inept for labor because of their "clumsiness and lack of reason and conduct." As in other guilds where similar quarrels had occurred, the solution to this concrete problem was to name two mayors: one a *bozal*, the other a *criollo* (Romero 1980, 22). In contrast to what happened in the *cofradías*, which excluded entire groups of blacks from official positions, the guild kept its occupational exclusion by dividing internal governance along racial lines.

In a more general sense, the criteria used to establish social relations were ethnicity, wealth, and legal status. Beyond the events within the Congos-Mondongos *cofradía* and the guilds, smaller-scale incidents embodied the tensions in society. Scuffles and street brawls between blacks, confrontations between neighbors, small purchases in corner shops, or broken street lamps could all bring about strings of epithets. And the worst insult was one that invoked a racial or economic condition inferior to that purported. In one such altercation, a woman named La Camacho called an acquaintance (a man who was perhaps more than a simple acquaintance) "a big black mule, and fists were drawn." Immediately, "La Camacho, [who] was a *zamba* by self-description, quarreled with the black mule's lover." Matters ended when the lover bit a finger off La Camacho's hand.[8] More than a few defamation trials were litigated and more than one angry black was presented with a hospital invoice for an amputated finger. However, what underlay all these seemingly insignificant quarrels were the deeply entrenched notions of hierarchy that prevailed among blacks. They were more than skin-deep.

On a different plane, social distances and hierarchies were also expressed in the city's geography and its slaves' work there.

Distribution of the Slave Population

Lima was and is a city of barrios with easily detectable social and economic characteristics. The barrios, districts, and parishes of wealthy people were easily distinguishable from the less white and less wealthy areas. Slaves moved about in all these areas because many lived outside the owner's household—depending on their trade and the work arrangements between them and their masters. The San Lázaro parish, for example, was considered to be an area of black residence, and we know that the links between slaves on the haciendas of Lima's hinterland and the residents of this parish were crucial elements of the trajectory between countryside and city. This parish appears to have been a place of arrival, residence, and meeting for blacks from all walks of life. Santa Ana, by contrast, located within the walls of the city of Lima, was a parish composed of whites but had a large number of domestic slaves.

A residential census of the Santa Ana parish, dated 1808, indicates that this parish housed 11,432 inhabitants of principally Spanish descent in 1813.[9] This census includes the number of slaves per household, which permits us to measure the distribution of slaves per residence and per owner in Lima or, in other words, the relative concentration of each group. Unfortunately, the census recorded only 3,460 persons, 30.0 percent of the parish's population, and 6.4 percent of the total urban population. The slave population makes up 22 percent of the total in this sample and might indicate that each fifth resident of Santa Ana owned a slave. The 3,460 inhabitants were grouped into 898 dwellings of which 187 housed 763 slaves (Table 9). Of the various types, houses and cottages (small houses) were large enough to hold domestic slaves (74.8 percent), whereas apartments, *interiores* (usually smaller rooms within a house, sublet to third parties), and single rooms (11.2 percent) were smaller, crowded residential units where slaves could hardly live with a master. The presence of market shops and stores indicates the existence of some type of mer-

TABLE 9. *Distribution of Slaves in Santa Ana: 1808*

Type	Household with Slave	(%)
house	113	(60.4)
cottage	27	(14.4)
store/shop	25	(13.3)
apartment	11	(5.9)
interior	6	(3.2)
single room	4	(2.1)
orchard house	1	(0.7)
	187	(100.0)

Source. AA, Sección Estadística, Santa Ana.

cantile activity involving slaves (13.3 percent); orchard houses were the parish's more rural element (0.7 percent).

Ascertaining the number of slaves per owner helps us clarify the dispersion and concentration of the black population in Santa Ana. Among the parish's households, 108 (57.8 percent) had one to two slaves, 44 (28.9 percent) three to six slaves, 10 (9.1 percent) had from seven to 12 slaves, 7 (3.7 percent) from 13 to 37, and one, Lima's mint, had 60 slaves (0.5 percent).[10] Thus it works out that 57.8 percent of the residential units counted in the 1808 census contained 19 percent of the slaves; 28.7 percent (small to medium units) had 31.3 percent; 9.1 percent (medium to large units) had 20.2 percent; and 3.7 percent (large units) contained 21.6 percent of the slaves (Figure 2). A high percentage of households in Santa Ana reported one or two slaves. This percentage increases if we add the medium-sized ones. Our bet is that the fewer slaves per owner, the greater the tendency to assign slaves to daily-wage labor, and the greater the dependence on slaves' earnings. Lima's nobility could most likely be found in the middle and upper categories of slave owners; although they too occasionally hired their slaves out in exchange for a daily sum, they usually considered their slaves part of their retinue and social status. Their slaves, therefore, would be placed in domestic service. If we extrapolate on Santa Ana's figures for the city as a whole, we would estimate that 20 percent of Lima's households had slaves, and that approximately 10 percent of Lima's households lived off the income earned by slaves.

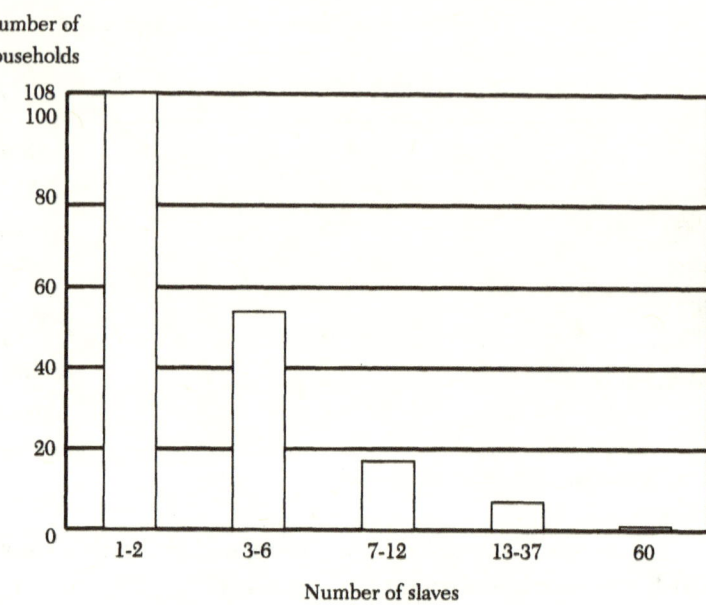

Figure 2. Distribution of slaves per household in Santa Ana: 1808.

Thus urban society included a high number of individuals who depended on slaves' wages for survival itself—even to the point of selling their only slave to avoid the anticipated disgrace of a pauper's burial.[11]

From the viewpoint of slaveholders—discreetly poor or prosperous—the hiring-out system was lucrative, though contemporaries condemned its "idleness." An owner's profits depended on the number of slaves, their age and health, the arrangement the owner made with those who were interested in hiring his or her slave, and profits hinged on the slave's "willingness" and aptitude for the given work. Despite the belief that a slave was a good investment (sometimes the only one possible), an owner knew its risks. Calculations for regions other than Lima have shown that the hiring-out system began to be profitable only when an owner possessed at least twenty slaves (da Silva 1988, 109). For Lima, the Defensor de Menores articulated the reasoning as he evaluated a father's hopes to invest money he had received to buy a slave whose daily wages would assure the rearing of the prospective owner's son in the capital. The Defensor de Menores evinced skepticism for several reasons:

The first is that when such daily wages reach no more than four or six pesos a month, it is not possible to meet the costs of food, shoes, clothing, and schooling [for the child]: The second that the daily wages of slaves tend to have the effect of causing debt, and much more so if women are involved. Given the uncertain outcome one cannot even consider that scant income: The third is that if it is necessary to pay for the treatment of the sick slave or if death accrues, everything will go to pot.[12]

With great assurance, the judge was dismissing the father's proposal. But can we take the judge's evaluations at face value? Mendiburu records a daily-wage arrangement that would yield annual interest—which fluctuated between 5 and 20 percent (1987, 39)—on an owner's investment equal to a slave's purchase price and comparable to earnings from other investments (i.e., in land, mercantile activity, factories). Several documents confirm that at the close of the eighteenth century the minimum daily wages given to owners by apprenticed slaves amounted to three reales. It has also been noted that the slave day laborers tended to work during the day—at jobs assigned by their owners or perhaps searching for employment—and returned at night to the homes of their masters, "to be of service to them in whatever capacity they might offer." The capital slaves acquired during holidays, which exceeded that earned during weekdays, was for the slaves' use and for the purchase of clothing. This pecuniary source allowed slaves some freedom; however, it also represented a way in which owners transferred a portion of their obligations to the slave. During the workday the slave ate in the home of his or her current employer. This meant that, especially when the day-labor contract was temporary, that whoever was exploiting the slave's labor power would have little interest in giving the slave an adequate diet; contracts of the time stated that "all of this is observed as firmly established practice and custom in all these kingdoms."[13]

In 1828 a daily-wage guarantee recorded before the notary Manuel Suárez noted that "According to established practice slaves are commonly obligated to pay their owners for the right of the daily wage only 1 real for each 100 [of their value]."[14] Thus, if a slave's *conque* listed his or her value as 300 pesos, then his or her daily wage would amount to 3 reales (see also Fuentes 1867, 191). And in this case 5 to 20 percent of a slave's annual earnings (as calculated by Mendiburu) represented 30–110 pesos each year—based on a daily wage of 3 reales and annual work of 300 days—which in turn equaled a slave's high average price of between 550 and 600 pesos; the average price for slaves in Lima was 280 pesos (Aguirre 1993, 102). The calculation suggests that in real terms slaves were paying more than 1 real for each 100 of their value. The earnings noted by María Baraona (from 4 to 6 pesos a month) would yield an annual income between 48 and 72 pesos.[15] Averaging both, we obtain an annual income of 65 pesos (70 pesos as calculated by Mendiburu and 60 as declared by Baraona). The proximity of the two values indicates their reliability and suggests that an owner could recuperate his or her initial investment—barring disturbances along the way—in seven or eight years. With the passing of the centuries, the recuperation period of this investment seems to have lengthened from the one Bowser (1977, 189) notes for the seventeenth century, when the owner of a specialized slave could—with a little luck—recover the value of his or her slave in two or three years. We might interpret the extension of the slaves' mortgage period as an increase in slaves' potential for accumulation, assuming that slaves kept a greater part of the earnings and the price of slaves had dropped. This outcome might, in turn, result from a real decrease in the profitability of the slave system except that other circumstances, such as the general state of the economy, explain similar outcomes.

We will never know precisely how many slaves earned daily wages for their masters, since we cannot measure the variations in daily wages over the course of the decades under consideration. Wages were determined by the arrangements between owners, or in their absence, between slaves and owners, and also by the slave's qualifications. In addition, slaves were not subject—despite contrary assertions—to regulations, but rather to the practices established in each particular case.

In spite of these limitations, we must hazard an approximation in order to understand the significance of daily wages in the lives of urban slaves and to illustrate—through the preponderance of wage labor—the exhaustion of the slave system. Three additional forms of evidence suggested by our data—of varying validity and weight—further corroborate the importance of daily wages to slaves. The first is the existence of San Lázaro as a parish in which freed and enslaved blacks lived together. They lived there because they had somehow found ways to leave the homes of their masters at night. As we will see, this option depended on the slaves' use of daily wages and of arguments about their rights to matrimonial and family life (such arguments before ecclesiastical courts gave Manolo Lasmanuelos the chance to marry Manola, a free *zamba*). The second hypothesis involves an analysis of the mechanisms through which slaves obtained freedom. Daily wages, along with robbery and eventually the lottery, were the only mechanism of accumulation to which slaves had access, especially in cases in which a slave was free of the owner's domestic control and the provided daily wages were both fixed and relatively low. The figures of the notarial record books entitled *cartas de libertad* (see Tables 1 and 8) help elucidate slaves' ability to accumulate and eventually manumit themselves.

If we base our calculations of the slave population's decrease on the censuses (1820, 1836, 1845, and 1850), we discover that from census to census the slave population fell at a rate that fluctuated between −2.4 and −2.8 percent annually (in absolute terms this rate is equal to an annual decrease of 143 slaves between 1836 and 1845, and 175 slaves between 1820 and 1836). If we project our statistical information for 1830 and 1840 onto these figures, we see that the manumissions recorded in the notarial record books represent 97 percent of the total slaves who disappeared from the statistical sampling between the first two censuses (1836–1845), and 74 percent between the second and third (1820–1836). This exercise reveals the reliability of the censuses and of the notarial record books and also demonstrates that slaves increasingly turned to notaries to record their freedom. Throughout all the years examined, the total percentages of manumissions through self-purchase or purchase by a relative (63 percent, 66 percent, and 68 percent respectively) were significantly greater than manumissions through the intervention of a third party or through a master's grant of freedom (37 percent, 45 percent, 41 percent), which—as we have seen—was not always easy to obtain (an assertion documented and valid for both rural and urban areas).

Beyond statistics, an examination of many slaves' daily life yields a third hypothesis about the prevalence and importance of daily wages amid the vicissitudes of urban existence.

Daily Wages: Part of Everyday Life

In 1819 a deceased master's testamentary wishes handed over a slave to his new owner, a priest.[16] From the convent he wrote to the archbishop, stating that despite the fact of his marriage he was forced to perform arduous labor and furthermore had been assigned on repeated occasions to work on the Monterrico hacienda close to Lima, and thus to abandon his wife. The response to the slave's first petition was that he should not be separated from his wife and children. The priest's defense revealed the range of negotiations in the case of—we should remember—a married slave: "He was placed in the kitchen to prepare the daily meals, however the difficulties that he caused owing to the vice of drunkenness were so frequent that the situation became intolerable."

It was the slave who immediately proposed to apply himself to "work, and contribute a daily wage so that the convent can replace the post with another hand." And, the priest replied, "I complied in order not to contravene the slave's wishes, and after living with free rein, because this class of people does not respect the sacred duties to which marriage is bound, his wife barely furnished me with a few reales, and he now owes me a considerable sum of money."[17] To understand how negotiations with masters were carried out, we must consider the implications of this brief dialogue.

What the slave argued was that since he was married, a transfer to another hacienda would interrupt his marital relationship. But the interference of alcohol sabotaged his kitchen labor; the priest's response illustrates that he did not wish to override the slave's wish. In short, a convenient solution for both sides was to use the slave's daily wages to pay for a replacement. In this way, the slave left the convent, sought day labor in the city, and demonstrated by the subterfuge of subverting his kitchen duties and the appeal to the Church's sacrosanct image of marriage that he could transform himself from a domestic into a day-labor slave. However, he did not keep his side of the bargain. As we see, the slave's initial negotiations were embedded in the context of the moral conditions sanctioned by the Church, a strategy that frequently led to success. Later, when a master's control had lessened, little could be done to make a slave comply with his promises. The priest argued that the wife—as he defined marital duties among slaves—was obliged to assume her husband's debts. But she did not: the male slave was deceitful, and the female slave was immoral since she did not understand her sacred duties. Yet both had succeeded on their own terms, something the priest, of course, failed to admit.

Others paid their daily wages and used their compliance to restrict an owner's arbitrary decisions. The court listened to these arguments and was inclined to favor the slaves. Manuela, a free black, lived with her husband in Bellavista. She claimed that she had punctually complied with the payment of daily wages (ten pesos a month) to her husband's owner, for which the latter allowed the couple to live together outside his household. One fine day, the owner decided to sell the husband in Pisco. Manuela would use the two-sided argument (of marriage and compliance with the payment of daily wages) in order to prevent this occurrence. And Manuela was successful in this endeavor.[18]

Marriage, family life, and daily wages appear together, whether to arrange a change of ownership, or to maintain a place in the day-labor market. Within the hundreds of records preserved in Lima's Archivo General de la Nación and Archivo Arzobispal are very few that do not explicitly refer to slaves' daily wages and marriage. This fact alone indicates their enormous reach and importance. Many of these cases were filed by owners demanding outstanding daily wages, and the owners' action tacitly gave slaves juridical personality: their response to owners' claims took place in the courtrooms.

Shrugging aside such cases, one owner declared, "It should be stated that there is no law that grants slaves the civil personality to make contracts or gives any consequent value to their contracts."[19] This statement, made at the beginning of the nineteenth century, underscores the fact that legal authority did not entirely cover the operations of day-to-day life. Both sides defended their interests in the civil and ecclesiastical courts. Slaves coveted their daily wages and sought to enlarge the degrees of relative freedom; owners tried to recover capital that the new arrangement forced them to collect.

Another gauge of the prevalence and significance of day labor were the cases that illustrate the amount of accumulation that daily wages made possible. As slaves became able to generate savings more quickly, a growing number of day-labor slaves were able to pay owners their purchase price. The slaves who encountered the greatest problems in negotiating margins of freedom, and thus in obtaining the sums needed for manumission, were those who we would generally suspect had the worst chances of earning and saving money: the *bozales*. This group of newcomers lacked the normal contacts and connections within the ranks of the slave and black population and could not make similar appeal to nonblack *padrinos*. Moreover, women—except wet nurses—also represented weaker links in the new economic and social network because they had only a remote chance of learning a trade. Although female labor was always needed, even in the midst of economic crises that contracted the male labor market, women's concentration in "female tasks" reduced their market flexibility and options, particularly because more free black women competed for the same tasks. Consequently, over the long run and the closer we come to abolition, slave women's potential for accumulation was reduced. Women and *bozales*, thus, represented fragile links of the slave-holding structure. And if it is true that both groups were successful at the urban process of accumulation, other groups with more experience and more contacts, and with varied and versatile occupational options, were even more effective in procuring their purchase price.

The tribulations of Luciana, born on the Bocanegra hacienda in 1753, are representative of the experience of slave women and their earning capacity. After five decades of work for two owners, Luciana had ended up in the hands of Doña Paula Almogera. For a long time she had contributed her daily wages to the maintenance of her owner, with whom she shared her small house. In 1810, at the age of fifty-seven, Luciana pleaded before the judicial courts that she be exonerated from the obligation of supplying her daily wages. In her appeal she enumerated her activities and sufferings:

During the years when I was at my owner's side, serving her in her own house, I gave birth to sixteen children of whom four remain, and for three of whom my said owner, Doña Paula, has collected 400 pesos for one, 350 for another and 300 for the third, renting out the fourth, who is a girl, for whom she would no doubt demand 500 pesos if she were to attempt to sell her. In addition to the hardship that the upbringing of my children has naturally caused me, I have had to undertake that of my owner's grandchildren, all of whom were put in my hands, and also the individual care for an orphan whom I nursed with my own milk, and for which my master received six pesos a month; furthermore I sell bread dough in the streets, from which I gain one real and a half per day, and finally I gave her fifty pesos last year toward my own purchase price.[20]

In the litigation pursued by Luciana, she enumerated the multiple ways in which her presence had been exploited—what we might call an amortization of self. Luciana stated that she had worked for her owner for sixteen years, and that practically each year she had given birth to a child. Of these, four had lived to reach working age and had doubled the owner's collected income. We can break down the slave's annual contribution to the household:

sale of children	65 pesos
daily wages supplied by one of her children	25 pesos
wet nursing for other households	72 pesos
wet nursing for the owner's household (or equivalent wages for a wet nurse)	72 pesos
sale of bread dough in the street (or annual wages equivalent to day labor)	65 pesos
Total	299 pesos

As we see without counting the slave's hours of additional domestic work, each year Luciana brought in a sum that equaled her purchase price. Luciana represents the case of a slave who went out into the neighborhood every day but remained subject to her owner's close control. The breakdown of the income supplied by the slave illustrates a degree of profitability beyond that of daily wages. Luciana worked as a day laborer on two levels: she was a bread-dough vendor and a wet nurse. Both activities amounted to 45.8 percent of the total 299 pesos. Additional sums derived from the children (the daily wages supplied by one daughter and the sale of the other children) represented 33.4 percent of the total. The remaining amount was at least equal to the value of the domestic labor. Even if the daily wage was the most significant percentage of the slave's total payments, it alone cannot account for all the characteristics of the slave system's profitability. Thus, what we have examined raises two fundamental issues: first, the profit possible in an urban hiring-out system beyond strict calculations of daily-wage contributions; and second, a slave's capacity to generate mechanisms of accumulation and surplus in the context of slaveholding. In spite of all the work and the beings—literally—handed over to the owner, in 1809 Luciana could still pay her owner fifty pesos toward her purchase price, which inevitably had to come from one of the listed activities: the sale of bread dough or wet nursing outside the house. Her capacity to accumulate was reduced by her specific circumstances, her status as a slave. In other words, a slave's earning power was quite impressive, although restricted by the master's control. As long as control was effective, it guaranteed the profitability of the hiring-out system, especially linked to other forms of slave exploitation. The lessening of authority, which the slaves fought for in myriad ways, would make the slave system useless from the viewpoint of slaveholders.

As Luciana's case reveals, slaves recognized that their owners rapidly amortized their initial investment through the great diversity of work slaves performed and through other benefits that accrued. Slave women's reproductive capacity, along with their work inside and outside an owner's household, made slave women more successful at bargaining for freedom. Sometimes, but not always, these arguments supported a ruling in the slave's favor, in the name of ill-defined but incipient notions of social justice within the slave system.

The greater the distance from a master's control, the greater the likelihood of channeling substantial sums of money into a slave's own pocket. A case of marital conflict between two slaves allows us to underscore this assertion and further illustrates the differences between men and women, the dynamics of strife over daily wages, and—as we are examining a *bozal* couple—the problem of the rate of accumulation even for those recently immersed in the turbulence of urban life.

In a petition dated 1806 Catalina, married to Miguel, related how—thanks to daily wages—she had managed to obtain the freedom of both:

> Last year, in 1791, being subject to the slave servitude of Doña Sipriana Palacios, I married Miguel Geronimo de Teruz, a black *bozal*, born and raised in the Portuguese Indies and then after we married and when he began to work with me, we reaped the fruits of our labor and he was freed first, and afterward we proceeded to liberate me. However, Your Most Honorable Sir should understand the conditions in which I did this: he being a slave and house servant, and I being a day laborer, who would be the one who worked to liberate both?[21]

Catalina and her contemporaries took for granted that they could purchase freedom with sufficient daily wages but were unlikely to reach their goal as long as they remained in domestic service. With her labor, Catalina managed over the course of approximately five years to free her husband and herself. Along the way, she had to hand over to the owner part of her daily wages; once one spouse was free and resided outside the master's household, the couple would assume maintenance costs for the freed slave, a minimum monthly expenditure of twelve pesos that decreased the couple's real income.[22] Even so, the total of slaves' daily wages given to the master, the costs of maintenance, and the additional accumulated amounts were by far more important than what the master contributed to the slaves' upkeep (food, shelter, and clothing). Thus *bozales* quickly learned to loosen their ties to the master's house and go out into the street to earn wages, and even for them the period of accumulation could be relatively short.

If we compare Luciana's capacity for accumulation with that of Catalina, we see what statistical information on methods of manumussion (Table 1) meant in real life. Luciana was able to save only fifty pesos over the course of thirty-nine years, or one or two pesos per year, whereas Catalina (with her husband's help) managed to save approximately six hundred pesos in fifteen years, or about forty pesos a year.[23] Catalina's rate of accumulation is very close to the seven or eight years previously recorded as the time in which masters could amortize a slave purchase. Thus in the best of cases, slaves needed twice the time to do what slaveholders did; in the worst of cases they died before they could finish payment of their purchase price.

As a consequence, the scale was tilted in favor of accumulation and freedom through the daily wage; it gave slaves increasing leverage against the slave system. In this sense the Defensor de Menores's skepticism was justified, though perhaps not for the reasons he gave to a father trying to recover the costs of his son's education. The purchase of freedom through a daily-wage arrangement could take an entire lifetime because daily wages came first and savings toward freedom followed. Yet this mechanism alone permitted accumulation, unless slaves could devise other strategies to lower their purchase price or obtain money outside the hiring-out system. The extreme alternative was to hide away and not pay the daily wages. But such an option could carry with it judicial persecution and possibly the enforcement of retroactive payment before delinquent slaves could purchase freedom.

If slaves had any incentive to reproduce, it was the fact that they could use children, as they could use marriage, to lower their own price—as Luciana did—or advance moral claims that would oblige masters to free their illegitimate offspring.

Children in Slaves' Lives

The situation of slave children and, more specifically, the political, legal, and philosophical discussions it generated serve as additional indicators of the importance of daily wages and of the possibilities for negotiation and accumulation that daily wages offered Lima's slaves. Slave children became a subject of contention among masters and slaves, specifically over the respective obligations of maintenance and the rights and privileges of the slave family. Children, like marriage itself, were part of a moral package dear to the Church.

In the residential census of the Santa Ana parish (mentioned earlier), of a total of 187 households containing slaves, only nine (4.8 percent) recorded the presence of slave children, an indicator at least as low as the one recorded for Lima's haciendas. The number of children ranged from one to twelve. Along with high mortality—we should not forget that the slave Luciana had given birth to sixteen children of whom only four reached adulthood (a fairly typical survival rate)—in the urban context, the type of residence outside the master's household was the key explanation for the low presence of children. Slaveholders were convinced that their slaves did not want to bear or raise slave children and that pregnant slaves would abort if they had the choice or the opportunity. On more than one occasion this resistance to procreate prompted contemporaries to describe slaves as simply clumsy, uneducated, and primitive. But matters were more intricate than masters perceived.

María del Carmen Breña, slave of a Lima merchant, purchased her freedom soon after giving birth. She left her owner's house and her child behind. In 1815 the owner demanded that she return to his house to nurse the child; however, María wished to move the child to her own house. The owner stated his conviction:

The [proposed] relocation exposes the infant to whatever might anger her mother, otherwise the slave will let the infant die through hatred of her masters, and to liberate the minor from slavery, with neither religion nor humanity to stop her, because owing to the uncouthness and ignorance of such people no rational consideration comes to their mind.... Being pregnant with another baby ... in another master's house ... she fiercely threw herself against a wall with the aim of aborting herself, and so that the fetus would not reach slavery alive. The black did this in the house of some masters who looked upon her with affection; what will she do when she comes up against the intentions of those whom she detests, and against whom she has litigated?[24]

What the owner argued here was that hatred of masters and desire for freedom were stronger than maternal instincts. To this perception we can add the fact that slave women who ceased being slaves often had a dangerous road ahead, particularly if they were to survive as single mothers. An infant, whom the master would safeguard in order not to lose a slave, at the very least had food and shelter. Moreover, it was no coincidence that freedom was granted to the woman after her child was born. A child born after the purchase of freedom would be free as well. María del Carmen's owner stated that in order to subsist, the slave mother "will have to spend all day in the street selling, leaving her daughter abandoned and exposed to all the accidents of her age. If she carries her on her back, the sun will be enough to kill her; and above all she is a *bozal* woman, so ignorant of religion, who was never convinced to go to church . . . to learn the Christian doctrine. Causing death to her child would be such an ordinary thing, like going to sleep, or something similar."

While the mother sought a livelihood and a new way of life, the child would have the owner's help and maintenance allowance precisely because the child was a slave. Occasionally—as in this case—such assistance would lead the owner's wife to nurse the slave's child. María del Carmen had left her child behind as she was unable to carry it with her as a free child; at the same time she was saving her child by making very literal use of the master's shelter and concern.

Apparently a very widespread practice, which helps explain the low presence of children, was the concealment of children. More than one female slave managed to run away from her master's house, give birth, and return. When asked what had happened to the baby, she would claim that it had died or been stillborn.[25] This alternative was possible when external links existed: loved ones or friends who would take responsibility for the newborn. Furthermore, if the slave mother lived with her masters, she would have to figure out how to leave in order to nurse her child or eventually find somebody to take her place. Claiming that children had died prevented an owner not only from designating them as his or her property but also from transferring children to another owner and separating them from the mother—a separation much more difficult to control because the slave mother would have a harder time tracing where her children were. The possible sale of children always loomed despite the Church's disapproval of the practice. Against the allegations of "clumsiness" that slaveholders imputed to their slaves we note accusations of "inhumanity" that slaves raised against owners.[26] Even if masters later realized that their female slaves had hidden children, time had passed during which the owners had not paid for the children's upkeep and thus the owners' property demands were weakened. Placement of children in a convent was a unique method of concealment. If an owner made a demand for the child in such circumstances, there was an entire institution behind the defense of the slave. The additional argument that the convent had assumed the child's maintenance would greatly decrease the child's price and facilitate manumission.[27] To give birth outside the master's control, to look elsewhere for day labor, or to abandon a child was to act well within the interests of slaves, given the impositions of the slave system. In such contexts as the ones described, and others—as we will soon see—it is difficult to find one sole rationale for slaves to express parental or filial love.

For slave women who did bear children in slavery, various options could at least guarantee that the slave family would not be arbitrarily scattered. Urban society offered nonmarried slave women with children alternatives that reflected its moral principles and sought to keep the slave family together without threatening the slaveholding system. A common practice among proprietary families was to make a prenatal partition of the slave children among their own sons and daughters. Contemporaries noted that "there is nothing more frequent in slaveholding families than parents distributing among their children the offspring of slaves."[28]

This distribution was seen as a portion of the inheritance, one realized "by womb" that increased the likelihood of greater equity among an owner's children. If the assigned slave died, it would simply be a matter of misfortune. But with luck, slave children would survive and as children would be assigned to serve specific members of the owner's family. Thus, while the master's children grew up they would have companions who would play with them, then wait on them, and much later accompany them in their departure from their parent's house to begin this cycle anew. Such mechanisms internalized slavery from infancy and partly explain the loyalty of slaves toward their masters.

For slaves who did not abandon their children in order to scratch out a bare living in freedom or give up babies assigned before birth to serve members of the owner's family, a vast array of negotiations existed to keep slaves' families intact and obtain their children's freedom. Slaves who lived outside the owner's household faced urgent questions of legal responsibility for the slave children: who was obligated to feed slave children—the couple, or the free spouse, or perhaps the owner? On the one hand, when slaves chose to live outside the household, owners would allege that they had to do without the services slave children usually provided—playing with their own children, doing minor chores of fetching and carrying—and that when slaves decided to live outside, they took on the parental duties and were obligated to nourish the children. On the other hand, slaves would say that the children were property that belonged to the owner who was therefore required to maintain the children. Maintenance costs, and the way in which they were provided, were at the heart of this dialogue. Both lines of argument furnished extensive matter for debate between two of the most distinguished lawyers of Lima's Audiencia Real at the start of the nineteenth century: Isidro Vilca who defended a female slave, and Pablo Ramírez de Arellano who represented this slave's female owner.

Between 1810 and 1814, the slave María Andrea had fought hard but failed to free two of her children from slavery. Five years later, Isidro Vilca would adduce in her name that the earlier negative judgment "also gives me the right to demand food for someone else's slaves [this was how the mother now referred to her two children] owing to the fact that I was not obligated to feed them. This petition is the most legal, just, and sacred of so many that may be filed in the courts of justice." The petition did not stop there. The owner's debt was specified: "The fairest sum that can be ruled for the sustenance of an individual is that of *two reales per day*, which makes *eight pesos per month*" (emphasis added). This sum is very close to that enunciated by hacienda owners intent on establishing their expenses, but it occurs here in a claim by slaves demanding retroactive payment.

María Andrea's oldest daughter was fourteen years old; her son eleven. Vilca's appeal continued:

In every court it is unquestionable and generally agreed that the owner should feed them. . . . No one is unaware that two reales per day is not sufficient even for the bare essentials, and even more so if one contemplates that we live in a country where in the last twenty years the cash supply has decreased and the price of the essential items has increased.

The total sum resulting from the petition amounted to 3,456 pesos. Announcement of the sum set off a cavalcade of arguments between the two lawyers. Ramírez de Arellano asked:

Who is the person filing a suit, and who is the one who has nourished these slaves? The same María Andrea who was owned by Don Eugenio, the natural mother of those children and who has benefited by her master's testament, obtained her freedom as well as that of her mother, María Jesús, and that of another daughter named Asención, a godchild to my party. With whose orders or capacity did she decide to assume charge of rearing her children? She did it all by herself because she wanted to do so as a mother, culpably and criminally swindling her master of his slaves.... After the violent extraction [of the children] from the owner's house, in which she would have never lacked food, with nothing to feed those two boys now, today she dares to demand food without honesty, owing to her rancor at her sons' declared slavery. This case is nothing more than a scandal.... She has done this because it pleased her, because she wanted to cheat her master, hide his slaves from him, feed them as if she had fed them as a mother. A popular saying tells us—and such attitudes are quite common among such people—that whoever gives bread to another's dog loses the bread and loses the dog.... [Furthermore,] it is indubitable that both boys at their respective ages, would have been capable of menial labor: in the house, accompanying their young masters to play and to school, taking care of the little tasks in their master's retail store for their own subsistence and for that of their master's children and family or of other jobs and tasks of this kind. From all these services my party has not benefited the least, but María Andrea has had them all to herself while the children helped her in the profession of preparing food.... Ultimately it must be said that obligations between masters and slaves are reciprocal.

In 1819 the owner agreed to sell the two boys and signed their *cartas de libertad*.[29]

In accordance with the legislation in force, an owner was required to feed his or her slaves. A slave remained a slave whether or not he or she lived in the master's household. If a slave couple had been given permission to leave along with their children, the slave family regained not only family unity but also—as in the cited case—the benefit of the children's labor; in effect the family deprived the owner of their labor. The defender of the owner's interests based his argument on this deprivation: the slave stole the children from the owner's house. Thus, the owner was freed of the responsibility of feeding them, and the mother, María, had to assume it. The fact that the lawyer revealed that María Andrea's demand was commonplace among "such people" corroborates not only our assertion that slaves could live with their children outside the owner's household, but also that conflicts over the obligations of parents and of owners were common and that these contradictions were frequently utilized by the slave population.

The amount María Andrea claimed was not small. Nonetheless, it tallies with what was minimally needed at that time for daily maintenance. Furthermore, it represents a decision by the slave family to feed itself and bear the costs of distance from the owners' house through daily wages. Tacitly, owners allowed familial slave life outside their dominion with the intent, once the children reached working age, of resuming their proprietary rights. When an owner did so, the loss for slave parents was double: they lost the granted maintenance allowance and were menaced by the owner's potential sale of the children. Lawyers for one such owner argued, "As the control of slave children belongs to owners, it is further just that during infancy these latter also furnish food and appropriate clothing until they [the children] are able to be passed into the hands of other owners."[30]

Law and reality clashed. While legislation stated that maintenance was an owner's obligation, many slave families chose to live outside the owner's household. Such a decision on the part of slaves presupposed the existence of mechanisms decisive to the attainment of freedom that could stop owners from selling their children. An extraordinary mechanism in the context of slavery—which relied on the apt intervention of the lawyers of the Audiencia Real—was a concrete calculation of the amount that the slave parents had invested in rearing their children, an investment that owners were responsible for repaying to the slave parents. The calculation simply followed the law. It safeguarded family unity even against owners' well-entrenched notions of private property. And in the case of María Andrea, it resulted in her son's accession of freedom.

Even so, however, the space claimed by the slave population remained—as inscribed by the definition of slavery itself—a transitional context. No slave's success was ever completely assured, and it is likely—as has been asserted for other areas as well—that this insecurity itself imparted particular traits to filial relations.

The supreme decree of 24 November 1821 reasserted that owners were responsible for feeding slave children, a ruling that gave slave petitions an even firmer basis. If the slave could prove that he or she had assumed these costs, it would be difficult for owners to recuperate their rights of property over the children. Thus the decree set up conditions in which slave children could live with their parents outside the owner's household.[31] The Defensor de Menores was the official commended to enforce this decree, and it is through his agency that slaves and slave children expanded their civil and legal representation.

For widowed and single slaves, and for those in situations such as the ones they have described for us, struggling to pay daily wages and at the same time to maintain one or several children, existence was a doubly demanding and toilsome task. The weight of this two-sided burden was also probably a key reason for marriages between slaves and arrangements in which, from the onset, one freed spouse lived outside the owner's household (see chapter 5). We observe the relative weakness of a single woman in the case of María del Milagro Solórzano, who was represented by the Defensor de Menores. María filed a suit against Doña Juana Murga over the freedom of her daughter, Micaela Bartola. The owner had placed María in the San Bartolomé hospital, where she remained for many years until she was well. In the hospital she was required to work; in other words, she paid for her own treatment with her daily wages. While in the hospital María gave birth to a daughter. When the daughter was only a few years old, the owner snatched Micaela from her mother's side and sold her, even though the owner had never made the slightest gesture to support the mother or the child. María set before the court the arguments of her use of daily wages to survive and her owner's failure to provide food or pay for her treatment, and attempted to take her daughter out of slavery and patronage. The judge denied the child freedom, despite the fact that María could even demonstrate that her daughter had been registered as free at her baptism.[32] María—so ran the counterargument—had not delivered daily wages to her master, which would have allowed the owner to provide food and medical expenses. Thus, the litigation turned the reasoning from wages against the slave. María was not married when she gave birth to Micaela, an additional fact that the judge might have viewed with disdain. Furthermore, the father of María's daughter did not admit his paternity or was at least unwilling or unable to help María out. Still, considering the decisions made in most cases, this judgment appears exceedingly arbitrary, and the Defensor de Menores must have appealed it.

What is certain is that slave mothers who had little contact with other persons, or who were not married, even if they might have managed to reside outside their owner's household, encountered the most difficulties in liberating their children. There were many women in similar situations who, with their "incessant work, industry, and economy," managed to amass enough money to manumit themselves and eventually their children.[33] In every case the slaves needed external support to strengthen and legitimize their demands. Sometimes the cogency of demands even led to physical confrontations between owners and slaves. At times the Defensor de Menores appeared; at others it was the slave couple who acted to free the children, especially when one of the spouses was free. Godmothers and godfathers (either black or white) also were decisive agents who intervened on the road to freedom.

In 1839 Marcos Esquivel, a disabled first sergeant of the Colombia battalion, filed a suit against Doña Isabel Espinoza, the owner of his mother and of his wife, Justa Torres. Justa and Marcos had given birth to two daughters, one eighteen years old, and the other nine. Marcos claimed his military salary had enabled him during all the past years to contribute a sum of twelve pesos each month to Justa, who lived with their daughters in the owner's house: "whom I have fed and educated since birth, paying for baptismal fees, clothes, and whatever they needed for subsistence."[34] Marcos alleged that because the owner had failed to provide for the children she had lost her patronage of them; he based his claim on the November 1821 decree. In December 1839 Marcos was imprisoned. The owner had appeared at his house in order to take away the youngest daughter.

And because I insisted that my daughter did not have to leave so soon, she raised the parasol that she was carrying in her hands, she hit me repeatedly, I prudently told her not to abuse me. Her furor increased and she continued to beat me with no respite; upon which I took out some small scissors that I was sharpening and gave her a small cut: the grocer Don José del Carmen Seco, the immediate neighbor of my workshop, was witness to all this.

The owner told the municipal governor what had happened, and Marcos, a free black, was sent to prison. The April 1841 judgment ruled that since Marcos had not convincingly proved that he had fed his children, the owner could recuperate the right of patronage. This episode shows the violence that could ensue over negotiations involving children: from scissor cuts to umbrella beatings and owners' visits to slaves' homes. All participants dreaded such actions and escalations but they did occur, despite attempts to mark spatial segregation. Violent encounters occurred and expressed changing social claims from Lima's black population.

Throughout the range of possible arrangements for slaves—from continuity within a fixed time and space to various demands for upkeep by slaves and ex-slaves who had gained a measure of independence—the elements of the situations we have depicted were the daily wage and the gradual distancing from an owner's control. The situations varied in rates of accumulation and in living arrangements, particularly those involving children. In a situation of womb assignment, children and the daily wages they produced were the property of the owner, even if a margin of accumulation (in Luciana's case, fifty pesos in fifty-seven years) existed. But a slave who had managed to purchase freedom but still had enslaved children had two options. Slaves might leave the children in the owner's house, thereby transferring the maintenance costs to the owner and risking the possibility of the later sale of the children. Or, gathering together all their funds, they might ask for the children back and consolidate the family unit. Conflict arose when both possibilities intersected: when an owner imposed his or her property rights and a slave demanded the ordained maintenance allowance. A successful outcome depended on slaves' skill in negotiation and accumulation.

As the price of slaves dropped and that of clothing and food rose, to leave the children under the temporary care of the owner was a way to accelerate accumulation. Rather oddly, the slaveholding system worked to the slaves' advantage in this situation because the value of slave children was, according to age, less than that of adult slaves. The calculations made by Isidoro Vilca, the lawyer of the Audiencia Real, represented the minimum amount necessary for survival—ninety-six pesos a year for the upkeep of a child. Thus, the cost of a child's maintenance for four years might equal the purchase price of an adult slave. Within the slave family's budget maintenance of sons and daughters was a considerable expenditure for slaves whose first necessity was to pay the daily wages they owed to owners. Because many slaves opted for family life, we conclude that they were willing to pay these expenses. Their decision to maintain a family outside the master's household delayed the attainment of their own freedom in order to negotiate the freedom of their children through the argument of maintenance. In calculating the profitability of the hiring-out system, we must add sums from daily wages to the maintenance costs of children. For owners, the strategy of leaving slave children with their parents meant reducing costs; yet for slaves, leaving their children with owners was a choice with the same objective. It was more profitable to wait until children grew up (and in the meantime avoid relocation outside Lima), and pay their purchase price when they reached working age. María Andrea's eleven- and fourteen-year-old sons assisted her with the chores of food preparation and strengthened the likelihood of their continued freedom. Freedom was a double-edged sword; for slaves, the final outcome depended on their place in the labor market. And success was skewed. After all, every nuance of any potential negotiation—including the payment of daily wages—was an expression of a slave system.

The circumstances of the slave Antonio described by his wife, Juana Pedreros, a free black originally from Angola, remind us of the brutal dimensions of slavery. When Antonio and Juana married, the master allowed the couple to live outside his household in exchange for the payment of six reales a day (twice what was currently stipulated). The couple had religiously complied with the payments for many years. One morning in 1812, however, Antonio hanged himself from a tree in the Alameda del Pino. Eloquent in its description of the reasons for this act was the declaration of Antonio's wife:

For some years she has been married to the black, Antonio, the slave of Don Ignacio Meléndez. Together they had five children. Her husband earned money as a water carrier, for which reason his master obligated him to pay the daily wage of six reales even if he did not earn them, and because of this contribution the declarant and her children had to pass many days begging in order to sustain themselves. Yesterday morning the black, Antonio, awoke at five to go to work and left, as he usually did, and a little while later she was notified that he was found hanged in one of the trees of the Alameda . . . that the reason that the black, Antonio, had hanged himself is the very obligation to his master who required from him the payment of six reales a day. . . . When he could not come up with the money he had to resort to borrowing. He mentioned this situation to his wife on several occasions. Added to all this distress was the illness of one of their children, and often they simply had no medicine to treat her, for which reason her illness worsened. Two months' rent was also owed to the owner for the room where the declarant is staying.[35]

Although the image of success overshadows the hardships on the journey toward freedom, some individuals could not face the dual exigencies of daily wages for an owner and bare necessities for a family. This compounded burden crushed their plans and desires for freedom and demonstrates both the fragility of the liberation process and the merits of those who crossed the threshold. For this same reason, it suggests that we must avoid excessive optimism about the possibilities of self-manumission.

The situations we have viewed lead us to three general points. First, the daily wage gave impetus to the development of an artisanal market for black urban labor. Second, owners benefited from their slaves' daily wages as the slaves gradually accumulated their purchase price. Third, the slaves' capacity to earn and save depended on their owners' circumstances and their own. The more slaves owners had, the less their dependence on slaves' earnings; the fewer slaves they had, the greater flexibility for slaves to negotiate spaces of relative freedom—circumstances that fit a significant percentage of urban slaves. The slaves' varying degrees of urban experience and real or fictive kinship ties shaped their opportunities and strategies for urban life. Over the long term and despite the enormous disparity in wages, the daily wage had not only the greatest influence on the organization of the master-slave relationship; it spurred the dissolution of the slaveholding system and the differentiation among slaves and the black population in general. For the slaves—witness Antonio's case—this transition was risky and hazardous. Yet slaves were ready and willing to take this risk and exploit all the small openings Lima's slave system provided.

We can confirm many of the tendencies we have analyzed by examining Peruvian slavery from another angle—from the perspective of the marriages and family life of slaves. Considering the debates about the vitality of the slave family and its importance in the construction of black culture, we must ask how slave family life began and flourished. Did an urban slave family often start with the birth of an owner's illegitimate child to a slave woman in domestic service? What disappointments and triumphs emerged from marriages between slaves and free persons and from other relationships that involved slaves; and how did all these factors influence conceptions of family life and slaves' marriages? Here are the questions we will explore next.

Chapter Four

Matrimonial Alliances and Conflicts

To a great extent, the course of slaves' marriages and family life was determined by the direct or indirect interference of owners. Because they were slaves, many women followed the expectations of their owners. In partial response to a question raised at the end of the preceding chapter, I believe that the sexual appetites of masters often set their slaves' choices for marriage and family life. For many female slaves in domestic service sexual relations with owners were all they knew of marriage and family life. But these relationships were not the only option for female slaves, nor was the matrimonial universe one defined wholly by owners.

Slave Women in Domestic Service

The day-to-day life of urban slave women took place in three different realms: within the master's household as a servant in residence; on the street as a day laborer but part of the master's household; and as a day laborer outside the master's household. Whatever the arrangement, the slave could be both a mother and a wife.

The statistics that we have indicate a relatively higher proportion of women in the urban setting, and the census figures show a more rapid increase of women from free *casta* groups than of men from this category, which may reflect women's greater success in the process of manumission. Between 1792 and 1818 the male slave population decreased 27 percent; the female population, 45 percent (Haitin 1986, 186). As we have seen, daily wages complemented domestic service, while residence with masters set up other mechanisms that help explain the results of this census. In the context of domestic service, emotional and social blackmail often became the basis for negotiations for the journey toward freedom.

Benefits and Dangers of an Owner's Household

The kind of work slaves assumed in the owners' households was closely linked to the owners' social status. A greater number of slaves meant not only higher social status for owners and slaves (and division of daily chores among the slaves) but clearly understood boundaries between owners and slaves as well. The proximity (or dependence) was less in households with fewer slaves where duties were multiple and a greater level of familiarity promoted inverted relations of dependence and such forms of male owner–female slave cohabitation as concubinage. Joint residence gave rise to affective ties. And only on rare occasions did owners use violence to secure sexual favors from female slaves or, if they did, would compensate for the initial violence with a series of concessions that female slaves would learn to use.

Lorenzo Rioja was a merchant and one of the municipality's *asentistas*. He was married and owned a slave named María Isabel who had been born in her master's house. Lorenzo had taken advantage of her for many years. When she reached fourteen years of age, María Isabel stated:

> It was his desire to have illicit intercourse with me; I was forced to yield for two reasons: the first because of the master's status; the second because . . . it being certain that the greater the interest of one's master, the better his treatment for us women. I sought my alleviation by faking pleasure when he reached out for me.[1]

The owner expressed his sexual interest in the slave and she consented. She perceived her master's status and knew that she could exploit it to receive benefits: clothing, good treatment, and perhaps freedom too. Alone and with no access to daily wages, a slave had limited means to change her condition. Yet within the immediate possibilities, such a transaction could ease her situation. The apologetic tone in her statement transferred the blame of moral transgression to the owner; he was employing his power as owner (and allowing her a chance to benefit). The attitude was not an isolated phenomenon; María Isabel was not speaking for herself alone. Female slaves talked among themselves and owners also exchanged opinions, as the statement of María Isabel's owner shows us.

> I am very certain, as are many more owners with even greater reason, who have suffered similar false imputations at the hands of their slaves and have experienced such fatal misfortune, that such kinds of demands are not new,

but rather very old, and very hackneyed, so that if the slaves do not manage to obtain de facto freedom, the least that happens is that the slaves become shameless and licentious, and live for a long time at the cost of presenting a false suit, ridiculing their owner.

Aside from elucidating an attitude common at the time, the owner shielded himself behind his position as owner: "There is no law that grants freedom to the slave woman because of a master's lewd treatment, and there exists only such a law that might consider the owners' wantonness to be spiritual cruelty."

María Isabel turned the argument around: "He is right when he declares that the owner's sexual intercourse corresponds to spiritual cruelty, but this is not so when rape and corrupted virginity are involved because this latter carries the punishment of freedom [for the slave], and even more so if there exists a pact or word that should be enforced with complete rigor as an example for rash owners who take advantage of their power."

A promise of freedom had been made, and the slave demanded fulfillment of the owner's word. The specific aggression or "spiritual cruelty" was not defined, and the slave—although denied juridical personality—invoked her condition as a raped woman. The law specified that if a victim could substantiate her claim, the offender had to marry her, pay her monetary compensation, or go to jail. Thus, a woman who petitioned to be freed was asking for a kind of monetary compensation and was demanding what society conceded to all women. María Isabel's response implicitly asserted that the courts should ensure the compliance of word and pacts, and that compliance should depend on a person's honor and integrity rather than on her status as a slave. Owners had defined themselves as honorable people and María Isabel was claiming that her master had not acted accordingly. The female slave assumed that she herself was complying with the standards of honor; the owner had transgressed his stipulated code of honor.

Other owners could grasp the dangers and implications of arguments such as María's: the assertions enunciated in her case might serve to obtain justice on a personal level and also become the principal postulates for others who suffered injustices, even if the final step of their litigation process was not successful.

For more than six years—until Lorenzo Rioja's death in 1814—the presence of his female slave fueled continuous disputes within the house, where not only Lorenzo and his wife lived, but her sisters as well. Lorenzo faced their repeated recriminations. Neither inside nor outside the house was his liaison with the slave a secret: on more than one occasion he had to turn to the services of a midwife, most of them black females who were known to disseminate the news of an illegitimate birth and of the newborn's racial features. When Lorenzo died, his wife would assume the litigation pending against the slave. Despite her efforts, María Isabel did not obtain freedom and was finally sold to another owner for two hundred pesos.

Emotional closeness between masters and slaves was greater when the master was a bachelor or lived apart from his wife. In these circumstances, many slave women were fully incorporated into their owners' households and assumed all the roles demanded of legitimate wives. They served as their replacements and in general cost far less to maintain: "Fear of poverty persuaded [owners] to remain unmarried" (Macera 1977, 312). Whereas a husband might pay out at least twelve pesos a month to support a wife, a female slave could supply her master with daily wages. Slave women carried out domestic chores, sustained themselves, and into the bargain often produced surpluses and eventually more slaves (through buying them or bearing them). We need hardly remind ourselves that in the event of conflict, while the female slave could be sold, the wife could not.[2] In such circumstances the only reason to marry was a woman's whiter skin or her ability to further aspirations of social ascent. However, choosing a female slave as a concubine had its costs: female slaves who had taken on the work and role of wives would not easily allow their owners to treat them as slaves, especially when they were lighter skinned (or so perceived themselves).

María Mercedes Oyague, the *parda* slave of a military officer who owned a cake shop, had helped rear her owner's daughter for one year. When the owner first requested María's services, she was working for another owner. María Mercedes stated that the military officer "desired with much resolve to provide the money for my price, assuring me that he needed a maid for the upbringing and companionship of a child, his daughter of minor age, since his legitimate wife, Doña María Encarnación, had abandoned him."[3]

He managed to convince her. The rearing of the child soon evolved into something more: "It always was the intention of the stated, my owner, as he did not have a wife during that epoch, to do everything to bring me closer to his lewdness. After he offered to grant my *carta de libertad*, I finally yielded to his desires, living by his side and in comfort."

Several years later the owner tried to punish María Mercedes, depositing her in a *panadería*. She deeply resented this attempt and insisted on obtaining the promised freedom or, in any case, a new owner. The owner experienced little inconvenience; the established facts show that he managed to retain María Mercedes by not appearing at the summons ordered by the civil court and by evading the delivery of her *carta de libertad*.

The dual role female slaves assumed makes it difficult for us to define their place in the slaveholding system and as one-half of a domestic couple. Their social articulation was rooted in daily, individual interaction that ultimately favored the slaves. Even if slave women represented a capital reserve for use in the event of an emergency or conflict, owners could not always exercise this option or assure their mastery by the usual mechanisms of punishment that threatened the slave population. Often what owners wished to secure was not simply property.

We see in the experience of Matea Neyra a version of the story of María Mercedes. Matea had also been "assaulted with the vehement impulses and promises" of her owner's husband. For a long time she was kept in "illicit friendship, and under the firm belief that the word [of freedom] that I had been promised was going to be fulfilled." But circumstances forced Don Juan Balada, the husband, to sell the slave without redeeming his promise. Matea stated, "I left his power and went to another master, however Don Juan soon returned requesting my return with great insistence, and telling me that if he had not fulfilled the promise it had not been for lack of love [!], but because of his scarcities, and that he now found himself in another condition, and that I should let him purchase me again; that I would soon be free as he had promised me."

The owner spoke of love, the slave of an illicit friendship that was preventing her from marrying a free man of "known industry and honesty, who proposed to me with perseverance, seeing my disposition for work."[4] Matea returned to the power of Don Juan and then, observing that he was breaking his promises (and we must remember that to grant her freedom, Don Juan had to relinquish her to another man), went to the marqués de Fuente Hermosa, a friend of Don Juan, to whom he had "confessed his crime." The marqués wrote a letter to the civil court endorsing Matea's version of the story. Nonetheless, Don Juan obstructed her emancipation from slavery by claiming that she belonged not to him, but to his wife.[5]

In these episodes was a chain of possible situations ranging from owners' startled responses at the accusations of female slaves to emotional commitments with these slaves; from slaves' awareness of the owner's supremacy to acceptance of their own weaknesses. And neither side was oblivious to what was taking place. Inverting the argument of female slaves—that illicit intercourse should lead to freedom—owners, as proof of their innocence, would then allege that the female slave "was not so stupid as to avoid seeking her freedom because of the mere fact that she had lived with her owner."[6] In many cases owners came out ahead, managing to seduce their slaves and later promising to free them if they could pay their purchase price.[7]

Occurrences such as those we have depicted were so frequent that liaisons with slaves were hardly ever a secret to the erring husbands' legitimate spouses. What did these latter think and feel when confronted with female slaves, especially when the relations involved deep feelings among all parties? And what occurred within the internal hierarchies of households if female slaves received better treatment than wives? As we shall see, the female universe encompassed not only master-slave relationships but emotional competition as well.[8] How did a wife react when her husband exhibited a clear preference for the domestic slave?

After five years of marriage Francisco Torquera, fifty-five years old, was in his house screaming at his wife. He reproached her: "What devils and demons did I have in my body to marry a sow and pig like you? It would have been better if I had married my maid Teresa who, more than you, deserves marriage to me and is the one I most esteem: compared to Teresa you are of no use to me."[9]

The ideal marriage was one in which the home and children were the legitimate wife's ordained field of action. The expenses of supporting a legitimate spouse were high—both socially and sexually—partly because a wife's education was oriented more toward religion than toward carnal matters. And from a subjective angle, a wife's upbringing must be one of the reasons underlying owners' predilection for female slaves. Torquera's description of his first days of marriage confirm this:

I soon recognized the lack of willingness and love that [my wife] professed to me, making it clear with the hundreds of contemptuous words with which she constantly reproached me, and most important because she denied me with no just cause to consent to what was owed, such that in the few occasions in which I made her comply with my requests, it was always with repugnance and in a very disagreeable manner. Thus it resulted that a few days after our wedding we were already divorced in terms of the nuptial bed, and the stated [wife] separated from my side.

By definition, carnal intercourse was to take place only within the confines of marriage; however, sex was both an obligation required of wives and an act tinged with sin. To remain morally and spiritually intact, wives had to resist and silence their desires. The presence of slave women filled this gap between desire and sin, a gap that female slaves recognized and used. This situation offered advantages to both sides, although on different levels, and it is evident that there were serious limitations to the effectiveness of ecclesiastical recommendations. For a man, his wife's sexual and affective rejection was an argument to legitimize his partiality toward a female slave. Many men sought neither pretext nor justification and more than one wife, night after night, perhaps did not see but at least heard her husband take the slave into his bedroom. For years Juan Gutiérrez Prio, a retail merchant, maintained relations with his slave while he beat his wife and openly admitted to her his fondness for the slave. Their matrimonial strife reached such an extreme that he was willing to return a large portion of the dowry to his wife to rid himself of her; the confrontation between slave and wife led to the slave physically harming the wife. Even after this altercation, the merchant decided to liberate the slave rather than punish her, as his wife requested.[10]

A society that left room for such possibilities would obviously open the doors wide not only to the so bewailed insubordination of its bottom layers but would also create immediate advantages for those who knew how to use them. Across all layers of urban society there was evasion of the rules of domination. The cases examined until now involved female slaves and male owners who belonged to the civil and military bureaucracy or who were petty merchants and shop owners, individuals who owned one or two slaves. Yet domestic service was the patrimony par excellence of the elite; nobility was not free from flaws. And when the penchants of the master of the house became public knowledge, rumors did not induce obedience among dependents. In some cases, the wife became an object of mockery and jokes, and within the household slaves began to take sides.

In a letter addressed to the archbishop Las Heras, the marquesa of Santa María expressed her complaints against her husband:

> Although I tried all the prudent methods to make my legitimate husband Don Fernando Carrillo, the marqués of Santa María, comply with his duties, they have not sufficed to obtain a social life that accords with the obligations into which we entered with the sacred tie of marriage. Your Excellency knows that before this time I found myself in need of withdrawing to a convent with the permission of Your Excellency in order to see if this action had a good impression on my husband. My heart always willing, with the recompenses that he promised me, consented to his suggestions, and thus I returned to his house; however as soon as I arrived I began to experience worse resistance, especially since I was without the presence of my uncle, the marqués of Casa Dávila. I begun to suffer from indifferent and insolent treatment. In matters concerning the household, I saw that a *chola* and three *zambas* were those who had the say, and that this [situation] arose from certain origins that modesty and moderation cause me to hide. For this reason, I was looked upon as a worthless person, as these [women] entered and left my presence without granting me any attention or greetings of courtesy.
>
> I endured these events so offensive to religion, and to my own honor, to see if my silence and discretion would bring an end to so much disorder. My new separation, although silent, brought to light the mismanagement of my husband: this consideration, and knowing how important our marriage was to his honor, and to the education of my children, obligated me to endure this flood of disorders at which I have only hinted, even at the risk of my conscience. However, they reached such extremes that I could not bear it any longer. . . . I see that because of my birth I cannot remain in this state, and that other circumstances must be sought for me. I have to look out for myself, given the liberty of this century. Even if I go on silencing this disorder as until now, I am still exposed to the gossip of the common people.

The marquesa again withdrew to a convent, from whence she initiated the judicial battle to recover her property.[11]

All the weapons that the wife had within her reach to make her husband "comply with his duties" (separation, the convent, intervention of a respected family member, silence) did not change her husband's conduct. This situation escalated to such a degree that finally the "maids devoted to him declared war on those at my service."[12] It is no surprise that given these experiences, a black slave would disobey both owners and set her own field of action with respect to daily chores.[13] Thus relations established through daily contact could be more effective than decrees to ease the oppression and abuses inflicted on slaves. Disagreements and conflicts in the family lives of owners—as we have seen in rural-urban relations—were used by slaves to expand their field of maneuverability and promote their own interests.

A distinct interaction within a household concerned relations between a domestic male slave and his female owner. Given the traditional subordination of women, we understand that examples do not abound, most likely because they were less common; similarly, the owners' feminine modesty probably inhibited them. In cases such as these, social and moral recrimination played a role. Was it easier for a male slave to obtain freedom because he could use social and personal pressure against his owner? The punishment imposed for rape was severe, and the rarity of this domestic situation despite the residence of male slaves and female owners in the same house suggests that intimate relations developed if the female owner encouraged them. One such case illustrates proximity and its consequences.

In the divorce case filed by Manuela Vargas Machuca and Francisco Bernardo Sánchez de la Concha after eight and one-half years of marriage, the husband accused the wife:

She gave herself to this slave with the greatest pleasure, so that he would delouse her, and strip off her stockings when it was time to go to sleep, he would take off her clothing, after having undressed her so she could sleep, he would return in the morning to awaken her; and finally, she preferred his service for these functions over those of the maid: whereupon she contributed to the situation, the entire crime of the consequences fall on her sole person, and thus the punishment should fall on her, and not on the slave.

Apparently, the relationship with the slave had preceded the marriage. The husband complained that his wife had not been a virgin, and his spouse, agreeing with this fact, stated that the perpetrator of the rape was not the slave but her lapdog. Don Francisco stated, "By concealing the accomplice in the rape, she places the crime of bestiality on herself." As we can see, after several years of marriage and the birth of a few children, anything was acceptable except a relationship with a slave.[14]

While the marquesa's partner accepted his wife's game of honor, withdrawal to the convent, and silence, even managing to convince her that he had changed and clearly improved, Doña Manuela's husband filed for divorce and exposed his wife's arguments one by one. For an adulterous wife, the worst response was to admit the adultery, but if it involved a slave, better to blame a lapdog. And here we see a husband willing to defend the slave and lay all the blame on his wife. What the wife should have done—according to the husband—was to accept the services of a female maid, not a male servant, especially when the demanded services were similar to those of Louis XIV's courtly rituals.

When relationships between a female owner and a male slave were discovered, the former could always claim that she had been raped. The moral (and physical) recriminations would fall on the slave in order to safeguard the woman's honor. Since by definition the husband was the guardian of his wife's property, it would be problematic for the wife to grant the male slave freedom even if she so desired. Only fears of social ridicule—which did not inhibit Don Francisco—would drive a husband to rid himself of a slave, and only if he could do so without going to court. Aside from the punishments imposed, such fears explain why we know so little about relationships between male slaves and female owners. Furthermore, the balance of power between men and women would be unlikely to encourage a male slave to pursue freedom by establishing relations with a female owner.

Certainly the presence of slaves in the domestic realm caused severe familial disturbances. Extramarital liaisons were facilitated by common residence. Concubinage and adultery were frequent. Although statistics on illegitimacy do not only refer to slaves, extremely high percentages of illegitimacy (around 22 percent—depending on the ethnic group) for the whole of *limeño* society corroborate such behavior.[15] Thus, we are only one step away from affirming that illegitimacy was a social behavior that gradually led to freedom. It was one more path of social ascent for the black population to follow. Cohabitation created margins for negotiation that varied for masters and slaves and also for men and women. The proliferation of such margins, as well as the harsh tones of owners' petitions for recourse against them from the courts and the interpersonal violence of their underlying tensions, were signs of increasing social unrest that was visible even within the domestic sphere. And this situation was apparently not particular to Lima. Equally dramatic expressions have been recorded for slave women in the United States, as Ellison assures us (1983, 56):

> They [slaves] fought unremittingly against misuse and brutality and refused to become mere victims. They sought to bend and undermine an iniquitous system so that they could win some degree of independence for themselves.

They often succeeded in making an intolerable institution more bearable and they evolved subversive techniques that were varied and devious enough quite frequently to make a mockery of the system itself. At the very least, they managed to alter slave laws and evade restrictions to create better lives for themselves and their families.

This assertion fits the actions of Manuela, Manuelita, and the many other female slaves we have encountered in the preceding pages. What we note in the final decades of slavery's existence is that the average percentage of all methods of attaining freedom (self-purchase, intervention of relatives or other persons, and grants of freedom) was much higher for women than for men. The average percentage for manumissions of women in 1830, 1840 and 1850 was 65 percent, a ratio of nearly 2:1 in favor of women.[16] This ratio corresponds to the average of urban female manumissions for Latin America as a whole (62–67 percent from Mexico City to Buenos Aires [Klein 1986, 227]). At the heart of these high percentages was the presence of slave women in urban life as domestics and wage laborers.

However, this was not all. An important component of the male owner–female slave bond were the children born from these relationships. Their presence gave the claims of slave women added force and complicated matters for the colonial and republican authorities.

The Children of Owners

Only in the mid-eighteenth century were genetic permutations that produced a black child from the union of black parents and one of lighter skin from a white and a black parent held to be facts rather than random occurrences; the observations led to the conclusion that both sexes participated in procreation. In 1854 the fusion of gametes in frog embryos was finally observed for the first time through a microscope (Tannahill 1980, 344 ff.). The Church opted in the meantime for the theory that the human being was reproduced by the decisive participation of the ovum, and thus legislators and slave owners would argue that slavery was inherited from the womb. Certainly the abolition of slavery in Peru owed less to theology or biology than it did to economic factors such as the growth of guano exports, yet perhaps the concurrence of the dates between the discovery of the fertility process and the abolition of slavery represents more than mere coincidence.

In a society as highly sensitive to differences of complexion and ancestry as Lima's, slave children were evidence of domestic realities and sources of additional conflict. Faced with the same few contraceptive options available to women at all levels of Peruvian society, slave women bore children inevitably. The prevailing legislation conveniently left the moral management of such cases to the authority of owners. Owners could recognize their children or not, feed them or not, sell them or raise them in their own houses. The decision depended on the emotions and prejudices (or ignorance) at work and, therefore, an important part of slave reproduction depended on individual actions. This fact placed the reproduction of urban slaves in a context distinct from that of slavery on plantations, whose owners weighted decisions for or against reproduction (the "buy or breed" dilemma) more by the profitability of the labor force and the market prices of slaves.[17]

Virginity, as we have seen in several previous cases, was a property valued by slaves as by other individuals; it offered slave women an ethical argument (of "corrupted virginity") to compromise owners before the courts. An owner who claimed innocence when confronted with this argument found his argument compromised if slave children existed. The opinions and feelings of a female slave acquired added weight if she could appeal to the values of the society in which she lived to persuade the court that the child or children were the owner's progeny. Given the lack of scientific information or definitive proofs of paternity, and amid contemporaries' determination to perpetuate a racially divided society and the social prejudices in force, slaves used the argument of miscegenation to obtain freedom.[18] One slave, Norberta, explained her understanding of the facts:

According to the rigor of the law he is obligated to grant me freedom because he has had illicit intercourse with me, a result of which was the birth of the mentioned daughter, Manuela; and furthermore Doña Teresa, the legitimate wife of my said owner, having come to know about her husband's criminal deed has punished me severely and frequently, not for my bad conduct in domestic service but rather for revenge after she ascertained the details of her husband's seductions . . . I should enjoy my freedom; and my daughter Manuela with much more reason; because no one could imagine, and nature opposes [such a possibility], that one's own blood be sold. If my owner attempts to do so, it is despicable and monstrous even to suggest this proposal because Manuela is his daughter. Well before claiming fifty pesos for my daughter, he is obligated to apportion her food.[19]

Along with her children, the female slave was vulnerable to the reprisals of the female owner because the latter now knew with certainty—because of the children's existence—that her husband was enjoying the favors of the slave. Added to this situation, which was part of daily family life with slaves, was the clear notion expressed by Noberta that it was unusual to wish to sell one's own kin. She demanded the acknowledgment of paternity with all its implications: freedom for Norberta and her daughter and a maintenance allowance. The female slave would not hesitate to turn to the courts. Laws did not define the obligations of a father-owner: they did not admit to the obvious because it was morally distasteful.

The courts' charge to settle these situations was not easy. First, it was necessary to know if a slave was lying about the owner's paternity, since many owners—as we have seen—were conscious that slaves often demanded freedom through this strategy. The only available method to evaluate the question was an informed comparison of skin color. But the prevalence of *mestizos* made pigmentation an unconvincing argument for paternity, and for this reason the reports written by Lima's Protomedicato were not scientific treatises but rather reflections of the father's status and of contemporary social conventions.

In the case of Manuela, Norberta's daughter, the inspection carried out by the Protomedicato circled warily around the possibilities:

We examined the mentioned Manuela with attention to the class of the mother, which is that of white *mulata, quarterona*; it was not easy to form a secure opinion of the daughter, given that, in the case of having been fathered by a Spaniard she would also be the daughter of a Spaniard; and if she originated from a black, or from a *mulato*, the said girl would be *mulata*, or *quarterona*, like the mother. It seems that these three possibilities, that is, Spanish, *mulata*, or *quarterona*, cannot be deemed in her appearance; the judgment remaining inclined that the mentioned Manuela might be the daughter of a *cholo* [darker-skinned person without clearly defined racial features] father. But as these conjectures are so fallible no final judgment may be ascertained.

A delicate question of conscience concerned whether a child whose mother was a slave could be declared a Spaniard if the father was known to be one. And nobody would think of suggesting that a Spaniard could be a slave. This tight spot in which the scientific and ecclesiastical authorities found themselves explained a necessarily loose ruling: Manuela was a *chola*. There were laws that determined the obligations and rights of the distinct racial groups, but *cholo* did not figure among them. Thus the owner, the female slave, the state, and the Church bore no responsibility. For some time all parties could rest peacefully. But as rumors about these episodes began to spread throughout the slave population and as claims put forth by female slaves were increasingly substantiated, the questions grew louder and more insistent.

Disputes persisted until after the abolition of slavery. In 1839 Archibald Smith, an English traveler, asserted that "Such is the influence which slave domestics exercise over the feelings and comfort of private families, and we would even add, over the moral and physical features of the community, that it would be impossible to give a correct picture of the state of society without first cursorily viewing the condition of the slave population in Peru" (1839, 1:106).

Given the social implications of the presence of slave children in owners' households, it is likely that only a fraction of such cases were aired in the courts. The modesty of wives and the trepidation of slave women encouraged silence, which often brought slaves manumission quietly and discreetly, to safeguard the family honor. Solutions within the four walls of the household were more feasible and less disturbing. These solutions did not necessarily end the relationship between the male owner and female slave. With varying enthusiasm, slave children would assume household chores and occasionally acquire the privileges of legitimate children. These alternatives emerged after slavery was abolished in 1854, in many cases that sought to demonstrate relationships of filiation. An example—with additional discord between slave siblings—was the case of Cesilio and his sister, both children of Don Felipe Alvarado and the slave Catalina Paniso.[20]

In 1857 Cesilio Alvarado filed a suit against the estate of his father, Don Felipe Alvarado, in order to prove that Don Felipe was his father. Cesilio claimed, "During my entire life I have worked only in the service of my father, even managing and having active say about his property." Prominent witnesses—among them several merchants and mine owners—corroborated Cesilio's assertions. The sister (according to Cesilio she was a child of the same father and mother) accused Cesilio of being a mere slave of her father and claimed that she was the only heir. Cesilio managed to prove his filiation with his *carta de libertad*, which stated that Don Felipe and Catalina Paniso had five children, two of whom were Cesilio and his sister Isabel.

In its manifold variations in an owner's family life, the presence of slaves was the source of continuous mistrust and rifts. Female slaves found ways to bring their demands to the attention of owners; many male owners experienced emotional blackmail as the consequence of easy sexual access to female slaves. And the presence of slave children within their owners' households had to be hidden, by wives or by husbands for more obvious reasons. Cohabitation of owner and slaves dislocated relations among all parties, whether on the haciendas of Lima's hinterland or in the urban sphere. But the greater the distance from an owner's control, the greater autonomy slaves had to formulate family strategies—where they lived, what they were able to save, how they survived as families.

Whatever slavery's conditions or nuances of arbitrariness and cruelty, the slave family was the unit that furnished a base of action and affective—sometimes even spousal—links. In many places the family was the predominant social structure among slaves. In contexts as disparate as the United States (Gutman 1976) and Martinique (Tomich 1990) some contemporary authors interpret the slave family as a mechanism of social articulation and as a tool slaves used against the impositions of owners; they describe the family also as an administrative mechanism that owners (especially planters) set up to distribute food, clothing, and shelter and to enforce discipline as well as to guarantee the reproduction of the slave population. Thus, they note the merging of nineteenth-century Victorian codes with a rationale derived from managerial practices and portray the family unit as the universe of social and emotional cohesion for slaves and free persons alike and, for slaves in particular, as defense against the arbitrariness of the power that slave ownership implied and which it gradually undermined—even as it worked within the context of slaveholders' interests and contemporary ethical sermons. (Gutman 1976; 1975, 88 ff.)

Yet I believe that we must look carefully at the specific situations of slaves' married and family life: the circumstances and the responses varied widely, expressing multiple links as well as conflicts. Slaves, and especially female slaves, knew many different marriage arrangements and family lives, often enough a succession of situations. Invariably an owner's interests—sexual, economic, political, moral—had an impact on slaves' construction of emotional bonds. But conflict in slaves' marriages did not always come from an owner's interference. What about slave families who lived outside a master's house, who had enough earnings that they and their children could survive, who had not undergone an owner's sexual assaults? If we find that conflicts within slave families differed from conflicts detectable in the rest of society, we can speak more specifically of the slave family and its peculiarities, of an intimate level of life reflected not only in the day-to-day existence of slaves, but also in the prevailing characteristics of gender domination.

The first point we must explore concerns slaves' patterns of gender relations and the diversity of their situations and responses, reflecting the heterogeneity of slaves' positions and intimate relationships as well as the divisions within black society. The conditions of slavery acted on individuals who were fathers and mothers, who worked to save money, who took part in community life. In the history of the Lasmanuelos family, we traced various patterns of marriage and conflict: in the first generation, the familial and matrimonial life of Manuel and Manuela, who jointly struggled over who would work in Lima and how to obtain freedom; in the second, the ethnic inequalities of Manolo and Manola that gave the wife greater earning capacity and the husband experience of banditry and maroonage, and that led them to separation and unemployment whereas in the circumstances of Manolo's brother Manolito, the needs of his wife's owner and the ups and downs of his own family determined their life.

These three sets of circumstances give us a context for reviewing the different expressions of conflict that slavery created in the private relationships—marriages and families—of Lima's slaves.

The Character of Matrimonial Alliances

In order to describe the character and significance of marriages between slaves and between slaves and free persons, I examined the records of all marriage licenses issued in Lima at ten-year intervals from 1810 to 1850.[21] One initial discovery was that the percentage of slaves who married (in other words, of couples with at least one slave spouse) was relatively high in contrast to the total number of marriages in Lima during this period (Table 10). As part of an agenda of social ascent, marriage guaranteed legitimacy, an important factor in terms of social respect and moral values. And as stated earlier, marriage could also be a step toward freedom.

If we compare the percentage of slaves' marriages to the rates of decrease of the black population during these five decades, we can

TABLE 10. *Marriages among Slave and Free Population of Lima: 1810–1850*

Year	All Marriages	Marriages involving Slaves (%)	Slave–Slave Marriages (%)	Slave–Free Marriages (%)
1810	386	138 (35.7)	118 (85.5)	20 (14.5)
1815	348	97 (27.8)	69 (71.1)	28 (28.9)
1820	241	64 (26.5)	48 (75.0)	16 (25.0)
1830	189	44 (23.3)	29 (65.9)	15 (34.1)
1840	168	16 (9.5)	6 (37.5)	10 (62.5)
1850	200	20 (10.0)	9 (45.0)	11 (55.0)

Source. AA, Licencias Matrimoniales.

see that, in relative terms, the numbers of slave couples who formalized their unions rose slightly, whether one partner was free or both were slaves.[22] Marriage augmented proportionally, although in absolute terms it decreased.

Of the marriages in 1815, twenty-eight (28.8 percent) involved a slave spouse and a free spouse, and sixty-nine (71.1 percent) involved slave partners. In 1820, sixteen (25.0 percent) were between a slave spouse and a free spouse and forty-eight (75.0 percent) between slaves. In 1830, fifteen marriages (34.1 percent) involved a slave with a free spouse, and twenty-nine (65.9 percent) were between slaves. The percentages for 1840 and 1850 were 62.5 percent and 55.0 percent for marriages between slaves and free persons, and 37.5 percent and 45.0 percent for marriages between slaves, respectively. Thus, a second finding was the much more frequent choice of a free spouse in these decades. From an overwhelming percentage of marriages between slaves (85.5 percent in 1810), we move to a percentage in favor of marriages between free persons and slaves (bordering on 60 percent in 1840 and 1850). Between 1800 and 1820 the same tendency appeared, in the parish marriage records of San Lázaro and Santa Ana: twice as many of the marriages among *casta* groups were between slave and free spouses as between slaves (Table 11). Undoubtedly, the choice of free persons as spouses resulted from the decrease of slaves in Lima yet also reflected the high value that slaves placed on the

TABLE 11. *Marriages between Slaves or between Slaves and Free Persons, Santa Ana and San Lázaro: 1800–1820*

Marriages	Santa Ana (%)	San Lázaro (%)
black–black partners	226	32
slave–slave	193 (56.3)	28 (59.6)
slave–free	33 (9.6)	4 (8.5)
black–*casta* partners	117	15
slave–slave	40 (11.7)	6 (12.8)
slave–free	77 (22.4)	9 (19.1)
Total	343 (100.0)	47 (100.0)

Source. AA, Libros de Matrimonio; further explanation of source is in chapter 4 note 23.

TABLE 12. *Ethnic Origins in Marriages within the Black Population of Santa Ana: 1800–1820*

	Free Man–Slave Woman (%)	Free Woman–Slave Man (%)
Spaniard	1 (2.7)	— —
mestizo	— —	5 (12.5)
Indian	3 (8.1)	9 (22.5)
quarterón	1 (2.7)	1 (2.5)
pardo	6 (16.2)	— —
zambo	11 (29.7)	9 (22.5)
moreno	2 (5.4)	— —
chino	3 (8.1)	6 (15.0)
mulato	6 (16.2)	4 (10.0)
black	4 (10.8)	6 (15.0)
Total	37 (99.9)	40 (100.0)

Source. AA, Libro de Matrimonio 3, Santa Ana.

state of freedom and on those means that increased the likelihood of its acquisition.

The higher frequency of marriages between free women and slave men documented in the parish registers of Santa Ana (Table 12) reflects the higher status of free women, the demographic imbalance between the sexes—an overwhelming majority of free *casta* women—and the fact that their children would be born free. Although in Santa Ana owners had more direct control over their slaves' marital choices, the discrepancy was almost nil with respect to the choices of slaves and free persons in San Lázaro, a parish in which—as we have noted—the black population had more capacity for mobilization and greater autonomy. This similarity most likely signifies that owners' wishes interfered very little in slaves' marital choices and that their option margin was quite wide and unfaltering. Another indicator that substantiates the same pattern is the frequency of marriages in both parishes. If we divide the number of each parish's inhabitants (in the 1813 census San Lázaro's population was 9,711 and Santa Ana's 11,432) between the number of partners to marriages between slaves and to those between slaves and free persons, we can verify a slightly higher incidence of marriage in San Lázaro (11.8 percent) than in Santa Ana (9.5 percent), a modest discrepancy that reveals some resistance to slaves' marriages. We will see later that the relative freedom of slaves' matrimonial choice expressed in such figures, along with the influence of owners, also fit into the broader process of the construction of families and conjugal ties.

The advantage of the parish registers is that they occasionally recorded ethnic origins for marriages within the black population's different subgroups. The figures gathered refer to the first two decades of the nineteenth century, and as in other matrimonial records, the data set is not always complete.[23] If we explore the same data for Santa Ana and San Lázaro, to elucidate the decisions of slave men and women to wed a slave or free spouse, we notice that among *casta* groups in Santa Ana, out of a set of 117 cases, 77 chose a free spouse and 40 a slave spouse. The partiality for a free spouse was even more evident in the smaller sample from San Lázaro, where out of a set of 15, 9 chose a free and 6 a slave spouse. Overall, including black and *casta* groups, about two-thirds of the recorded marriages involved two slaves (Table 11). Variations in skin color within the black population may well explain the choices of the free men and women who married slaves.

Free men often married *zamba* and *mulata* slave women; free women most often chose partners outside the black population (Table 12). Slaves married to *mestizas* and indigenous women accounted for

35.0 percent of the Santa Ana sample, a choice that probably reflects the legal status of any children their wives might bear, since slavery was inherited from the womb. Aside from this quite visible emphasis, we might conclude that legal status was more important than actual skin color because the distribution was nearly equal with respect to other factors.[24] As we have seen, this assertion had a parallel expression in the election of *cofradía* queens.

A still larger perspective shows us that urban slaves usually chose spouses from the same ethnic group, a pattern that applied to all the urban racial groups. The percentage of marriages in which each partner belonged to the same ethnic group amounted to 64.4 percent in the parish of Santa Ana, and to 61.1 percent in San Lázaro from the marriages recorded between 1800 and 1820. Both these percentages are lower than those Haitin (1986, 293) reports for the period between 1790 and 1810, starting one decade earlier with the 1790 census. The gap between the percentages might indicate a greater opening toward interethnic marriages as the nineteenth century progressed, an option that was certainly also related to the *casta* population's increase and the slave population's decrease.

Therefore, several clear tendencies emerge despite differences between the parishes. Over the course of the first half of the nineteenth century more and more slave couples organized their lives and their families around their marriages. Status itself had more weight in marital selection than pigmentation: slave men wed free women or chose their partners from other subgroups within the black population such as *mestiza*, and especially indigenous, women.

Once they were married, slaves often found themselves in two universes—the households of two owners (if each spouse belonged to a different owner), or one inside and the other outside the owner's residence. In both spaces owners had some bearing on the couple's life, although in one case more than in the other. Given the frequent presence of one free spouse, conflict often involved mixed situations as one partner worked and lived in the owner's house while the other earned daily wages and lived independently in the urban area.

The Role of Owners in
the Married Life of Slaves

To marry in the nineteenth century, a man or a woman needed the father's consent. Contravention of paternal power meant exclusion from the inheritance (Gilbert 1947, 38–39), although (as Seed [1988, 7 ff.] demonstrates for colonial Mexico) the patriarchalism that controlled matrimonial alliances as a powerful ideology in the era of Enlightenment was in no way monolithic. A growing stimulation of individual freedoms began to break down the all-powerful paternal authority (Mariluz 1960, 94). Many men and women who married in the nineteenth century had no living parents. Life expectancy in the general population hovered around the age of fifty-five. For slaves, an owner's authority replaced patriarchal supremacy because in their case the likelihood of having a father living or present was lower: parents and children were separated by the Atlantic trade, owners divided up slaves with successive sales, and the life expectancy of slaves was even shorter. Although the free choice of a spouse was an established right dating back to the seventh century (Goody 1983) in colonial Lima as in Europe, other interests often stood in the way.

Even though the parental consent recommended for slaves was never officially ordered, it was exercised (Konetzke 1946, 20). As the Catholic church struggled against sinful cohabitation, immorality, scandalous life-styles, and superstition, it actively supported claims by slaves in the name of marriage and matrimonial life. Confronted with the accusations by slave women in domestic service against owners who "committed sin daily," the Church offered less decisive aid than in cases involving married slaves. In one case it would favor the owner's authority and in another, divine law and the right of choice and consent. Sexual life should take place within the boundaries of marriage; anything else was sin.[25] Nonetheless, ultimately it was up to the discretion of owners to follow these moral recommendations or not. Individual convictions and conscience, and possibly social pressure, were the only forces that promoted the acceptance of these suggestions.

Owners—who as we have seen were generally uninterested in the reproduction of their slaves according to Catholic law—did not always understand why the authorities should enforce social morality at their expense.[26] Slaves needed their owners' consent in order to marry; if owners resisted, slaves had to request the Church's intermediation. In the Santa Ana parish in 1808, of a total of 763 slaves living in 187 households, 132 (17.3 percent) were or had been married,[27] a percentage much lower than the 35.7 percent that represented the number of marriages between slaves and between slaves and free persons in Lima in 1810 (Table 10). This statistic suggests that slaves who actually lived in their owners' households had to overcome resistance in order to marry and indicates that a higher percentage of married slaves (the difference between 35.7 and 17.3 percent) lived outside their owners' households, probably contributing day wages.[28] We may infer the resistance of owners in Santa Ana from the matrimonial age of slave men and women, which was slightly higher in Santa Ana than in San Lázaro.[29]

Owners always had the upper hand over slaves but less absolute authority over them once a couple married. The Church was very interested in maintaining the marital unit and often intervened to prevent the arbitrary relocation of a married slave from one place to another, least of all out of Lima; the sale of a married slave proceeded only with the ecclesiastical court's approval. Marriage gave slaves a way to acquire more freedom in their relations with owners and to expand their means of defense before the courts—even though it brought the Church into their lives and into owner-slave relations. Once married, they had to follow the same moral obligations as the rest of Lima's inhabitants. Measures such as the annulment of marriage for noncompliance with required formalities applied to slaves, as did decrees prohibiting marriage with a second or third spouse when the death of the previous spouse had not yet been confirmed and when the Church could suppose bigamy or any other encumbrance.[30]

On the margin of a possible annulment for nonfulfillment of required formalities (including an owner's consent), slaves—who could not be castigated with exclusion from the inheritance—had almost greater liberty than other couples to choose their spouses. Nonslave newlyweds who lacked parental consent faced social reprimands and forfeiture of any family legacy. However, slaves could ignore nonconsent of an owner without grave consequences. The only punishment conceivable was nullification of the marriage.[31] An owner who opposed the marriage of his slaves was not complying with a divine precept, and certainly slaves did not find it too difficult to renounce their inheritance. Once married—with or without permission—the slave could be unwed only if the other partner appealed a slave's false claim to be free;[32] the owner had no say in the matter.

In extreme cases slaves defied an owner's power to stop the marriage. For example, to circumvent a master's right to interfere, a slave might argue that at the age of twenty-five he should have the same freedom from parental consent that the rest of the population had. Thus Rafael Astorga, a slave of the Caucato *panadería* whose owner refused to grant his consent for Rafael to marry the *parda* slave Petronila Torres, simply alleged that "the contracting party having reached the age of twenty-five years does not require the consent of the parents, *and much less that of owners for their slaves.*"[33] Using this argument, Rafael and his betrothed obtained the ecclesiastical court's permission to marry.

Underlying this constellation of strategies invented by owners and slaves alike to grant or deny or evade consent was a fundamental contradiction between slavery and free spousal choice. Freedom of action and of free will appeared in slaves' arguments when a thoughtful individual asked: "Although slaves might not wish to leave the house, will they be sold whether they like it or not just because their master might wish to sell them? Is there any justice that prevents them from being sold or experiencing any extortion? . . . Masters are owners of the slaves in terms of the money they pay for them, but not in terms of their will."[34]

Within the margins of slavery, responses to the resistance of an owner fall into four categories: direct intervention by the ecclesiastical court, escape, search for a more compliant owner, and nonacceptance of the owner's authority over marital decisions, which often—as the slave we quote explained—involved not property rights but rather the right to exercise authority over a slave's will and conscience.

Another way to evade an owner's obstruction was manumission, a response situated outside slavery and within the opportunities offered by daily wages. Pablo Salazar, a free *mulato*, succeeded in convincing the archbishop of Lima that the arguments the count of San Miguel was using to prevent his marriage to a slave woman were arbitrary. The archbishop entrusted a religious attorney to "cut at the root the scandal that stemmed from the opposition." The count argued that the female slave had eloped with the *mulato* and deprived the count, her owner, of daily wages. Later the slave woman returned to her owner's house. She was pregnant. While Pablo filed litigation against her owner, the count deposited the slave woman in a *panadería*, an act that according to Pablo had no other end but to "deprive her of communication with him." The ecclesiastical court intervened again, requesting that the pregnancy of the slave be certified. We do not know the end of this story, but we know that the owner's attitude shocked the archbishop, since before the escape Pablo had offered to pay the count the purchase price of the female slave.[35]

Here was a typical case: a free man who wished to marry a slave woman and was willing and able to pay her purchase price. He was outside, while she was inside an owner's household. The master did not let his female slave marry, yet against the property right the *mulato* opposed an economic argument (payment of the female slave's purchase price), a moral argument (marriage with the pregnant slave), and an ecclesiastical argument (spousal communication).

For male slaves as well, *limeño* society offered various alternatives. One such slave who recognized and took advantage of all the opportunities before him belonged to the priest Custodio Montesa. The slave's mother belonged to the same master and the slave had escaped. Repenting the escape, he requested that the priest take him back. Shortly after he returned, the priest gave him thirty pesos to purchase materials and learn the profession of shoemaker. Once established, the slave proceeded to get married without his owner's permission, telling the vicar general who recorded the marriage that he was of indigenous origin. He fled again and this time when he returned, he "proclaimed himself to be a soldier," of nothing less than the royal regiment, and "defined himself as a free man."[36] Apparently, changing ethnic status was possible and advantageous depending on the objective. The slave entered and left the master-slave relationship when he wished; it was almost as if he used a return into his master's care to catch his breath, rest, and then continue on. Neither did the change of legal status appear to be too complicated, which indicates that the legal barriers were blurry. Neither the state nor the Church had the authority or the means to control the adventures of this slave. The owner remained alone in his attempts, and he was the one who—with his slave's baptismal certificate in hand—would end up asking the viceroy for a refund.

This male slave simply completely avoided the opinion and consent of his owner: the female slave's situation was more subject to negotiation and suggests that owners exercised greater control over female slaves. The contrast between the two cases is even more striking because in the first case the owner was also a woman, whereas in the second it was a man, a man who as a priest perhaps found that care for his position allowed him less room to maneuver in the city than his slave had.

Apparently within approximately half a century two factors had reduced the authority of masters: the decisive intervention of the Church and the advancement of the demands formulated by slaves. For example, in a case similar to the one described, a free man who wished to marry a slave woman in the 1750s had to deploy a complex strategy to get his case heard before the court and make it stand out from the plethora of similar cases: "He must arrive at the dissolution of slavery in this particular case without allowing [the case] to seem to attack the idea of slavery in general" (Trazegnies 1981, 156). Fifty years later, an owner's resistance to a slave's married life, to granting his permission, and to receiving payment for the female slave would be interpreted as "a scandal" that could provoke the intervention of Lima's archbishop.

Yet owners, in order to prevent slaves from using such stratagems to force their consent, had their responses, which the courts and slaves knew well. Owners could raise a slave's price or seek a new appraisal; either expedient made it difficult or even impossible for a slave to purchase his or her freedom or negotiate a transfer to another owner. Owners could put forth real or false accusations of robbery or other criminal offenses. They could—as in the case of Pablo—argue that they were owed daily wages. The simple announcement that a slave wanted to marry seems somehow risky, given that owners faced with such a decision might take precautions as severe as depositing the slave in a *panadería* (which would make it difficult to find a new owner) or attempting to sell the slave outside the city.[37] Nonetheless, these appeared to be isolated incidents.

We have observed some rather significant variations in owners' willingness to grant consent. They usually gave permission for both spouses who were slaves, and slightly more often for male slaves who wished to marry free women of other *casta* groups. Both tendencies

TABLE 13. *Owners' Consent and Status of Partners in Slave Marriages: 1810, 1815, and 1820*

	Marriages (%)			
	1810	1815	1820	Average with Owner's Consent
one owner (both slaves)	94.2	100.0	76.9	90.3
different owners (both slaves)	94.2	94.5	83.4	90.7
male black slave–black free woman	100.0	54.5	90.0	81.5
female black slave–black free woman	90.0	71.4	83.3	81.5
nonblack free man–female black slave	75.0	100.0	71.4	82.1
nonblack free woman–black slave man	—	75.0	100.0	87.5
Average	90.6	82.5	84.2	85.6

Source. AA, Licencias Matrimoniales. Three-year sample.

indicate that owners knew that permitting a slave to marry a free person would generate problems and convert their slave property—given the greater capacity for accumulation that living outside the owner's household afforded—into a possession with a dubious future. And such tendencies suggest that owners preferred to keep greater control over slave women, perhaps because in many senses they were more useful. Yet whether slaves chose free or slave partners, most owners were quite willing to consent to the marriages. In the great majority of the cases (85.6 percent)—with or without pressure—owners granted their consent (Table 13). Delay was possible but over the long term a marriage was difficult to prevent.

Familial and Marital Life: Freedom with Conflicts

Slaves demonstrated their desire for a married life in their strategies such as the daily wage or seeking the Church's support against owners unwilling to give their consent. Similar arguments based on economic achievement or on the sanctity of family bonds helped slaves avoid relocation outside the city as well. In all the cases in which slaves protested their owners' intention to transfer them outside Lima's gates, the ecclesiastical court's final decision mentioned the existence of marriage and required owners to maintain the couple's unity.[38] And some slaves, who had been separated for a few decades, used the argument of marriage to be reunited in the city. The judgment was the same even when the owner claimed that he had not known that his slave was married.[39] In this case the owner, who had sold his slave without declaring the slave's "flaw of being married," eventually had a suit (*juicio de redhibitoria*) brought against him to cancel the sale. Owners clearly felt that a slave's marriage worked against their interests, especially when the spouse lived outside the household.

The task of obtaining an owner's consent was doubly difficult for a female slave who had maintained sexual relations with her owner. Depending on the degree of the owner's emotional proximity to the slave, a confrontation between two men over one woman might unfold. From the slave's perspective, "illicit intercourse" with the owner was an argument to use before the ecclesiastical court to forestall the owner's decision. A ruling in favor of a slave in this situation was plausible if the future bride had a judgment against her owner pending in court.[40]

When owners could not prevent a marriage, they often attempted to impose restrictions on the married life of their slaves. Using tactics similar to those we observed on Lima's haciendas, owners tried to regulate the frequency of spousal visits when one of the spouses lived outside the owner's house or belonged to another owner. Apparently, the established custom was that a free or slave man would spend Saturday night in his wife's place of residence.[41] However, even given these restrictions, there was no dearth of different commentaries to indicate that married life continued along lines not controlled by owners, even if these constraints could force a slave husband to hide under the kitchen table until his wife's master had retired to his own bedroom.[42] What is interesting is that when owners inveighed against such strategies in court—protesting slaves' nonobservance of the rules of game— the complaints were often dismissed because judges found them too insignificant, or perhaps too widespread.

When both slaves lived under an owner's roof, the circumstances of their marriage gave the owner a way to monitor their conduct and perhaps to ensure the production of future slaves. Slaves recognized this other face of marriage. Francisco Carabalí, slave of Don Manuel Bittar, in a letter to the archbishop, stated that his owner had purchased him for domestic service, and "I have fulfilled my obligations without remark; to further ensure my person my stated master made me take the sacred vow of marriage with Dominga del Cristo of the Mina tribe and also a slave of the said owner." Married a short time, Francisco would complain because his owner had moved his "good *compañera*" to Pisco, "infringing the precepts of the sacred Church, making me commit sins against divine law." If his wife did not return to his side, "I might perhaps commit some blasphemy and lose my poor soul, which so cost the Creator; Your Highest Excellency is my protector, because it is clear that what God our Creator united, there is no power nor hand that can undo it. I expect consolation from Your Excellency."[43]

Therefore, while masters viewed residence within the same household as an efficient way to comply with ecclesiastical precepts and satisfy slaves' marital longings, slaves realized that this was not necessarily a just solution. Residence with the owner under the same roof could represent a permanent trap for slave women. We have seen how owners abused their female slaves; many owners did not bother to respect slaves' matrimonial ties. And certainly no slave husbands wished to witness their wives suffer rape or abuse. Francisco Ramirez, slave of Señor Portocarrero, revealed that "I find myself unable to agree that my owner bring my wife into the same house because many times we, poor slaves, living as a married couple in one house, are stifled when the owner punishes our wives. For natural reasons a husband feels fully like a man and this is the just reason for my wish that he not purchase my wife."[44] Being in the same house meant not only incurring the abuse an owner could inflict on a female slave but also submitting to the emotional blackmail that an owner's rules of conduct could impose. In a similar vein, slaves knew that dependence on a sole owner isolated them from contact with wider networks of jobs and assistance. The more masters slaves had, the greater the likelihood of patronage for individual slaves and of protection for couples and slave families.

In an increasingly emphatic manner, slaves demanded the right to a married life. Ultimately, the formulations and arguments they used questioned the integrity of ecclesiastical officials and gave wider currency to the slackening of the slaveholding system that affected other sectors of the urban population as well. A certain Domingo explained his reasoning with honest indignation:

When I sold myself it was with the condition that I could always see my wife, and thus I did not leave Lima. Now, for what reason should something granted by our holy Church such as the sanctity of marriage be denied without any other reason except that masters are even greater despots than the Church superiors, causing such scandalous divorces, which here and now only emerge in very criminal cases. . . . I do not ask that my expectation be completely satisfied, nor that my wife's master be left without her services. The only thing I am requesting is to be permitted to be with her in my spare hours, without interfering with her duties.[45]

In a similar fashion Antonio Marris, another married slave, contended that "it is well known that owners do not have despotic control to dispose of slaves however they please; neither should any slave be harmed. However, provided that the slave supply them the money for his purchase price, they should agree, without assigning them the condition of place, unless they have [committed] some crime. Yes, sir, my wife has not committed any atrocity to be banished, nor should she be deprived of her husband, since I cannot follow her, also being a slave."[46] Testimony in the case stated that common practice obliged owners to accept the money of a slave's purchase price and liberate the slave. Hence Antonio was clearly aware of the way in which the rest of society expected such situations to be resolved, though he lacked the money to manumit his wife. Once he provided it, it canceled further material losses and the rights of ownership. Antonio carefully added that he did not wish to harm the owner's interest. Furthermore, given all these conditions, a slave would aptly be supported by the argument of marriage. The logic underlying the slaves' agenda was summed up by Pedro José Iturrizaga, a *limeño* slave, in a petition dated 1818:

If we the poor slaves were to understand at the time of marriage that we were not the perpetual owners of our bodies for our entire life but rather the victims of the arbitrariness and cruelty of an owner, who wants no part of responsibility and all the rest before God (for the harm and many evils of soul and body, for which they are the responsible party), I believe that no slave would ever marry.[47]

This argument was blatant blackmail directed at the Church. If marriage were not respected, slaves would not marry . . . and would therefore live in sin. The force with which this reasoning was constructed and the circumstances in which it was formulated reinforced married life and gave slaves an effective way to gain freedom.

Finally, slaves challenged not only morality—which was validated by Church and society—but the rectitude of the social structure. On this level of argumentation, a slave could show up the ignoble behavior of a member of the nobility and repudiate being treated as an animal. In 1803 Manuel Góngora, a free black, was married to María Aparicio, a slave who lived in her owner's house in the parish of Santa Ana. Being married, they had a child who died a few days after birth (or so the owner claimed). María became ill after labor, and it was Manuel who had to pay for his wife's treatment. Manuel then demanded that his owner pay him back for these expenses. Instead of fulfilling his duties as owner, the latter rented María out as a wet nurse. "Who would believe that a subject who flatters himself as a noble would behave in this manner, he is nothing," stated the slave. María's duties as wet nurse made it impossible for Manuel to see her. And as a last cruelty Manuel accused his owner of having hidden his child, that is, the child could not have died: "He completely denies me access to his home so that I may not find out where my wife is. . . . He greedily wishes to make use of his female slave in a manner in which animals are usually treated. Their offspring is hidden in order to extract milk from their mothers."[48] Beyond challenging sexual abuse and fear, Manuel's clear aim was to vindicate human rights, to expose slave owners who tended to treat slaves as animals. He clearly indicated that his paternal rights were as strong as any father's right and that only a base and ignoble noble could deny the righteousness of such feelings. In other words, slave fathers and mothers alike furnished arguments that conformed to the way in which all Lima's citizens perceived paternity, maternity, and conjugal love.

Such powerful and eloquent testimony might lead us to conclude that the slave couple represented a unit able to oppose the schemes of owners. And in fact, marriage was a weapon of war, even if the outcome (we must not forget Antonio, who hanged himself) did not always demonstrate success. But the story does not end here. In spite of slaves' ability to use the prevalent moral principles in their own interests, slaves' marriages often replicated the patterns of behavior dominant in society at large. Marital disappointments and violence could lead slave women to seek refuge with their former masters.

A set of 622 cases of matrimonial conflict recorded in Lima's Archivo Arzobispal from 1800 to 1820, and from 1840 to 1860, included fifteen cases (2.4 percent) in which one or both spouses were slaves.[49] Of these cases, fourteen took place between 1800 and 1820, which could indicate several things. Perhaps slaves no longer appealed to ecclesiastical intervention (of their own accord or because they were denied access), or slaves' marital conflicts decreased, or the number of slaves decreased (a fact that we can confirm).[50] Overall, conflict was less than that recorded in other ethnic groups because slaves had access to a wide array of solutions other than annulment or divorce.

With the aim of acquiring the permission and support of the Church, slaves—perhaps believing more in marriage's form than its content—tried to imitate the marital and familial behavior of the upper layers of society: fulfillment of matrimonial rites, separation between respective spheres of public and private life for men and women (which for some female slaves meant refusing to do menial work), and finally the differentiated treatment of children, by parents as well as siblings. However, to keep this ideal intact required daily monetary expenditures. A husband had to pay his owner the owed daily wages. If the wife abandoned her job, the debt doubled and occasionally intensified the tensions in the slave family. Slave husbands demanded "good behavior" from their wives (or rather, the behavior they observed among other women). Slave women, for their part, asked their husbands to comply with standard marital obligations—such as a maintenance allowance. Often such expectations contributed to conflict because slaves could not afford such luxuries.

Camilo Rosales, a soldier in the *pardo* army and proprietor of a coach-building shop, saw his marriage in this light. His aspirations for his wife most likely related to his incursion into the military and his profession—fabricating coaches for the urban elite. He married a slave and related that after having been married for eight months "in accordance with an order of our holy mother the Church" to the stated María Candelaria, he had given "her the respect and assistance that I have earned in my profession as coachmaker and each month paid the four pesos and six reales of her daily wages to her owner, the cited Doña Francisca." Camilo, however, could restrain neither "the bold and chimerical temperament of the mentioned, my wife, nor more important, the adulterous tendencies that have been noted in her, with a *mestizo* whose first and last name I do not know, but who has been seen in the room of the referred Candelaria and for whom she cooks and washes clothes."[51] Camilo had not verified the circumstance of adultery; others had mentioned it to him. And here the inference of adultery from the acts of cooking and washing clothes for another man denotes the fragility of the marital relationship, which was summed up in Camilo's pointed reproach: he had to continue to pay only to receive an unfair compensation. Camilo managed to prove his wife's adultery and requested a separation. She, an indigenous *zamba*, returned to the house of her female owner.

In another case a free husband, a cartmaker, sold his house for three hundred fifty pesos in order to liberate his wife, a *morena*. After a short time the *morena* left him, and he reprimanded her not only for the investment in her manumission but also for the expenditure of more than one hundred pesos on her wardrobe before she abandoned him.[52] The supposition behind this reproach was that the purchased freedom carried the price of submission and eternal loyalty.

At the other extreme were those cases in which the woman was free, and the man a slave. In relationships of inverted economic dependence, we should expect greater equality between the couple. Yet what we find is the presence of more violence because as slaves they were unable to fulfill gender roles. Greater impotence on the part of males led to more broken bones and bruises, and perhaps monetary losses as well. One free *bozal* whose husband was a slave stated her complaint:

[As I slept,] he got up at midnight to take the key to my room and rob me of the personal labor that sweat and fatigue had earned me; he did not only do this to me but also to people in the street; in the plaza of this city he was at law for having stolen from the site of a butcher shop a quarter of meat, and he has cruelly beaten me for admonishing him for these and other excesses.

The wife, María Luisa Nieto, brought a claim against the owner hoping that he would discipline his slave. She alone could not reason with her husband for fear of physical reprisals. The owner promised to sell the slave outside Lima's gates. Nonetheless, in this case—and against María Luisa's will—the ecclesiastical court intervened in order to salvage the marriage. The vicar general stipulated that only "if the violence about which the wife complains recurs and is not tolerated by any person possessed of better education, and knowledge than corresponds to a woman of this class," would the court allow the owner to separate the couple with the sale of the male slave.[53] Owners intervened similarly in the relationships between slaves and their children. The decision not to free a child was a way to chastise slaves and to regulate a child's behavior if the child "has turned out to be disobedient, and ungovernable, so that in all conscience we are absolutely advised not to consider his freedom."[54]

Slaves encountered a gap between what they desired and what was possible: a fundamental contradiction between the urgencies of slaves' psychological and intimate universe and the absence of alternative forms of collaboration and resistance against owners. Further compounding this situation for women was the struggle for authority between their husbands and their owners—a situation inherent to the slaveholding system itself.

Legally married men were the administrators of conjugal property, a right based on the duty of a husband to maintain his wife and children. In the case of slaves, the boundaries between the authority of husband and master often overlapped. Slaves did not own property (at least legally); they themselves were property, and female slaves worked for their masters unless someone—as sometimes happened—would assume payment of their daily wages. In principle, the owner distributed the food, clothed the slaves, and commanded their obedience. Arrangements were less complex when slaves resided outside the owner's household and furnished their own livelihood with daily wages. However, this latter option tended to increase economic hardship and tensions within families. Although domestic violence was not only the patrimony of the slave population, it became almost inevitable within this dysfunctional arrangement of rights and obligations. Whereas in the rest of society clearcut relations of economic dependence determined the authority within the family hierarchy, in the case of slaves fists occasionally imposed subordination, particularly among families who subsisted on the earnings of women, free or slave.

The many hostilities and situations of conflict that could arise from the superposition of two authorities merge in the history of a woman who was neither free nor slave. When Manuela Matallana and Tomás Venegas decided to get married, she was the slave of Doña Paula Villegas. Tomás sold lottery tickets and was a mayoral assistant. He decided to free his future wife. "Having money to spare, loving my wife, and not wishing to dishonor myself by marrying a slave," he gave the owner a portion of the price asked for Manuela. Her price was 380 pesos; the amount paid by Tomás amounted to 200 pesos. Once the couple married, the honeymoon did not last long. Tomás would soon accuse Manuela of adultery with a *pardo* slave and state that despite having liberated her from slavery, "today she pays me back only by committing adultery with a bachelor."

To punish his wife's immoral behavior, Tomás asked the authorities to deposit Manuela in a convent for correction. Such a placement cost money but he was not willing to provide it. Consequently, Tomás initiated a long series of petitions directed at Manuela's female owner, to decide who would be in charge of maintaining Manuela in the convent—Tomás or the owner. As a solution, the ecclesiastical court offered to relocate Manuela to the San Bartolomé hospital, "particular to that same class of people . . . as a prisoner entrusted to the nurse so that she is not allowed to leave the hospital, threatening her with shackles that will be put on her should the need arise." Maintenance expenses in the hospital would be lower but someone would need to pay them. Shortly after, Manuela was transferred to the Amparadas *beaterio* (an institution resembling a convent, administered by nuns, in which girls received education and divorcing women found refuge); her owner paid the expenses. The owner stated that Manuela "has now been placed in the Amparadas *beaterio* by her husband, a barbarous and extremely dim man; he has not complied with his principal obligation: to feed, treat, and clothe her . . . on the said person, my slave, he always inflicts severe abuse." In addition the owner claimed that only a divorce suit would resolve Manuela's case, "so that this woman remain in peace, and so that the acts of violence inflicted on her daily and permanently involving her in legal suits be cut at root."

The reason behind the owner's altruism was that Manuela had fallen ill in the *beaterio*, where it was impossible to treat her, and the owner feared that sickness might incapacitate Manuela and cause the owner to lose the remaining 180 pesos that she was demanding in court from Tomás. Finally, when the divorce complaint was presented, Tomás alleged that no marriage had occurred and thus no annulment was necessary. He claimed that when the couple married, he was convinced that his wife had been liberated from slavery, and since this premise was false, the marriage was void and the divorce petition obsolete. He demanded, in exchange, the 380 pesos he claimed he had paid. Several witnesses, among them Manuela and her owner, were able to prove that Tomás had paid only 200 pesos. Given the body of evidence, the ecclesiastical judge revalidated Tomás and Manuela's marriage and ordered payment of the missing sum to the owner.[55]

Each party turned to the most convincing and convenient arguments when the fulfillment of responsibilities was concerned. The punishment imposed on an adulterous slave (wife or husband) would be placement in a *panadería* or sale outside the gates of Lima with consent of the other spouse and previous permission of the ecclesiastical court.[56] As we can see, moral transgressions by married slaves were punished in the same way as any other crime. A female slave would never be placed in a convent or *beaterio* for any reason; such institutions were reserved for nonslave women. In Manuela's case, the *beaterio* was an option because she was a half-slave. A monthly allowance had to be paid to a wife in a *beaterio*, and a wife—unlike a slave—could not earn daily wages or work to pay for her expenses. But the question circled, unresolved: who should provide an allowance to Manuela? Husband and owner searched—each within the context of his or her respective rights and duties—for ways to free themselves from the obligation. Though Tomás admitted having more than enough money, he relied on the owner's interest in a healthy slave and had no wish to make more payments; he assumed that Manuela's daily wages had completed payment of the amount needed. The owner had more at stake; she wished to keep the slave alive and recover the amount Manuela's husband owed; she interpreted the payment of daily wages as part of Manuela's obligation to her since the husband could not furnish the remaining 180 pesos. Given these attitudes, the slave chose to testify against her husband and return to the house of her owner. Her husband's abuse, as well as the experience during the separation, made the personal protection her owner offered the only choice possible. Thus Manuela bore the brunt of both relationships. The experience of marriage brought her neither freedom nor happiness.

Modern readers might wonder what divorce (the owner's suggestion) would have brought Manuela. Divorce, or annulment, was difficult to obtain; but if the ecclesiastical court had decreed divorce—on the argument that one spouse mistakenly believed the other to be free—Manuela would have received one-fourth of her husband's assets. In the circumstances, Tomás argued that there had never been a marriage. He allowed Manuela to slip back into slavery by evading the issue of the marital bond and of economic obligation as well.[57]

The opposite situation, in which the woman was free and the man a slave, is one the authorities must have found particularly puzzling, especially when it was the male slave who provided food and clothing to his spouse. Bonifacio Cuellar, a slave owned by Micaela Cuellar, was one of these slaves. In 1811 he complained before the ecclesiastical court about the disorderly conduct of his wife, Isidora Casaverde. Isidora had been the recipient of "the daily livelihood, underwear, and clothing that she needs along with all other necessary assistance," and she had developed "many bad habits," incessantly increasing his debts to third parties. Yet after eight months of marriage it was Isidora who ordered that Bonifacio be sent to jail, claiming that the owner had requested his imprisonment. The owner then intervened in order to save the slave from the harassment of his wife, who had supposedly been influenced by her stepfather. Now the slave requested that his wife be deposited in a *beaterio*.[58]

When marital conflict arose and the husband was required to fulfill his matrimonial obligations, being married to a slave had its advantages, even though fewer and fewer marriages involved partners who both were slaves (as we observed in Table 10). Responsibility for the slave's upkeep could be transferred to an owner, and divorce tacitly took place when the couple physically separated; a speedier and simpler kind of divorce than prolonged years of litigation before the ecclesiastical courts. When conflict emerged, and the husband—a slave—was paying for his wife's daily needs, the woman could order his imprisonment. Such requests were not uncommon, since slave status diluted a husband's authority, nor was the decision of a female slave, even if halfway to freedom, to shut herself up in her owner's house.[59] For some slaves, marital altercations (especially if they escalated to physical attacks) might mean a return to the owner's house after reaching a daily wage arrangement.[60] The paradox of this situation was summed up in a court sentence ordering that a slave "should be put free . . . by being delivered to his owner."

In spite of the fact that we are dealing with a small set of cases of slave conflict (which unfold mainly in the first two decades of the nineteenth century and thus show no long-term changes), they do exemplify the main sources of marital discord between slaves. The presence of owners often occasioned conflicts, but incompatibilities within couples played a key role. In fourteen cases of conflict between 1800 and 1820, four of the male litigants lived in their owner's house, whereas only two slave women did. In other words, of the twenty-eight persons involved in marital conflict only 21.5 percent were subjected to the vicissitudes of residence with owners;[61] the rest lived outside.

In eight of the fourteen cases, the accusation against the spouse was followed by a counteraccusation. Abuse, adultery, abandonment, and lack of food were the most repeated complaints, accusations common among the rest of the litigants in Lima's courts. Six of the fourteen cases involved adultery, five of them accusations against wives. This trend is also visible in the cases discussed earlier; accusations against wives might point to marital strategy rather than fact, since judges would pay more attention to moral arguments than to ones of personal economic convenience. Only (and perhaps surprisingly) two male slaves complained of abuse by their wives. Although the ecclesiastical court permitted temporary separations in cases of marital conflict, none of these cases reached a judicial ruling. The most frequent options it presented were agreement and return to married life or the owner's intervention in the resolution of the conflict (four out of fourteen). Sometimes intermediation meant a tacit marital separation, for example the transfer of a slave to a hacienda outside Lima. However, even if this possibility existed, the Church preferred to rescue the marriage rather than yield to spousal complaints or the exhortations (justified or not) of owners.

A slave woman might endure a beating by both her husband and her owner: the husband to vent jealousy or impotence; the owner to enforce property rights. In such a circumstance, to have a relative nearby who could echo her laments was certainly an enormous relief. When the slave Mariana Espinoza, who—"suffocated by passion"—was relocated to a hacienda in Ica, she was forced to marry a *pardo* ("a monster!" in the words of her sister). Beyond the forced marriage Mariana received prodigal whippings from her owner. In Lima, Mariana's sister presented a petition to the vicar general in her name, claiming that this double hardship was untenable "because hardship has its limits, and if both [husband and owner] mistreat her, she will be a capital victim of cruelty and a creature worthy of utmost compassion."[62] Similar help came from family members in two of our fourteen cases (14.2 percent) and perhaps occurred in other disagreements that did not reach the courts, through the intervention of the slaves' extended families or from the wider black community.

On the whole, married life presented difficulties for couples if one or both partners were slaves. At the outset newlywed slaves might evade an owner's consent, choose to live under the same roof (which under certain circumstances multiplied the potential conflicts between a slave husband and a master), or negotiate the contribution of a daily wage in exchange for residence outside the owner's household. In any of these situations, the slave couple would not escape the marital discord prevailing in society at large, and its resolution often demanded the presence of the owner and the ecclesiastical court. Even though slaves displayed creativity and ingenuity in dealing with stubborn or unreasonable owners who would not consent to slaves' marriage or grant immediate manumission, they could not transcend the limits of the existing system: more violence occurred among unhappy slave couples because solutions to their dilemmas did not exist. There is no case of a slave husband who returned to a former owner to parallel the case of the abused slave wife who returned to slavery. The wife's case embodies and illustrates the precise limits of the social creativity permitted and realizable in the slaveholding system beyond what contemporaries would call the "natural subordination" of women, and the search through all social channels to resolve a fundamental contradiction between husband and slave. Translated into simple terms: for slaves, marriage was a viable route out of slavery; if matrimonial conflict ensued, for a slave woman it was often safer to return to the refuge of her master—to remain a slave.

Chapter Five

Slaves and Their Owners

Property and Freedom

Inevitably the relations between slaves and owners took many forms. One salient feature was the interdependence that grew from the lives of owners and slaves—lives both shared and parallel reflecting their respective goals. Owners defended their property interests or simply their survival. Slaves worked toward manumission (those who had the ingenuity to bring their hopes to fruition) by gradual degrees from within an oppressive system whose flexibility or weakness they were often able to exploit, using accumulated experiences passed down from their grandparents or established through other social connections. So the members of both groups lived, in the countryside and in the city. To highlight the specific interactions we need to focus on the elements and opportunities that owners perceived as the weakness of the slave system and the unruliness of the slave population, and that slaves experienced as both misery and openings for negotiation.

Property and Negotiations

Slaves maneuvered in three spheres: as laborers in the countryside, as artisans in the city, and as servants in their owners' households. In each sphere the highly differentiated conditions of their work determined the negotiable degrees of freedom. Final success almost always depended on a fair share of luck and on the slaves' individual ability to present cases and arguments before the civil and ecclesiastical courts. Because the use of abuse and physical punishment was illegal, slaves from all walks of life frequently demonstrated that they had been victims of cruelty or mistreatment in order to force an owner to grant his or her consent for their relocation or purchase by another owner, or perhaps to compel the owner to accept their payment and issue a *carta de libertad*. A slave had to prove that he or she had been the object of abuse, and this was not always an easy or inexpensive task. Witnesses had to be summoned and convinced that they should testify against someone who generally occupied a superior social position. Moreover, a lawyer willing to file a suit had to be retained. Despite the obstacles, there was no lack of witnesses among the slaves themselves: another servant, a neighbor, an occasional visitor, or a godfather—each willing to testify in favor of a slave—as well as certain lawyers and bureaucrats who believed that slaves had to be defended and often subsisted on what slaves paid them for their services. In addition, the courts contracted with forensic experts who were in charge of verifying the visible marks of mistreatment. When a slave succeeded in assembling witnesses and obtaining a medical report, an abuse trial began.[1] The Caroline Code and the Cádiz courts prohibited mistreatment and cruelty. However, even individuals who did not directly witness abuse increasingly rejected corporal punishment as a form of correction. Since neither the laws nor the community at large sanctioned abuse, the doors to the courts were wide open to slaves. Charges of abuse became a strategy that slaves employed to change their owners or free themselves. However, since this recourse was common among slaves and their defenders, an individual could increase the chance of a favorable outcome even by an accusation of some religious or moral lapse that offended *limeño* society. The content of "abuse" extended to encompass more subtle infringements, which made slaves part of a wider "moral community."

When the slave Gregoria Santos appeared before the courts in 1811 requesting to be transferred to another owner, she claimed that aside from the abuse inflicted by the present owner, he was "a British individual perhaps foreign to our religion." Given the popular link between hostility to the British and dislike of non-Catholics, nothing was more effective in attracting the courts' attention than adducing the impiety of one's owner. This placed the slave on the side of the majority, and the owner on the side of a minority viewed with suspicion. In Gregoria's case, impiety was one of the arguments most revered by the judicial authorities, and it prejudiced them in her favor. A second argument that Gregoria used was that the owner's wife agreed with her. Both arguments—although with different objectives—were buttressed by public opinion. The slave would claim:

During this space of time I have been excessively oppressed, I have suffered infinité wrongs under the imprudent and inexperienced management of Don José Ignacio, who punishes his slaves excessively and for no reason. It is not necessary that I state or explain his general unseemliness nor that I divulge his atrocious conduct and unprecedented acts because Doña María Pontejo, Don Ignacio's legitimate wife, said of him that he was ungovernable, deceitful, audacious, and indolent and anyone else would say so.... And if his own and very good wife, who could with these words state that Don Ignacio was as evil as I made known in the proceedings... no one can doubt how much I must have suffered in these years because everyone is fully aware of Don José Ignacio's rashness and vehemence.[2]

An additional argument was added to those of impiety, public opinion, and his own wife's judgment: his youth, implying that owing to his scant experience the owner was not capable of adequately managing relations with his slaves. These arguments displayed a whole array of experiences and prejudices that were well known to the populace and authorities. The individual case vindicated Gregoria; her allegation was not formulated as a protest against the system but rather as personal experience and bad luck, reinforced by an abstract public sentiment that the authorities recognized as legitimate. As a system, slavery did not come into question, because it was "not deplorable in itself but rather became so when one was subjected to a capricious and mean owner."[3]

Witchcraft, sorcery, the evil eye, or in this situation British citizenship were arguments that complemented assertions of cruelty or emphasized the uniqueness of such cases and augured swift success before the judicial courts. Lacking arguments other than abuse, steps toward freedom because of inflicted mistreatment passed through legal channels that slaves and owners alike followed easily. All such steps by the slaves had to respect the bond of property and the rights of owners. Before slaves could search for a new owner, they had to deposit with the current owner a sum of money equivalent to the daily wages that would be lost during the quest for another owner. It was not easy for individual slaves to find a new owner; this process required time, and taking time off work placed the contribution of daily wages in jeopardy. When a slave did not possess money for a deposit, he or she had to turn to a guarantor: and, for a slave without a network of established social connections, it was difficult to obtain a guarantor. As Gregoria would say, "being black is enough so that no one wishes to stand surety for me."

In this context the *cofradías*—as we have seen—could serve as an alternative channel. *Cofradías* represented a possible source of credit, yet seeking their support could be risky. They lent money. If a slave's attempt at manumission failed, the *cofradía* would recuperate its investment by selling the slave at a higher price in order to cover the slave's initial value, the surety, and potentially contracted diseases. But other less compromising alternatives existed.

Within a slave's social network, relatives and friends might stand surety or at least offer help in the search for a new owner.[4] If it was difficult for owners to hush up a slave's flaws and recover the money invested in his or her purchase, for slaves to do the same was a genuine feat. Slaves had to face additional expenses such as obtaining a sum equivalent to the deposit of outstanding daily wages, had no immunity against possible diseases, and in general had to earn their own livelihood during the period between the old and new owner. All these circumstances called for a rapid solution, especially when the slave was not in a position to pay his or her purchase price. Thus, another way to obtain a guarantee was to secure the interest of a new owner who might be willing to give the slave his or her entire purchase price in exchange for a commitment of labor until the incurred debt had been paid. Such covert tactics prolonged slave status or in any case made slavery into a kind of debt-peonage in which the slave temporarily gave the new owner his or her *carta de libertad* as insurance and recovered it as soon as his or her debts had been settled.[5] In this way the surety guaranteed by legislation perpetuated slavery in a more sophisticated manner—under the liberal mandate of property. It was a way of reaching a truce with a still weakly defined liberal ideology without prejudicing the "interests dear to the nation" (i.e., to slaveholders).

To be on the safe side, so that the slave would not flee once he or she had expressed his or her desire to leave the owner's control, some owners placed their slaves in *panaderías* until the transfer had finally been arranged. Consequently, slaves would be faced with more problems and have less time to track down guarantors or new owners and more complications, a situation that in the words of the slave Pablo Calero was "very unjust, as [in this case, his wife] does not have a person who will carry out the stated proceedings for her, since I am a slave and unable to separate myself from my obligations for one instant, only running the risk of finding myself in the same state [deposited in a *panadería*]."[6]

The lower the slave's price, the greater the possibilities of obtaining a new owner and also ultimately of freedom. An efficacious way to lower one's price—aside from testamentary negotiations, emotional blackmail in the context of domestic relations, or claims of good service—was to possess "defects": to be a habitual runaway, a drunk or loafer or thief; to be sick or to claim that one was either too young or too old for a certain job or duty.[7] In other words, inversion of the moral code to claim ineptitude could be a path toward freedom. But owners also used the device to rid themselves of a slave in failing health whose treatment meant expenses. In some cases, self-accusations and feigned illnesses were strategically utilized by slaves and supported before the courts by persons interested in purchasing the slave. Both parties—slave and new purchaser—would secure benefits. For the former a lower price meant a smaller payment for the purchase of freedom in a foreseeable future. Moreover, the transaction (the change of owner and the price) would figure in notarial record books that offered documentary proof of the slave's value, critical in a legalist society such as Lima's to restrict the new owner's arbitrariness. And the new buyer would gain, simply because he or she had to pay less for a slave. This silent complicity had concrete expressions.

For example, after his slave Juan de la Cruz Zapata had asked to be sold, Doña Rufina Trevino stated that "sickness is a pretext to lower his own cost and thus more easily purchase his freedom."[8] These arguments could be a double-edged sword. Owners countered with the same reasoning, which bordered on social and religious hypocrisy in more than a few cases. Judges often heard counterarguments such as the one by Luciana Josefa's owner, Doña Paula Almogera:

Especially when she brings this suit against me just because I ordered her to come to my house as a servant, and because other persons are enjoying her services. These persons incite her to file this suit that they uphold in her name, trying to make me believe that she is sick; and this is another reason why her request to be transferred to a new owner or gain freedom should be denied, because her health should be discussed first, not her freedom. What advantage will the new buyer derive from a supposedly sick slave? Would it not be inhumanity, after the distinguished merits and benefits that she says she has provided for me, to demand public compassion because her owner grants her freedom when she is sick and cannot be of service? Never, Sir, will such a thing be stated of me, I do not agree nor will ever agree to such nonsense. I wish to treat and assist her, if she is sick; and if she is well it is necessary that I seek protection of the property that I have of her service, of which I cannot be stripped because I own her.[9]

We can assess the sincerity of Doña Paula's declaimed humanitarian sentiment from what took place. She allowed the slave to die in a hospital rather than yield to the petitions formulated by the interested parties and the slave. And none of the other interested parties were willing to pay for the slave's treatment. Luciana assumed the costs for a sickness so grave that it ended her life in the midst of the legal proceedings. Sickness, then, was not always a lie to lower a slave's price. Nonetheless, slaves turned to similar arguments with such frequency that owners used this assertion before the courts as a convincing allegation against slaves. An authentic sickness might impel a poor owner who lacked money to pay for his or her own burial to sell an old and faithful slave.[10] Furthermore, in some cases genuine illness can explain why a slave clung to an owner; it was the only guarantee that the costs of illness would be financed. Before the courts slaves could invoke the Catholic mercy of owners, insisting upon the moral and religious accountability of masters. In extreme cases their eloquence persuaded the Church and state to intervene in order to condemn—on the basis of a broader social critique—an owner's evil intentions.[11]

Owners were required by law to pay for their slaves' treatment and for injuries and thefts their slaves caused to third parties. Only rarely could they add the costs incurred to a slave's price. On the contrary, the more widespread the rumor that an owner had ordered a search for a maroon slave or the more often a slave was seen in neighborhood bars and cantinas, the worse his reputation and the lower the price to be obtained for him. For owners, ridding themselves of slaves—male or female—known to be drunkards or runaways was the most desirable option. Rumors of a slave's misdeeds could cause disaster to an owner's pocketbook. As soon as flight and stealing became the topics of gossip buzzing throughout the city, the likelihood of selling a slave waned considerably.

Given the spread of fears and accusations, we might well imagine that these were a subjugated population's passive mechanisms of resistance or its careful invention and utilization of strategies to obtain freedom. What could an owner do with a slave who gave himself over to continuous intoxication, who simply did not wish to work, who stole, who escaped for days and nights ... or perhaps even combined all these attributes?

An order for the slave's retrieval from the *pulperías* (small shops that were both taverns and grocery stores) or a search for him or her by the rural or urban police also involved expenses, and the costs would be in vain if the slave were not found. Neither was sale necessarily the best solution because if owners decided to be frank with the new purchaser, they risked losing money; if they were not honest, the swindled buyer might sue to cancel the sale. In this last case the deceived purchaser would receive not only the entire value of the "defective" slave but payment for the damage, theft, delinquent amount of daily wage, and legal costs as well. Similar conflicts between owners and slaves were the order of the day; insults and even street scuffles resulting from the actions of slaves were part of daily urban life.

In 1817 Doña Jacoba Centurión ventured to sell a "faulty" female slave to Don Martín Gonzales, without informing him of her defects. The wronged party complained:

That the mentioned slave, aside from the vice of drunkenness, also suffers from that of maroonage, and she has suffered from these for many years, even though she has on several occasions been placed in various *panaderías* by the stated Doña Jacoba, thus, that for this reason, as well as her continual drunkenness, she is incapable of service, principally when she goes so far that for twenty-four hours or more she remains completely unfit and incapacitated to work in the kitchen or prepare food, or [do] anything else useful.[12]

The owner's laments were confirmed by witnesses who had observed the slave in "continual disputes in the *pulperías*, intoxicating herself, and almost all the time she stayed outside her house in the *cofradías*, so that Doña Jacoba Centurión, her owner at that time, frequently ordered that she be sought in those places." Doña Jacoba had to return the total amount of 300 pesos to Don Martín. In the meantime both owners had lost daily wages, and Doña Jacoba would be doomed to continue losing them. Apparently no type of control that owners were capable of exercising was sufficient to prevent the slave from getting drunk or obtaining money to purchase liquor.

But Doña Jacoba had more luck than José Ignacio Palacio, the owner of Pedro Piélago. Whereas owners of drunken slaves lost daily wages, in the case of thieves and maroons, apart from the loss of daily wages, they had to assume responsibility toward third parties and conceivably loss of the slave as well. Don José had purchased Pedro Piélago for 250 pesos. After a few months, between the persecutions the slave had managed to avoid, and the costs of his retrievals, as well as his pilfering along the way, his value had increased to 425 pesos. As we can see, the expenses were higher than his initial price. The owner used this argument before the courts to request that Pedro's *conque* be rescinded, so that he could sell Pedro to a hacienda or ask the court's assistance in selling him for 425 pesos. To the owner's surprise, the slave paid his purchase price with his own resources.[13] Within this logic, misdeeds were an obviously rentable commodity, even if owners occasionally took reprisals against the slave's relatives still under his authority.[14]

The more defective a slave, the more determined a fugitive, and the less willing a worker, the greater was the powerlessness of owners and the higher were their losses. The events that surrounded the slave José Gregorio summarize almost all the possibilities and malefactions of a slave in Lima. Reading his adventures, we can only conclude that in his comings and goings and in the manner in which he managed to get himself out of scrapes, he tricked all those with whom he had dealings. Furthermore, his case shows us the weaknesses in the mechanisms of control, the powerlessness of owners, and not least significant, the visible ruin of the slaveholding system. Therefore, his adventures merit description in great detail.

Doña Manuela Gonzales purchased José Gregorio from the widowed countess de la Vega. Using some excuse, the countess avoided showing the new purchaser the bill of sale, which stated that the slave could not be sold for more than 400 pesos, nor "outside the gates [of Lima]," and that his purchase price should always be accepted as long as he could provide it—whether to purchase his freedom or to change owners. As soon as Doña Manuela received the slave, her problems began.

Soon after José Gregorio entered into my power, I put him to work for his clothes and board, since he arrived almost naked and with nothing to cover himself up at night. The slave having offered to earn daily wages, I set him up as a water carrier at an expense of over 100 pesos in mules, materials, pipes, and other necessities. In the first week he wore down and mistreated the mule and returned without the pipes, stating that the mule had been stolen and that he had left the pipes at the pot maker's shop to be mended. I ordered he be given a second mule so that he might continue the work with other pipes; which had no effect because he fled and remained a fugitive for close to two months, at the end of which he was seized one night by Don Ignacio Negreiros and soldiers of his command in a store on Juan de la Coba street where José Gregorio along with other criminals of his class congregate to dance and spend what they rob from their owners. Quickly placed by a verdict in the supply house in the plazuela de San Francisco belonging to Don Juan Sisneros, without any work or punishment, as a form of reprimand, I made him go to the Chuquitanta hacienda managed by Captain Don Pablo Josef de Albarado, two leagues away from this capital, where he was treated with the greatest leniency and without the infliction of any harm through the favor that hacendado granted me.

I released the aforementioned after some time, believing him to be corrected; however the correction was stealing the water carrier's equipment, several books, a pan, and other items without sparing even the trimming scissors, paper, and penknife from the table. He again fled and after much time as a fugitive he was seen in the house of Señor Conde de Villar de Puente where, feigning my consent, he rented himself out for the service. He sent a *mulato* to ask me if I would be willing to sell José Gregorio, and my husband answered that he was willing to sell him but warned the buyer that José Gregorio was a thief and maroon in order to protect us from a suit to annul the sale by the stated count, whom the black had deceived. A dependent of the count then forged and produced in the name of José Gregorio the petition included in this file.

This petition stated our willingness to sell José Gregorio, with the condition and pact of being discharged from any claims to annul the sale. However the slave gave no respite to conclude these negotiations, because stealing new saddle gear and other articles, according to what the count stated as he withdrew from the sale. Instead of—as I insisted—putting José Gregorio in a *panadería* or directly assuring he would be delivered to me, the count just threw him out of his house.

The black continued as a fugitive, robbing whomever he could, for which I received several complaints principally about two dozen boxes, two ponchos, a pair of stockings, and a mule. At this time he wanted to marry and sent to me his fiancée's owner whom I warned about his vile deeds and bad conduct. Then he tried to hurt a black from whom he had stolen some bottles, on the occasion of helping him carry several large boxes of bottles from the warehouse to the purchaser's home.

One of the last nights of September, he broke into the house after midnight with the idea no doubt of cleaning out what was mislaid; his bad intentions manifested something worse, as evidenced in the fact that he came accompanied by another *zambo* or black of his class. On 27 September the stated went to the Chuquitanta hacienda claiming to have already been sold by me and convinced his new owner to transfer him to the nearby hacienda of Naranjal so he could recover from a sickness he did not have. On the morning of the 29th, about the time of mass, José Gregorio forced down a door, and breaking the lock he entered the yard and took the two best horses from the stables. While he was stealing them he was surprised and placed in the pillory. In order to avoid work and punishment for his infamy, he feigned stomach pain and claimed to have two or four fistulas on his body. He was examined and nothing was found. Being returned to the pillory, he broke and splintered the roof from where he escaped, taking along with him a new pair of shackles.

The days before this last escape he was on the hacienda, and when he was put to work with two warders he pretended to be near death, turned his eyes white, and finally made them take him to the house exclusively to sleep and eat. At this time he had the boldness to fiercely cudgel with a solid stick one of the warders who opposed his escape.

After escaping in the described manner he associated himself with a certain *zambo*, slave of Don Josef Basurco, to whom he gave some reales so that he would act as a sponsor and return him to me. No doubt, he was preparing another swindle in an imperceptible manner. That night I attempted to secure him. Nevertheless, he jumped down the roof of the compost dump and could not be found either because he hid himself in the irrigation ditch or escaped by climbing on the neighboring roofs. However, the spectacular thing was that after this he returned to the kitchen when everyone was sleeping, he lighted the fire, heated something to eat, and after satisfying himself he dirtied pots, taking as he left half a hen, a hat, and a shirt from a boy who had just contracted smallpox.

He remained a fugitive until a few days ago when with the accustomed expense, some soldiers imprisoned him and placed him in the Santa Ana *panadería*, from where he was then moved to the *panadería* at the San Francisco plazuela, where he is now.

The black José Gregorio is the uttermost thief and maroon that can be imagined; but he is even more sneaky than a thief or maroon. I will not hide his defects from anyone, and there is no one who upon knowing them will give me one peso for him. Neither should he forever be in the *panadería* nor is it reasonable that he remain there ready to kill or be killed. Neither he nor his brothers are able to procure or arrange to find someone willing to purchase him. To his price of 400 pesos, 200 pesos or more from his thefts and other detailed vile acts should be added. It is necessary to make a firm decision in order not to lose everything.[15]

Unless we assume that the owner had an exceedingly active imagination, we must marvel at the slave's remarkable skills. They brought slaveholders and authorities to a standstill. The only alternative was to sell José Gregorio outside Lima. But we have come to know José Gregorio and other slaves like him: surely such a ruling came to nothing and he became another of the city's free black inhabitants.

Owners could buy and sell slaves; slaves could purchase, rent, and also sell themselves. For this final option, a possibility was to go out into the streets to search for a new owner, sometimes with the aid of a friend, sponsor, or other loved one. Another option was to do what owners did: appeal to slave brokers, key intermediaries who were at work when the colonial period began (Bowser 1977, 125). A slave broker could set up a dialogue between different purchasers and perhaps also a way for slaves to escape difficult circumstances. As agents of intermediation, slave brokers at times found themselves suspected of complicity with slaves, and intermediation most often became a thankless duty for persons belonging to *casta* groups. In negotiations between a not so meek slave population and owners dependent on slave labor and willing to perpetuate the slaveholding system, sometimes intermediation backfired on brokers.[16]

Owners and slaves could appeal to the services of brokers in exchange for payment of a commission that they would set. Owners did so in order to avoid suits to annul the sale and to obtain a good price for the slave. And the slaves did so in order to locate a new owner, especially if their former owner did not permit them to do so independently. The brokers, for their part, sought to assure the quality of their commodity and investigated the reasons why a slave wished to change owners. Once the slave had stated his or her reasons, the broker consulted the owner regarding the slave's possible defects (typically, being too old or young, ill or drunk, or a fugitive) and the more general stipulations of the *conque*. When the broker contacted potential buyers, he might then claim to have good references for the slave. Sometimes, the broker took the trouble to make additional inquiries among the slave's previous owners and acquaintances. A slave's social image was important.

In the quest for buyers, brokers helped one another or shared out the brokerage. It was not unusual that even as brokers worked, slaves made their way through streets and into residences, searching for owners on their own. When an interested party was found, the slave remained "on trial" while the purchaser verified the flaws and attributes of his recent acquisition, including a medical exam. This trial period usually lasted no more than a few days, depending on the seller's impatience or the slave's eagerness to change owners. In the case of illness—including mange, which was widespread—or other defects, it was possible to renege on the sale and thus the cycle began again.

While the transaction was in process, the intervention of the broker demonstrated the will—whether of the owner wishing to sell or the slave to be sold—to reach an agreement and could ease strife between owner and slave. This intermediation engendered expectations on both sides for a speedy agreement. An intermediary could absorb tensions and possibly impede the slave's escape. However, the final objective was not always attained. When the proceedings with a broker stemmed from a slave's discontent with his or her owner, and the new purchaser made a negative decision after the trial period, the slave was likely to resist a return to the former owner's house. Some slaves took the opportunity to flee, especially if the potential buyer had directly communicated to the slave the decision not to purchase. The slave would not wait for the broker's return to fetch the slave in order to deposit him or her in the former owner's hands. Either possibility clearly depended on the treatment the slave received and also on the slave's initiative. And it hinged on the expertise of the broker, who at all costs would have to guard against the slave's discovery of the owner's decision.

If the slave managed to flee (or refused to return to the first owner), beyond an accusation of the broker's complicity with the purchaser to the detriment of the former owner's interests, an owner had little recourse against a less than honest broker who entered into direct negotiations with the new owner: in exchange for declaring that the slave had fled, the broker received money and hid the slave or transferred him or her to a hacienda. Or a broker might connive with the slave (for example, offering to lower the slave's price). Finally, a broker could claim that the former owner had lied by stating that his or her slave was not a maroon (however, as soon as a slave fled, he or she became a maroon, or bandit) or that a slave was an inherently risky commodity, a "commodity with feet." Some brokers were jailed for such occurrences, and when the broker had relatives among the black population, he could even end up in a *panadería* until someone paid his surety. In this way, brokers played the role of articulator and lived off an increasingly obstructed discourse between property and freedom—synthesizing the conflicts at the core of slaveholding that justified their services and allied them with slaves.

More broadly, the speed with which slaves changed owners was an indication of their mobility, added to that of their daily wages. Lima's urban slaveholders found ways to assure that slaves remained with a proprietary family—for example, through arrangements such as womb inheritance or promises of future freedom—and in return slaves engaged in a more visible strategy of negotiation, the continual switching of owners. There would always be an owner interested in acquiring a slave under the best possible circumstances, which above all meant a low price. There were very few *cartas de libertad* signed by the master into whose hands the slave had been born, rather, specifications about the identity of former owners confirm that the same slave often passed through frequent transactions. In Santa Ana's residential census of 1808, cited earlier, only in one case did members of a slave family spanning three generations live together with their owners. The parallelism between the lives of owners and the lives of slaves had limits dictated by the conquest of greater spaces of freedom and of freedom itself. Switching owners could be a way to improve living conditions and in the long run could also serve as a supplementary instrument of negotiation.

To a greater or lesser extent—and using additional arguments—slaves on haciendas, others with daily-wage jobs, and ones in domestic service fought their own battles along lines similar to those of José Gregorio. Each interstice of the society left room for an original response, which over the course of the years freed individuals from slavery and made the contradictions of the whole society resoundingly obvious. There were more than a few cases in which the dominant sector experienced internal fissures as a consequence of the actions and the ingenuity of their slaves. Nevertheless, up until the final years of slavery owners wielded mechanisms and entities of control. Some were overt, such as the variously mentioned *panaderías*; others such as unfilled promises made to slaves were more sophisticated.

The Other Side: Mechanisms of Control

The ease with which slaves—and certainly other groups as well—moved about the city suggests questions about society's mechanisms of control. Generalized disorder and the absence of a reliable and well-organized police corps can explain much of slaves' easy mobility. However, society's forms of control were multiple and sometimes extremely complex. It is difficult to know where they began and ended. They ranged from very individual mechanisms such as the owner's whip to more sophisticated mechanisms of broader yet more diffuse social control, which were manifested through expectations of social ascent, racial prejudices, and dissension within black society.

As in all cities, Lima's inhabitants knew that some places were more dangerous than others, where rowdy and disorderly characters met for various purposes. These places were usually associated with the consumption of alcoholic beverages; for the period we are examining these places were taverns and *pulperías*. Such locales abounded, in spite of the complaints voiced by neighbors, and offered amusement and diversion for some sectors of the popular classes. It was not unusual for Indians and individuals of black ancestry, including women, to be the proprietors of these establishments, many of which sprung up without the consent of the municipal authorities. In 1816—in response to yet another neighborhood complaint and upon the initiative of the taverners' guild—the municipal council ordered the "closing of the taverns of this capital not possessing a license." Although this decree existed, many managed to remain in business by pretending to sell other goods or by barring street access.[17] More than one villain found asylum and refuge in these places. Taverns and *pulperías* were one facet of the image of urban disorder bewailed by contemporaries.

From at least the close of the eighteenth century, commentaries about urban social malaise were heard, ranging from robberies to the physical disintegration of urban space. Lima was "a Babylon." Confronted with this situation, Jorge Escobedo, the inspector general and superintendent of the Peruvian viceroyalty, decreed Lima's division into districts and barrios. An edict dated 17 April 1785 established *alcaldes de barrio*, to be elected from "persons of distinction." Each neighborhood mayor would be in charge of a body of *serenos*, who would protect the peace of the city. The *serenos* were authorized to use arms after ten at night, the slaves' curfew hour.[18] Notwithstanding the authorities' vigilance, problems about the inefficiency of the urban police subsisted until at least the end of the nineteenth century. In 1827 the indictment about the ineffectiveness of the neighborhood watchmen recurred, but apparently the underlying problem was the lack of jails: "The lowest common citizen holds that inspectors in the practice of their post are nearly worthless bodies because they cannot order the apprehension of anyone, even if caught red-handed, because there is no place to deposit them and it is for this reason that every class of crime is repeatedly executed" (see also Távara 1855).

Widespread violation of another ordinance—which decreed that each resident had to have a light at the entrance of his or her house—made darkness the refuge of robbers and thieves. The meager salary of the *serenos* came from the city's residents, who seldom paid their assigned quotas. Consequently, *serenos* did not take their job very seriously.[19] Another reorganization of the police force was ordered in 1835. Yet the panorama was the same: every day wrongdoers were up to their tricks in the streets of Lima. This time it was ordered that the district governors, neighborhood inspectors, guards, *serenos*, and other employees of the police come under the jurisdiction of the Tribunal de la Acordada. The Tribunal, for its part, would rely on a squadron of armed police to be distributed "as suited public security."[20] A new reordering of the urban police was recorded in 1854, under a ruling by the ministry of government.[21] This time the authorities wished to form a battalion of *serenos*, independent of the police, with its own chiefs and officials. It was to be composed of five companies, corresponding to the number of city districts, and under the control of the district inspectors and Lima's prefect. The guards became the executors of the inspectors' commands, and the *serenos* now fulfilled another daily function of ensuring public cleanliness and clearing the streets. A new figure emerged, that of district commissioner, to whom the inspectors were to lend their support if requested.

The image that remains with us is one of the weakness and lack of mechanisms of control to regulate urban life systematically and efficiently. Those mechanisms aimed at the subordination of specific groups were better organized, such as *beaterios* for nonslave women and *panaderías* for slaves. The *panaderías*, as we have seen throughout many of the personal histories, were a place to deposit slave men and women as punishment for some crime (such as robbery, homicide, maroonage), or for nonfulfillment of obligations (such as nonpayment of daily wages). And slaves themselves would use internment in a *panadería* in order to resolve familial conflicts. The *beaterios* were places of confinement for women in the process of divorce, within which whites, blacks, and Indians attempted to settle quite similar marital problems.

The most obvious places of punishment were the prisons, reputed to be unsafe; for this reason they were less and less used in the years following independence. In eighteenth-century Lima three jails existed: they belonged to the court, the city, and the Inquisition (which ceased functioning in the 1830s with the recess of the activities of the Holy Office). In 1790 the two remaining jails sheltered 194 delinquents, of which 103 were in the court facility (Flores Galindo 1984, 163). Even in 1796 the city's royal jail (or that of the court) housed 59 prisoners, of which 15 were white and 12 *mestizo*;[22] in 1854 the number of prisoners had fallen to 35 (Távara 1855). At both times, the number of slaves among the prisoners was insignificant. A slave's imprisonment deprived his or her owner of the slave's labor power but placement in a *panadería* allowed the *panadería*'s proprietor or *mayordomo* to pay the corresponding daily wages to the owner and benefit from the slave's labor.

Beyond institutionalized penal sites, many complaints, cries, and laments from slaves who had the misfortune to anger their owners never reached the ears of the authorities. It was not uncommon for an owner's whip to exceed the number of lashes permitted. Corporal punishment did not cease to be part of the daily experiences of slaves. A slave's cost made replacement difficult, and because the number of slaves rapidly decreased the slave's last weapon was blackmail, the threat to take his or her own life. Arguments based on blackmail might even obtain a favorable judgment in legal suit, for example, when a slave pressured the authorities to allow him or her to search for a new owner. In the words of Ana María Murga: "If the master wins the case, and Your Excellency orders that I return to his service, I am determined to commit suicide, and he will lose his money just as I lose my life."[23]

Slaves were cognizant of what was taking place. Ana María Murga was returned to her owner and she did not commit suicide. Yet the possibility always existed and might take quite dramatic form. The punishments imposed on slaves, as well as actions carried out against their will, always had two faces. And reprisals were not just a means of retaliation. There was a possible margin of negotiation, even if in the ultimate extreme, negotiation or open confrontation accompanied suicide or self-exclusion, as was often the case with maroons.

Between both extremes of *panaderías* and prisons on the one hand and of suicide and banditry on the other, a possibility of additional punishment was relocation from the city to a hacienda, in other words, the conversion of a city slave into a hacienda slave. Transfer to a hacienda hung threateningly over the heads of slaves, even if it rarely took place after oral or written promises of permanent residence "inside the gates" or of marriage. The gamut of these options in some way represented the universe that tightened the most immediate confines of the daily life of slaves.

The Continual Threat: Transfer to a Hacienda

As we explore the mechanisms owners devised to move slaves from city to countryside and those slaves used to avoid the transfer, we notice additional weak points of the slaveholding system. One point derived from the most central aspects of the system's control: the treatment of slaves as objects and their distribution, which varied according to the profitability of the slave labor force. Lima's slaves often evaded their owners' attempts to transfer them to the countryside, offering in practice a corollary to the argument that the survival of slaveholding relationships and an increase in slave profitability came from placing the slave labor force in those realms or sectors where there was no other labor force, and where the exploitation of the labor force could be maximized.[24] Because the unrestrained geographic shifting of the slave labor force was not possible, one of the most pivotal elements of the slaveholding authority crumbled.

In 1809 Apolinaria Ontañón presented an appeal in her daughter's name that she be moved from her place of work. The reason for this petition was the mother's fear that her daughter might be relocated to a Chancay hacienda, owned by Doña Ventura Espinoza, "because they portray her as vicious and full of defects." Until that time the owner, the mother, and the daughter had lived in Lima. Accusing the slave of real or supposed defects before Lima's civil authorities was an argument used to alter one of the stipulations of the slave's *conque*, which stated that she could not be sold outside Lima's gates. In the cited case, the owner agreed to the slave's searching for a new owner, as long as she provided surety of her person, "because my intention is not to oppress her." The owner, after having deposited the slave in a *panadería* as punishment for committed misdeeds, placed her in the hands of a broker so that he could find her another owner. However, when a new owner was located, the slave fled. The reason for the slave's attitude was that she lived apart from her husband. She had switched owners three times in one year alone. The owner concluded, "Your Excellency will discover the perverse nature of these people of servitude and will wisely agree to a judgment that ensures my rights." A few days later it was decreed that the mother should grant surety in two days. If this were not done, the mother would be placed in prison until she surrendered the daughter she had supposedly hidden.[25]

Many owners attempted to transfer their slaves by contending that they were disobedient and rebellious. They had to prove such accusations. And a way to accumulate evidence against a slave was to deposit that slave again and again in a *panadería*. Owners knew that they were staking all that they had: if the judgment went against transfer to a hacienda, as we have seen it, later sale to another urban owner would be impossible. And even if an owner took on this risk, he or she would still have to face protests from the slave's relatives. Families had access to the *panaderías* and could verify what was taking place; some family members learned from personal experience what deposit in a *panadería* meant. In 1810 the mother of Julián, the slave of Don Francisco Riobo, the owner of the Nazarenas *panadería*, complained about the lashings inflicted upon her son "almost to the point of murdering him, tearing his buttocks to ribbons, with no attributable reason." The mother went to the judge ("as a loving mother turns to the source of Your Excellency's mercy") after Julián recovered from the beatings and managed to flee. The judge verified Julián's condition and ordered his placement in the hospital. If frequent deposits in the *panadería* could be used as evidence of the slave's disobedience and thus become an argument to transfer the slave to a hacienda, whippings (and thus, treatment within the *panaderías* that the owner entrusted to the administrator of this institution) were an argument to request a change of owner, as well as a way to find a new owner who had no intentions of relocating the slave to a hacienda. In this case the slave's mother immediately suspected that the owner wished to relocate her son to a hacienda and she intervened in order to prevent this. She requested that she be allowed to search for an owner for him in Lima. The judge ruled that no relocation of the slave should take place until the circumstances surrounding the abuse were clarified.[26] In this case the dual argument, brutality and transgression of the stipulations of the slave's *conque*, gave the slave's relatives means to paralyze the owner's pretensions. The abuse received was in this context an action that worked for the slave, as it allowed the family to keep him in the city. The law supported and recommended lenient, paternal, and Christian treatment; and society punished transgressing owners, sometimes with the forfeiture of a slave.

If the slave was married, ecclesiastical authorities intervened when they witnessed the breakup of a marriage: they wished to see slaves married and united in order to avoid sinful cohabitation and misbehavior. Apparently owners internalized this moral exigency to such a degree that when they managed to demonstrate that the best alternative was to relocate the slave to a hacienda owing to his or her unruliness, vices, or idleness, they went to the trouble of notifying ecclesiastical authorities about the impending transfer. And even then the Church would make sure that a slave spouse would be given the chance to follow his or her mate.[27]

But slave women were not obligated to follow their husbands; only if they so desired—whatever the owner might think about the other spouse—would they work together on the hacienda. As we noted earlier from the vantage point of the haciendas, women were the first to leave, which meant a tacit separation. For the same reason they were not likely to follow their husbands to a hacienda. I found no case in which slaves chose this course, men or women. Therefore, there were open channels for relocation to haciendas but few ways to prove that this course was necessary. Only in two cases were owners' measures successful. In all the other attempts, there was resistance by the slave or, even more frequently, the assistance of a loved one or spouse and the Church's support.

Complaints by parents who wished to avoid the relocation of their children were less effective. Generally, the *conques* of slaves born into the hands of a master did not specify the conditions of sale, which were established when the slave was sold for the first time. Moreover, the slave matured, and using the argument of investment in his or her maintenance and clothing, the owner usually raised the purchase price when the slave reached working age. José Llanos was the slave parent of María del Carmen Marín, who at the age of two or three was sold to another owner, Doña Juana Daga, for 130 pesos. When the girl reached thirteen years of age, Doña Juana wanted to sell her outside the capital. Confronted with the parent's insistence, the new owner gave her mother permission to find another owner for her daughter in the city. However, the owner now asked 450 pesos for the slave girl. In the appeal for a court decision, the argument to keep the girl in the city revolved around the price. The mother asked for an appraisal of the girl, alleging that 450 pesos was a price that would not allow her to find a new owner and that owners were not free to randomly assign prices to their slaves. Precisely, she stated, because the slaves "acquire an important right in order to attain the sad consolation of moving from the yoke of slavery, which would be imaginary if owners were to retain the power to impose capriciously the price they wish." In other words, only respect of the *conque* and moreover, of the slave's stipulated price, assured the slave's free mobility and consequently the possibility of loosening the ties to one's owner. The owner in this case very clearly felt the obstacles that such an interpretation placed on her pretensions of property. Her response was emphatic: "An owner is free to assign a price to his slave, without any previous appraisal being required of the former, unless the slave is found defective or if the stated price is exorbitant. The price of 400 pesos is common in this city."[28]

Reappraisal of the price, therefore, was a way to make residence in the city difficult even if the owner formally agreed to the slave's request to search for another owner. This appeal was tested particularly with children who had not been born with their *conques* in their hands and whose first sale took place before their adulthood. Given these situations, the legal appeal was usually to request that the slave's appraisal be performed by experts and in a context in which former and prospective owners could reach an agreement. Thus, appraisal in order to avoid relocation outside Lima's gates could also turn into a mechanism through which slaves—with the mediation of the judicial courts—renegotiated their purchase prices. As we have seen, the likelihood of lowering one's price was even better if defects or illness existed.

Even if only rarely urban slaves went to the countryside, the possibility hung permanently over their heads. The mechanisms of resistance not only reaffirmed slaves' determination to stay in the city or return but also fit into the privileges granted by legislation and the Church: marriage in the case of married slaves; the *conque* and price in the case of children. Transfer to the hacienda was not an effective threat. Neither the fear of urban rebellions nor the varied profitable rural jobs for slaves were forces great enough to resolve the pressing problems of the labor force with urban-rural slave migration.

Despite the determination of slaves to defend the occupational and social spaces earned in the city, it appears significant that there were slaves who voluntarily went to the countryside and, moreover, were content. Given the previously described patterns of behavior, this happiness had only one basis: the enormous fluidity between countryside and city. The mobility of slaves between rural sites adjoining the city and the city proper must have been quite great, enabling a slave from the Aucallama hacienda (200 kilometers from the city of Lima) to walk through the streets of Lima often enough to win the heart and favors of Bernardina, the slave of Doña Fermina Garcia, and bring her back to the hacienda.[29] For this couple, the hacienda served as a refuge until the abolition of slavery succeeded in finally rescuing Bernardina from the persecutions of her owner in Lima. In other words, only love and not a criterion of profitability can explain the inverse road from the city to the countryside. But far more often marriage—or rather, love—was the weapon of choice. The simple suspicion that an owner was contemplating the relocation of a slave to a hacienda was enough to bring the slave's immediate protest. Almost without exception, the argument of marriage secured a judgment in favor of the slave.

Panaderías: *Prisons and Meeting Places*

Placement in a *panadería*, the use of shackles, and the length of stay depended on the crime a slave had committed. As we have seen, owners put slaves there for several reasons, typically when they did not know what to do with their slaves or wished to prevent slaves from having their way. Then with the aid of a *sereno* they brought slaves to a *panadería*. Some owners put slaves under the control of a *panadero* and collected the daily wages directly. Given conduct such as that of José Gregorio, the combination of daily wages and imprisonment was a preferred way to control the slave population. This "practice grew so extensive that the many *panaderías* could hold no more slaves or keep them under irons."[30] On occasion the parents of a black, *pardo*, or *zambo* attempted to educate the child through internment in a *panadería* because they found the child too frivolous or wayward.

In 1803 various complaints of excessive abuse caused a thorough inspection of all Lima's *panaderías*. A fragment of this inspection, written by Dr. Baquíjano, remains with us. It referred to the nine *panaderías* of the fourth district and noted if the persons who worked there were from "outside" (deposited by outside owners) or "local" (owned by the *panadero* or *panadería* administrators).[31]

Panaderías had almost as many people from outside as from local sources. Outsiders represented a highly unstable component. They came and left according to the inclinations of their owners (or family members). Since this inspection also recorded the length of stay of those convicted, we can see that at the time of the inspection the average length did not exceed two or three months. There were two obvious reasons for this: owners did not want to be without their slaves' services for a long time, and the arduous *panadería* labor wore slaves out and might destroy their value. Local residents had longer internments and were typically maroons; some, such as the slave Esteban, had a long criminal history. In 1853 the owner of the Siete Hormigas *panadería*, Don Francisco Ramírez, recounted the slave's misdemeanors:

A year and a half ago Esteban almost stabbed a woman, a servant of the *pulpero* on the corner, and because of the complaint she made to me I placed him in prison: after three days in prison he hurt two of his cell mates, and he tried to do the same to me, for which reason I restrained him and called the police. He hurt the warder. . . . Reported as corrected, he was returned and I had him again at my service and on the day cited he purposefully caused me to lose a batch of bread, and with the permission of the commissioner I flogged him three times.[32]

Esteban's deeds were crimes—as opposed to José Gregorio's petty thefts—and there was no way to control him other than send him to a *panadería*. Thus, slaves from outside with extended stays in a *panadería* tended to be individuals with a long criminal record, even representing a menace to the owners. Other reasons for imprisonment existed (Table 14). Clearly the most serious offenders in *panaderías* were maroons, followed by robbers. Imprisonment for not delivering day wages was trivial, even though, as we saw, it was a perennial complaint of owners. The number of women deposited was much below that of men: a ratio of approximately 1:10 because alternative sites to deposit women were hospitals and, in exceptional cases, *beaterios* or convents.

Not everyone in a *panadería* was a slave. There were also free *mulatos*, *pardos*, and *zambos* who had been accused of being maroons but might not actually be slaves. Sometimes the term *maroon* was synonymous with vagrant. The inspection explicitly documented the person's status as a slave (Table 15); in others only ethnicity and perhaps the type of crime was noted.

We can see that most of the *panadería* population was free, a ratio of approximately 2:1. Local slaves were few; slaves who came from outside numbered twenty-five and there were ten free outsiders, who

TABLE 14. *Reason for Placement in the* Panaderías *of Lima's Fourth District: 1803*

Reason	Owner Outside	Owner Local
maroonage	17	27+2[a]
family dispute	2+2	1
theft	2	6+1
debts	3	—
non-payment of daily wages	1	—
no information	7+1	+1
Total	32+3	34+4

Source. BN, D 10130, Contiene la visita de las panaderías de la comprehensión del cuartel cuarto, hecha por el Sr. Dr. Don Baquíjano de la Real y Distinguida Orden de Carlos III. . . . Los Reyes, 10 de mayo de 1803. 12 ff.
[a]The numbers that follow the plus sign refer to slave women; all other slaves deposited in the *panaderías* were men.

TABLE 15. *Origin of Slaves and Free Persons in the* Panaderías *of Lima's Fourth District: 1803*

Panadería	Slaves		Free Persons	
	Owner Outside	Owner Local	Owner Outside	Owner Local
Guadalupe	6	—	5	5
Sauce	3	—	—	2
Ormeño	1	—	—	1
Chacarilla	1	—	1	3
Recoleta	—	—	—	5
Brabón	4+2[a]	—	+1	7
Animitas	8	+3	1	3+1
Bellavista[b]	—	—	—	4
Bellavista	—	—	2	4
Total	23+2	+3	9+1	34+1

Source. BN, D 10130, Contiene la visita de las panaderías de la comprehensión del cuartel cuarto, hecha por el Sr. Dr. Don Baquíjano de la Real y Distinguida Orden de Carlos III. . . . Los Reyes, 10 de mayo de 1803. 12 ff.
[a]The numbers that follow the plus sign refer to women; all other individuals deposited in the *panaderías* were men.
[b]One Bellavista *panadería* was owned by A. Aldón, the other by L. Carrillo.

were usually the ones assigned to bake bread. The explanation for this distribution is twofold: owners attempted to avoid depositing their slaves in *panaderías* regardless of the disturbance they caused and *panaderos* were reluctant to accept slaves because they knew that those who ended up in their hands were the worst of the lot, the most difficult to control and the most contumacious.

Owing as much to the composition of the *panaderías'* labor force (free persons and slaves, and many ethnic hierarchies within black society) as to the fact that in the *panaderías* the least submissive members of society existed in the worst imaginable work conditions, rather violent episodes took place. Excesses ranged from mistreatment that merited a hospital bed in San Bartolomé, to the rape of slave women by some *mayordomo* or bread distributor.[33] Revolts were not uncommon since *panaderos* often had trouble keeping their slaves in order. They could not achieve greater control through harsher corporal punishment. Civil suits initiated by the state against unscrupulous *panaderos* revealed the shrewd eye of owners determined to defend their interests and of free family members concerned about deposited slaves. In cases that depicted mistreatment and execrable working conditions, judicial action tended to defend slaves, penalizing *panaderos* with fines.

In 1818 the criminal prosecutor and count of Vallehermoso filed a suit against Don Francisco Gómez, the proprietor of the Sauce *panadería* (in the fourth district), for excessive punishment inflicted on two slaves for the crime of leaving the *panadería* to go shopping. The criminal defender stated his opinion regarding the happenings:

The punishment given to two blacks who were moved to the San Bartolomé hospital has been excessive and since the governmental edicts . . . impose a fine of 200 pesos on *panaderos* the first time that more than twelve lashes are given to a slave in their homes, and the court has barely fined him the fourth part, the *panadero* should not be allowed any appeal.[34]

The law was categorical. The only danger of a very high fine was that the *panadero* could choose to let the slave die, a less expensive solution than payment of the penalty resulting from a complaint. State authorities intervened on behalf of slaves even when the charge was neglect or sabotage of their assigned duties (for example, putting too much or too little flour in the bread dough, ruining the containers, or perhaps attacking the work foreman).[35] In these cases the judge's ruling was limited to stating that the slave should quickly be transferred to another owner or if the slave was local that the *panadero* should give the slave his or her *carta de libertad*. Slaves from outside often belonged to *hacendados* known for their readiness to transfer unruly workers to other owners. Slaves with urban experience could be a headache for owners, particularly since the correction of a stay in a *panadería* usually strengthened stubborn and rebellious natures.

Authorities took complaints against abusive owners and administrators seriously, not only because the property of owners was in jeopardy, but also because urban residents knew well what happened within the walls of the *panaderías* and depended on the daily production of bread. Those with loved ones deposited there were doubly alert. In an episode that took place in one of Santa Ana's *panaderías*, a slave from outside, Antonio Lara, was whipped. A free black, Juan Daga, a cobbler who lived on the corner of Cocharcas street and worked in a shop alongside his cousin, Antonio's brother, heard screams and ran to the mayor (the marqués of Torre Tagle) to warn him. When the mayor's emissary reached the establishment, the slave had already been transferred to the Serrano *panadería*, probably to hide the evidence of the lashes. The *panadería*'s administrator described the slave's offenses, which the bookkeeper confirmed and accused the slave of possessing a knife that he used to escape. In fact only the intervention of the other slaves in the *panadería* forestalled a "fatal outcome" because—so they said—Antonio had tried to hang the administrator.[36] Those outside were completely clear about what took place inside; those inside kept Antonio's frenzy from ending the administrator's life. And this was the same mistreated slave who initiated a suit against the administrator for cruelty.

As the inspection showed, persons from varying social backgrounds met in *panaderías*. For some, the place became a "hidden dungeon," "the whole of all misery," or "the representative symbol of all pain."[37] Yet for others life seemed quite tolerable. They enjoyed privileges, such as the right to tips or permission to leave the *panadería* in order to purchase articles (in this case, tobacco) for personal consumption. Conditions and complaints varied even within a single *panadería*.

In the inquiry after a riot that took place in the Santa Clara *panadería* in 1809, several inmates complained that "the administrator gave workers small tips when he wished and not when he should," that they slept underneath mats, and that the ration of food they received every twenty-four hours was very meager. Others said that they had nothing to complain about because the treatment and maintenance received were reasonable, that they even ate from the administrator's table and could come and go as they pleased. Those with privileges were aware of the different treatment and stated that "those who should complain are those who are imprisoned in the kneading room and are fed from the frying pan." The conditions in which this disturbance took place were significant: it was Sunday and the *mayordomo* was celebrating his birthday. Everyone participated, and the *mayordomo* "gave *aguardiente* [an alcoholic beverage made from sugarcane] to those free and shackled in the kneading room as well as those in the cold-storage room, so that everyone got drunk."[38]

In light of the severe measures that authorities took against any signs of indigenous rebellion, their attitude toward the black population might seem surprising. In this situation, as in earlier disorders, the public prosecutor believed that the rioting grew from abuse and noncompliance with ordinances; therefore, the suit did not "call for further support." Officials preferred to forget the incident and the admission by one of the instigators, the slave Domingo Larreguerro, that the whole affair had been planned and that its timing "seemed fitting to them, given the inebriated state of the *mayordomo* who was alone because the administrator of the Paceo [*panadería*] was in the town of Chorrillos."

Contemporaries understood that *panaderías* were places where conflicts were likely to ignite over differences in treatment and background—but authorities did not consider that such outbursts threatened the social order. Fights broke out not only between proprietors (represented by the *panaderos* or their administrators) and slaves, but also between members of black society. Their rough conditions and the frequent interference of alcohol often led inmates to turn their aggression against other workers in the *panadería*.[39]

The years immediately after the inspection saw no change in the conditions or opportunities within the *panaderías*. Two decades later, in the 2 November 1822 session of congress, a report of the commission in charge of inspecting the *panaderías* was read, which showed concern about "the abuses that have been observed in the stated houses, with regard to the treatment that is given to some slaves who are placed in these houses as a means of punishment." In 1821 the congress had decreed an amnesty—intended to include the slaves imprisoned in the *panaderías*—and had made proposals to correct abuses. The commission noted that the decree had not been posted in any of the city's *panaderías*. In other words, there was official concern but no translation of concern into slaves' and owners' behavior.

We have witnessed the presence of *panaderías* in the histories of several slave families, including the Lasmanuelos. Everyone in Lima knew about conditions there but beyond nonenforceable good intentions said or did nothing. In spite of their potentially explosive character *panaderías* continued to exist and fulfill their functions during the abolition of slavery. Many of them hid an owner's arbitrariness or fit the distinct objective of securing a surety, bending the will of a slave woman who felt the right to be treated as a wife, or preventing a slave's marriage. However, we have also seen that slaves increasingly objected to the reasons for their deposit. Still the mechanisms of control within the *panaderías* were very loose.

Given this panorama, we easily understand how and why slaves defined the fields of negotiation in terms of interpersonal relations. The state, along with other sources of control, interfered little in matters between owners and slaves. Legal channels gave both groups means to appeal those situations that personal relationships could not resolve. Trials allowed intermediation that eased social confrontation and perhaps muffled voices of dissent against oppression. Yet some figures and rumors provide accounts of uprising attempts. Labarthe (1955, 18) believes that Lima's slaves were well treated, even spoiled, and mentions that in the epoch of Gamarra's government (around 1835) some conspiracies and intentions to seize power were uncovered. Contemporaries talked of conspiracies to overthrow the government and assassinate whites in Lima. The leader of this plot was Juan de Dios Algorta. In 1827 the black candidate to replace the president was Bernardo Ordóñez, the bankrupt owner of a small shop in Guayaquil. When the plot was unveiled "meeting records, orders, appointments, and so forth were found," which according to Labarthe "demonstrated either enormous stupidity or an absolute security on the part of the conspirators."[40] Such adjectives could easily fit many nonblack and nonslave conspirators. It was an era in which many caudillos dreamed of becoming president. Given the entirety of day-to-day experiences, who would wonder at slaves who also held such dreams? Weren't the dreams attached to the price of freedom?

It is difficult to know what was behind such plots and conspiracies or what their magnitude and objectives were. Yet given the patterns of behavior we have recorded, and the interpretation proposed by Blanchard (1990) of an uprising by blacks in Chicama in 1851 organized by outsiders, we must posit only limited effects and propagation for these "presidential conspiracies." The panic of urban whites over the anticipated arrival of a tribal chief on a slave ship to spark a potential revolt of urban slaves never had any real foundation, but it signaled their collective urgency and despair—or certainly showed their imagination. And slaves had a decisive part in it.

Final Episodes

Slavery did not end in 1854. It ended both before and much later. Before, because it was a system undermined from within. Later, because the slaveholding system created racial prejudices whose wounds remain open, and more directly because the formal dismantling of slavery in *limeño* society after official abolition lasted at least two more decades. Cluttering the years after 1854 were suits by owners who sought to recover slaves mortgaged to other persons and to collect sums set by the official manumission council.[41] Civil suits dragged on for many years to limit the mobility of ex-slaves. Other owners, having sold their slaves or holding partial payment of their purchase prices, now pretended to be proprietors in order to collect the 300 pesos offered as compensation by the state.[42] Contemporaries decried the slow pace of this process of change or clung to their cherished ideas that correlated slave with black and black with manual labor and robbery.

Perhaps a final story will help us clarify the long transition from slavery to freedom. According to his baptismal certificate, Manuel del Espíritu Santo Real, a *moreno* of sixteen years of age in 1855, had been born free. He was raised in the house of Don Eusebio Carrillo. Through a public deed, Manuel was placed with a shoemaker to learn the trade. Soon after, several pairs of shoes vanished from the shoe shop. The owner of the shop immediately accused Manuel and two underlings of having stolen the shoes. Claiming that it was of no concern to him whether Manuel was a slave or not, he deposited Manuel in the Pescadería *panadería*, ordering that he be whipped and shackled. This not sufficing, Manuel remained in the *panadería* for a few months and the daily wages he earned (six reales a day) were contributed to the shoe shop owner in payment for the supposed theft. In this situation the shoemaker offered to sell the slave to the *panadero*. The latter requested the *conque* and the only record that the shoemaker could show him was the deed that placed him as an apprentice. The *panadero* knew that this document did not furnish proof of slave status and withdrew from the proposed sale. The shoemaker told to the *panadero* that it did not matter if he did not wish to purchase the slave, since he already had another buyer, a *hacendado* from outside. While the shoemaker insisted on Manuel's sale, the latter's defender alleged that the shoemaker should indemnify Manuel 100 pesos for each lashing inflicted and that for shackling him for the period of three months, he should pay a fine of 500 pesos. He added that even if the robbery had taken place the police intendant had no jurisdiction, and the real crime was treating him as a slave instead of sending him to prison and filing a civil suit.[43]

Thirty years after the republic was founded the combined tensions and confusions of slavery and bureaucracy generated an atmosphere that included such possibilities as using an apprentice contract to sell a slave or a convenient *panadería* to punish an artisan and demanding indemnification for whippings and accusations of participation in robbery. Contemporaries generally regarded blacks as more delinquent, even as others sifted through criminal statistics in order to dismantle common prejudices. In 1855 Santiago Távara took the daily criminal column published by the police in the newspaper *El Comercio* as a point of reference; he compared crime rates for the first six months of 1854, when slavery existed, with those for the first six months of 1855, after its abolition. The crime rate had decreased (from 36 prisoners in 1854 to 30 in 1855), although murder had risen among the reasons for imprisonment. This increase of homicide in 1855, explained Távara (1855, 35–36), came from the increase of military troops: many of the murders were committed by soldiers who were not black. "It should be warned that in both columns the blacks receive very little space: because when a member of this class commits an offense, the police usually uses the words, 'the so-and-so *moreno*,' a phrase used only once in the column of 1854." However, the majority of Távara's contemporaries did not know how to read and the minority continued to cling to the construction (and necessity) of hierarchies that allowed for the essentially primitive construction and reproduction of interests.

This social image of the black had its economic counterpart. The guilds that had weathered political separation from Spain were gradually dying out as new urban jobs opened up for *castas* and slaves (Haitin 1986, 108, 118 ff.). Later on, with greater sophistication in consumption and higher revenues from guano exports, the unskilled black population found fewer places within the traditional artisanal trades.

> The guilds, which survived a few years of republican life, did not last long. . . . Their rules were seen as strangling, based on exigencies too impossible to fulfill such as the obligation that their members know how to read and write, even though national illiteracy reached 90 percent. Apprentices disappeared. The new small industries were in the hands of foreigners. Articles as easy to make within the nation such as doors and windows came from abroad. There was no place for the artisan and manual laborer in the workshops. (Romero 1980, 41)

This loss of jobs resulted from slavery, not only in the racial perceptions it included but also in the ways slaves emerged from it. To pay for manumission, they spent savings that otherwise might help them perfect an apprenticed trade or procure work tools to compete with imports. In the struggle to survive many ended up without savings or skills. And they and their more fortunate contemporaries existed in the economic context of a state that did not, could not, and would not see the disastrous consequences of its policies. After abolition became official in 1854, those who protested the state's blindness were not members of the black population but artisans, *castas*.

> The guild of cart makers, comprised wholly of people of color, tries to sabotage the construction of the railway between Lima and Callao, which deprives them of their occupation. Shortly after, the carpenters (people of all ethnic combinations) burn the doors and windows that this train transports and for forty-eight hours they fight against the troops sent to subdue them, producing casualties and fatalities in the struggle. (Romero 1980, 41)[44]

Artisans' protests, as well as banditry and rural laborers' uproars, continued in a fragmented struggle for power and self-assertion. However, British pressures, racism, and inefficiency were more powerful than the protests of artisans. We recognize here the long-term effects of the reality and experiences of the slave system that we have explored—and within it the hiring-out system, the ethnic occupational structure, and the dissension among social groups—as a continuing inheritance and, most important, a pattern very particular to the form in which slave life developed in Lima.

Conclusion

Lima's Slaves and Slavery

As individuals and as members of social groups, slaves and slave owners interacted on a daily basis. Since each group contributed to this interaction, in assessing slavery and the varying and multiple processes of manumission we must take account of the heterogeneity of their perspectives that make up the dialectical nature of the slave system and encapsulate its contradictions. Mintz (1969, 27–28) suggests that even though slavery created the most comprehensive kind of fracturing of human relations, it was still "in every historical instance a way of life, a conception of the human condition, an ideology of society and a set of economic arrangements, in short, a cultural apparatus, by which slaves and masters are related."

Relations among slaves, masters, and other individuals all took place within the same social fabric. "Europeans and Africans encountered one another through the unequal relations of slavery and engaged in a day-to-day struggle, sometimes implicit, sometimes overt, over the organization of work and the norms and values it entailed. . . . The ability of the slaves to adapt to the routine of the plantation, to organize their own capacity for collective activity, and to physically carry out the tasks assigned to them . . . discloses the contradictory process at the heart of New World slave systems" (Tomich 1990, 216). In this sense, a plate of spoiled food set before an owner was equivalent to a whipping endured by a slave: both actions represented facets of the complex universe of the slaveholding system that grew from daily interaction.

When we grant that slaves were part of a continuous dialogue—which although skewed did exist—they become visible historical actors within a social group that constructed its own destiny and participated with other groups in the destiny of the society around them. Such an analysis not only views historical processes from different angles but also emphasizes a perspective that starts with the daily trials of slaves; in this widely neglected genre of history the creation of a black culture assumes a more important role than the action of political forces per se (Morrisey 1989, 13). And it is the creation of black culture in this very wide sense that makes up power, politics, and policies. The focus on black culture, as Gutman (1976, 31) indicates, is not slavery's effects on slaves, or external modifications in slaves' behavior, or owners' treatment of their chattel. Its interest centers on the many resources that allowed slaves to survive, a process that Mintz aptly calls "the repertory of socially-learned and inculcated resources of the enslaved." Lima's slaves expressed these resources in a multiplicity of ways.

Two of the long-standing characteristics of slavery in Latin America hold true for Lima: the importance of the Church in the lives of slaves, and miscegenation. As Tannenbaum recognized several decades ago, religion was a central component of Latin American slavery. Although the Church was a decisive agent in creating slavery, it also provided the institutional mechanisms to express and defend slaves' moral personality. Thus tradition, law, and religion were key elements in the definition of social relationships and of slavery itself. The system based on such traditions was receptive to possibilities of freedom, even as slaveholders fiercely defended their property rights over slaves. In this context, one of our central conclusions acknowledges the importance of Church and religion and, more broadly, the existence of prevalent moral codes that helped slaves attain freedom. This more general pattern not only gave owners a mechanism to profit from individual manumissions but also, and most significantly when slaves took the mechanism into their own hands, enabled slaves to negotiate both their conditions within slavery and—ultimately—their freedom.

The concepts of love for humanity, marriage as a sacrament, and broader notions of justice and ethical obligation, all intended to be valid for members of polite society rather than for slaves, became arguments that Lima's slaves used to generate compassion, exemptions, and support from judicial and ecclesiastical authorities. Without asking permission, slaves incorporated themselves into a society that claimed to stand for moral equity and impartiality. These values became those of the slaves themselves and shaped the language in which slaves conveyed their messages to their masters. It was moral breaches—codified into law and prosecuted in the courts—that gave slaves the strongest arguments against their masters. If sexual transgressions against women were unlawful, why not punish a master who forced a woman into sexual relations and who abused his authority? If the separation of the family would produce moral deviation, why tear apart slaves' families? At the core of such allegations lay the defense of slaves' family life. The Church mediated because it wished to correct immorality (in slaves and perhaps in their owners as well) and the slaves manipulated this aim in order to fortify their family links and concomitantly widen their possibilities of freedom.

Miscegenation—the other feature that distinguished slavery in Latin America—meant that over time the equation of black with slave lost its meaning. The existence of *mulatos*, *pardos*, *zambos* and an increasingly complex choice of marriage partners not only made it difficult for medical experts to determine the filiation of the offspring but encouraged slaves to view themselves as slowly merging with the white population. In their eyes, whitening distanced them from slavery. We encountered two extreme expressions of this process: slave women who bore their masters' children and questioned the justice of enslaving "Spanish" children; nonslaves in the black population who were themselves owners of slaves or perhaps intermediaries between owners and slaves. Probably what best illustrated the simultaneous process of approximation and estrangement were the power struggles within the black population of the *cofradías* or the guilds and the *gracias al sacar*, a document devised by the dominant society to confirm the whiteness of its purchaser. These institutions and the *gracias al sacar* were similarly "directed toward the *castas* to reward individual merits and at the same time to give some the possibility of social mobility to disentangle them from their fellow group and thus alienate possible leaders and generate an increased willingness to pay taxes" (Olaechea 1961, 228–229).[1] Masters in Lima were both originators and victims of the black population's racial diversification. Street frays, matrimonial conflicts, and hierarchies within institutions governed by *castas* and blacks (guilds and *cofradías*) depict the active role these distinctions played in the minds of the black population and their white owners. In extreme cases, blacks and *castas* even resorted to white judicial intermediation in order to manage the hierarchies in black society that observed racial and economic lines.

Impulses toward miscegenation were greatly related to the numeric relation between the white and black populations, as well as to the ratio of men and women within each racial group or subgroup. According to Genovese (1975, 427–428), in places where blacks predominated, whites erected an intermediate sector of *castas* in order to strengthen their power. As a result this intermediate group, both in racial and economic terms, typically expanded and used this enlargement to activate a whole set of subterfuges and strategies, creating a "*casta* society." Such societies were more open to gradual adjustments, ongoing negotiations, and racially homogenizing tendencies than societies in which economic and racial segregation prevailed. Intermittently, societies with a strong inclination toward miscegenation would reinforce racial prejudices in order to accentuate racial and economic divisions in the hopes of lessening the trend toward homogenization and reestablishing social hierarchies.[2] But such behavior characterized not only black-white relationships in *limeño* society but those within black society as well. Thus we observed one effect of a continuous process of miscegenation, the simultaneous emergence of many cleavages that undermined potential political alliances.

If we believe the arguments of Lima's landowners that there were too few slaves, how are we to understand why, instead of remaining hard at work on plantations and haciendas, slaves were able to engage in a diversity of trades—with the free population and among themselves? Since slaves were successful in relocating to the city and staying there against slaveholders' expectations, they did so by creating mechanisms resilient and sturdy enough to counter their masters' desires. Furthermore, rewards, rather than punishment, opened more and more bargaining space to slaves and became the only way for owners to keep enough slaves under their control. In rural areas slaves cultivated truck gardens or used commerce and barter of slave produce and the possibility of leaving the hacienda either to find a new owner or simply to buy tobacco at the local *tambo*. And what they achieved in Lima's hinterlands was even easier in the city itself, where the most successful slaves lived out of the reach of their masters, had their own families, and still maintained savings for their own purposes. Yet not all slaves—as we have seen—were so effective: some found themselves snared by the dual imposition of slavery and the family's upkeep, which often fell completely to a slave as part of the agreement with an owner. Some slaves collapsed under the burden; others took their own lives.

Slaves often tacitly acquired civil rights although society formally denied them. Slaves also learned to create or implement their rights, using resources from family relations, culture, and daily life. Fields (1985, 52) synthesizes this process: "Where slave and free workers are volatile substitutes for one another on the market, there slavery has become an attribute of individuals, not any longer of the system that organizes their labor." Through recognition of their moral personality and through repeated efforts to be valued as individuals in all spheres of life, slaves paved the way for their conversion into free persons. All the strategies slaves employed, ranging from obtained promises of future freedom to spatial mobility, had a single goal.

The integrated portrayal of the lives of slaves and other members of the black population in the previous chapters has given us a sense of the essence of slave life in Lima. From the experiences of the Lasmanuelos family we gained a concentrated and microscopic view of the meaning of family life for slaves. But we also looked beyond individuals to slavery's broader and more insidious effects on the family. By breaking down the experiences of the members of the Lasmanuelos family, we explored the most human aspects of slavery during that era and set out a theoretical framework for additional arguments. There is a thread of continuity in the lives of slaves that transcends the turmoil of this historical period. Lima's slaves had wide margins for negotiation. But every negotiation was also an overt power struggle of some kind. Many slaves had no choice but to resort to intermediaries or assert themselves violently (for example, by stealing) to make their voices heard. Slaves could bargain, outwit, and exasperate their masters. With sympathy and admiration we watch their progress: three steps forward and two back.

Over time, marriage became an exceedingly significant aspect of slave life. Many more slaves married in the first decades of the nineteenth century than in earlier eras.[3] Approximately 60 percent of the slaves in Lima's hinterland haciendas were married to slaves living on the same estate or *chacra*; the parochial registers (from Santa Ana and San Lázaro) show that about 20 percent of all marriages involved slaves. But matrimony did not necessarily mean family, and there were few children in either rural or urban areas. Thus, few slaves carried on a family life in their masters' households or in the hacienda's *barracones*. Owners might allow parents to free their children in order to avoid the high costs of maintenance. Sometimes, even before parents managed to raise the money for their children's manumission, they assumed the expenses of child rearing. These kinds of filial arrangements later allowed slave parents to allege that an owner had not fulfilled his or her obligations and no longer held property rights over individuals he or she had neither fed nor clothed—part of the cautious construction of doorways to freedom through which slaves could eventually pass. Such strategies help explain not only the rapid diminution of Lima's slaves but also their urgent need to build wide social networks in the city and with other members of black society, the fluidity of urban-rural connections, and the desperate struggle to free at least one of the slave parents (as we have seen, usually the woman) from rural bondage.

Slave family members were slowly reaching the city and attaining freedom, each at a different pace and in a distinct condition. This temporally staggered and geographically dispersed pattern created a very peculiar family life, which could range from a situation in which a slave woman would abandon domestic service and leave her child behind to be wet nursed by her mistress to a situation in which a slave woman would take her children with her on frequent and long journeys from the haciendas to the city, sometimes visiting other family members who were still unable to leave the hacienda, and finally to the situation in which a slave committed suicide under the simultaneous burden of wages for the master and food and medical expenses for his family. The fight for freedom unified slave families around a common goal that sustained and permanently reinforced their bonds. Yet stress and anxiety were the perennial companions of slaves and often made owners wary of their every move. At no time in their family history did all the members of the Lasmanuelos family live together under one roof, eat at the same table, or even possess the same legal status.[4]

Gutman (1976, 273) asserts that family solidarity among slaves in the southern United States did not rest on the solidity of religious or civil norms granted by national or regional culture, but that slave marriages obtained their vitality from norms within their own culture. In Lima, however, marriage became a strategy to attain freedom, by which slaves simultaneously opposed and were assimilated into the system. Female slaves would argue that they were not sexual objects and that their masters were obligated to honor their virginity as they respected that of their own sisters and daughters. A master who was not willing to listen or abide by such codes could not be considered a gentleman; social morality repudiated such scandalous behavior because good and honorable masters should not behave so.

Given that family and marriage were so critical to the development of slavery in Lima, it is not surprising that slave women took an especially important role. They were the primary link among slaves in the most intimate realms of life. But we must not conclude that slave women were matriarchs or that their predominance in household chores proves the existence of a matrifocal slave family: to do so would be to confer on them more power than they actually had (Bush 1990, 166). Although it is true that female slaves were of paramount importance on the family's road toward freedom, and that it was they who organized the marketing of truck garden produce and of their own reproductive tasks, this situation was more the result of how slavery was constructed and production organized. Since male labor was more valuable on the haciendas, slave women were the ones who went to nearby markets and took care of the family plots. Older women were in charge, tending to and cooking for the few children on the haciendas, thus enabling their mothers to labor on the hacienda.

When women made up their minds to leave the hacienda, they could usually base their decision on a *hacendado*'s preference that the women pay their purchase price and search for a new owner in the city. From the slaves' point of view, the decision reflected wider occupational opportunities for women in the urban sphere. The universe that Lima's female slaves were defending was a family universe, not a female universe. Only later, when female slaves were in the city, would a preponderantly female network evolve, a network that responded to shared female activities: selling food together in a market stall, meeting in the *cofradías*, babysitting one another's children. But there were also quarrels over husbands, bouts of jealousy, street insults, fights, and competition within community organizations (such as the *cofradías* or guilds). In other words, women's personal conflicts compounded the racial and economic strife within that sphere of black society where mutual aid was of such crucial importance.

Occasionally such gendered confrontation went beyond the boundaries of black society and involved whiter women. In the British Caribbean, "as opposed to white women who were accorded a status on par with children, black women had far more independence of actions and a greater degree of equality with their menfolk. The jealousy white women exhibited toward their 'inferior' rivals may have been motivated as much by envy of their relative 'freedom' of action as by their husbands' philanderings" (Bush 1981, 259). In Lima, black house servants felt the rage and resentment of their mistresses. Yet on more than one occasion such conflicts proved—perhaps in a slave's involuntary alliance with a master's wife—that a master had impinged on his moral and authoritative duties. Enraged wives desiring divorce were unexpected witnesses whose testimonies favored the arguments of female slaves in court. Many white women were aware of their own subordination and asserted that some of them were treated more harshly than slaves; occasionally husbands admitted that, despite potential ecclesiastical and social recrimination, they preferred their slaves or were unwilling to relinquish the slaves' sexual favors.

Whether circumstances in Lima did indeed allow black women "the opportunity to rank and order themselves and obtain a sense of self [that] was quite apart from the men of their own race and even the women of the master class," (White 1983, 254), is a debatable issue. Lima's female slaves were neither matriarchs nor asserting selves. Their combined options showed success, yet they opted to play by the rules set in place by the system, their owners, and their husbands.

The relationship between female slaves and masters was much more complex than that between masters and male slaves, unless—as in an exceptional case that we saw—a slave became the lover of his mistress. Sexual tensions and conflicts over gender issues and property rights were the central components of this intricate universe.[5] Their ubiquity leads us to believe that female slaves' amorous relations with their masters was an important facet of the mosaic of slave family life in Lima and contributed to the particular nature of its organization. Sexual liaisons not only transgressed moral codes and influenced slaveholders' authority but, even more significantly, permitted attempts by female slaves to secure advantages and small privileges and even to manipulate their way out of the system. Although these relations were not a solution in the same sense as marriage, they nonetheless built up personal and even affective bonds. Many female slaves had long-standing ties with their masters and never sought husbands within their own ranks. Given the existence of these intimate bonds, it is difficult to imagine how masters could simultaneously achieve their goal of augmenting the available labor force and increasing labor productivity without condemning their own offspring to coerced labor. Such a rampant contradiction, in Lima and elsewhere, could but signal the end of slavery (Morrisey 1989, 10). Aims that highlighted this incompatibility were formulated by Lima's slave women and wittingly used to blackmail masters.

Christian marriage was more than a strategy for freedom: both female and male slaves continued to work after the wedding. Nevertheless, the mutual expectations of slave spouses were very explicitly drawn from what other members in society determined to be the proper behavior for each gender. Furthermore, this behavior bore a clear resemblance to that demanded from society as a whole. Slavery made the fulfillment of this goal almost impossible. Out of this discrepancy arose conflict, which even in its manifestations, such as domestic violence against women, did not stray very far from the sufferings of women of other classes.

Thus, family and marriage also represented a social web from which women found it difficult to disentangle themselves. Slave women could not selectively choose only the convenient aspects of marriage (such as an argument to obtain freedom), they had to take the whole package and live in a situation where they tried to achieve moral ends that their slave status made impossible.

For slaves in Lima, as compared to other areas, it was much easier to purchase the freedom of family members because the Church backed both institutions of marriage and family and because slaves there were able to work and to save.[6] The greater the number of family members who could escape a master's control or even manumit themselves, the higher became the chances of freedom for the remaining members. Self-purchase contained its own dose of acceleration. What Lima's slaves did was to negotiate or manipulate their purchase prices so that it would eventually approximate what they were capable of amassing. Not only did slaves evade their masters' attempts to raise their prices but also used any subsequent transactions, negotiations, or even changes of ownership to gradually reduce their price. The lower the price, the closer the goal. Nothing obligated an owner to accept a slave's purchase price; but social pressure, custom, and expectations dictated that once a slave was able to pay, it was the duty of an owner to give the slave her or his *carta de libertad*.

Ultimately, as we search among the complex mechanisms that slaves used to obtain freedom for an increasing understanding of slaves' actions, we must look beyond the explanations of religion or miscegenation or family networks to the economic arena in which these negotiations took place. Success or failure on the road to freedom depended on highly subjective circumstances that were dictated by the working environment. Freedom was closely tied to the rate of accumulation.

In many different regions in which plantations and slaves existed, masters allocated plots of land to their slaves. From the point of view of masters, this tactic was particularly profitable in those areas where the price of food was high. By granting slaves subsistence plots and allowing them to cultivate them on certain days or for specific hours, masters reduced the costs of maintenance required for their slaves' upkeep. Furthermore, the tactic gave owners ways to secure and retain the labor force as links were created that bound their slaves to the plantation. The sizes of plots varied; in this sense, allocation controlled the labor force through the establishment of low levels of differentiation among slaves on the plantation and incentives for "good" behavior. After a slave or slave family was actively reaping products from a plot, means and ways to commercialize the produce would follow. To a great extent, success depended on the availability of excess crops and on the proximity of a marketplace. In Lima, small estates were the norm, and many slaves worked on *chacras* in Lima's immediate hinterlands. The smaller the unit of production, the greater the relative autonomy of slaves to determine production and even marketing. Although these slaves did not own the means of production, they tended to act like peasants. In some places, processes homologous to those in Lima have been interpreted as the fundamental impetus for slave peasantization, from which—after abolition—a black peasantry would evolve (Cardoso 1988). Given the pace of manumission in Lima, peasantization was well under way long before abolition and became a vehicle for self-manumission.

Urban markets in Lima were open to slaves, whom we observed preparing and selling food there. From this process of monetization developed more diversified occupations. Although we have scant quantitative evidence for Lima, as well as other regions, which directly refers to these mercantile and service activities, travel accounts substantiate their unparalleled importance for urban life. The memoirs of voyagers and visitors suggest that the participation of slaves in markets was as important for Lima as it was for Martinique during the middle of the nineteenth century, where some slaves amassed two to three times their own value (Tomich 1990, 278). However, in contrast to Martinique, Lima's slaves rushed to purchase their own freedom, instead of hiring or even buying other slaves to assist them with their work. Similarly in Cuba, "Reading through the daybook [of the Angelita sugar mill], one gets the sense that relations within the plantation were shifting as slaves, particularly women, found ways to buy their freedom and as the plantation increased the use of monetary incentives." Most of the money slaves used for self-purchase probably came from their frequent sales of pork and crops to the plantation or to nearby marketplaces: "a circuit of money exchanges had now been introduced to replace a relation of direct control—and not necessarily entirely at the planter's initiative" (Scott 1985, 106).

For Lima there is no evidence that slaves sold their produce to the plantation or adjoining estates. However, given the propinquity of town markets and the city market, as well as the advantages of a higher consumer concentration, slaves probably preferred to sell their produce in urban markets. The additional gains from such a decision included the proximity of other slaves and free blacks and the distance from the reach of one's master. The slaves' urban jobs not only meant that they had access to money but also meant increased spatial mobility and protean and subtler levels of social interaction. In this sense, the rural-based experiences of slaves were very comparable to those recorded—for example—in Brazil, where the "relations of production were typified by the large plantations, but in reality neither the majority of slave owners, nor the majority of slaves interacted within that context" (Schwartz 1982, 87). The more intense and diversified the slaves' participation in the market, the greater the alternatives and opportunities to obtain freedom. By the final years of slavery, about one-fifth of all manumissions occurred in Lima's hinterland; over the course of time the rhythm of accumulation increased, essentially as a result of slaves' widening market participation.

Another component in the sequence of varied forms of accumulation was the artisanal and service skills of slaves as well as the hiring-out system, which was much akin to systems that have been detailed for cities as disparate as Buenos Aires, São Paulo, or Caracas. Often, artisan skills had already been fostered within the rural setting, but occupational diversity was much greater and more sophisticated in the urban sphere as a result of the organization of city life.[7] Lima's slaveholders were very aware that the positions of their slaves in the urban occupational structure and their consequent accumulation hindered owners' capacity to control the slave population and thus put the existence of the slave system itself into jeopardy. From the point of view of slave owners, even though the hiring-out system permitted the slave labor force a higher degree of spatial mobility, it also guaranteed the profitability of that system.[8] Thus, while slave owners sought to adapt slavery to a changing economic situation, they were also undermining the slaveholding structure. As we consider the lucrativeness of the slave system, Scott reminds us, we must not forget that slaves participated in determining how, when, and where wages were given to their owners. Lima's slaves document an enormous variety of possible agreements and arrangements: a slave could reside in or outside the master's household, sign a daily, weekly, or long-term contract, reside with or without children, work with or without tools, have a master who decided where and with whom a slave could work or who relinquished this decision to the slave. The wide spectrum of possible combinations of all of these options can also explain the diversity of outcomes: from the most expedient of self-purchases to suicide.

In contrast to Brazil, where apparently wages and the hiring-out system did not allow for a widespread process of manumission, accumulation by slaves through this system can help account for the decay of slavery in Lima.[9] As we have shown, the particular denouement of slavery in Lima partly resulted from the process of parallel bargaining on behalf of the slave's price. By using a vast gamut of mechanisms to reduce their price, slaves managed to narrow the gap between accumulation and price. Overall, and in comparative terms, Lima's slaves were very successful at accumulation, even despite the disparate outcomes of individual cases. Their success not only gives us an idea of how busy judges must have been on their benches, but—more important—the tremendous impact that self-manumission had on the abolition of slavery. No rules existed that precisely defined how, when, or under what condition slaves could be hired out; as in other slaveholding situations, concrete behavior was determined by common practices and long-established traditions.[10]

By suggesting that wages among urban slaves represented a process parallel to that of slave peasantization, Nogueira da Silva (1988, 116) proposes an interpretation of the hiring-system as a process in which the monetization of the relations within the slave system illustrates the contradictions inherent to slavery. Departing from such a global perspective, we can use daily wages to suggest that slaves' efforts even more than masters' desires for profits fueled abolition. Repeatedly, it becomes clear that Lima's slave owners very much wanted (and needed) the daily wages earned by their slaves, but that they also were increasingly unable (and unwilling) to keep track of how these wages accrued. In Lima, individuals like José Gregorio (mentioned in chapter 5) gradually came to dominate the streets as slaves gained increasing control of the hiring-out system and daily wages, transforming the relations between slaves and masters. Beyond accounting for self-manumission, their greater control also explains slaves' effectiveness at avoiding transfer back to a hacienda or plantation.

On their way to self-manumission, Lima's slaves displayed manifold expressions of protest, from rebellion and banditry to what is now termed "passive resistance" (that is, refusal to work, inefficiency or laziness, witchcraft, even suicide). All these faces of dissent complemented other strategies aimed at the acceleration of manumission—ways to persuade masters that the only reasonable option was to accept their terms. Concretely, these attitudes or actions brought transfer to another owner, replacement of an administrator or *caporal*, better working conditions, less anxiety, or support from a wife against the master of the house. In short, "more than fight overtly, slaves negotiated" (Nogueira da Silva 1988, 112).

The ultimate proof of slaves' success at manumission emerges from statistics. From a total of 375 manumissions for three years (1830, 1840, and 1850) in Lima, an average of 125 slaves obtained their freedom each year, a number that, if multiplied by intercensus years (18 slaves between 1818 and 1836; 9 between 1836 and 1845), suggests a notarially recorded manumission frequency of Lima's total slave population of 1.24 between 1818 and 1836, and 1.14 between 1836 and 1845. Thus, we can see that only a small percentage of liberated slaves was not notarially registered and this percentage decreases the closer we come to the year of abolition. These calculations also indicate that during the first period about 31.3 percent of all slaves became free. In the second period this percentage comes to 21.9;[11] it is equivalent to approximately one out of three between 1818 and 1836 and to one out of five between 1836 and 1845.[12] The closer we come to the year of official abolition, the smaller Lima's slave population became. It was an irreversible process despite the contrary and influential argumentation of slaveholders.[13]

One of the questions we have tried to answer is why slaveholders let slaves buy their freedom, or better yet, why they could not prevent them from doing so. The dependency on slave labor, the distribution of slave ownership, and the slaves' agency lies at the heart of an answer to this question.[14]

When in chapter 3 we analyzed the distribution of slaves in the Santa Ana parish we found that about 20 percent of its inhabitants had at least one slave, and that most of them had one or two slaves.[15] This distributional pattern shows a diffused ownership and widespread reliance on slaves' wages, even among members of black society who owned slaves or those fewer slaves who owned slaves. In other words, the relative concentration of wealth in slave form was low. The dependence increased the potential for conflict in individual relations but also fragmented owners as a class, making them unable to reaffirm their reliance on slavery. Thus, to ensure the continuation of slavery there were no staunch interests emanating from a concentrated pattern of slave ownership but rather individuals, urban slave owners and their rural counterparts as well. As individuals, they bargained with slaves and set up relationships that gave the slaves potential for maneuvering and relative success. Open insurrection was unnecessary.

Within this schematic explanation of Lima's slave system we should not forget to stress the absence of state-based control mechanisms.[16] In Lima, the only way to punish a slave but still receive a daily wage was to send him—more frequently than her—to a *panadería*. The *panaderías* soon became overpopulated; for quite obvious reasons, administrators and owners of these establishments preferred to sell bread baked by their own slaves rather than by slaves who had already exhibited predilections for incorrigibility and protest. In a similar vein, slaveholders feared the contamination of their own slaves by the bad example of other slaves and the diminished working capacity, health, and value that arduous *panadería* labor would bring the slaves. Thus, possessing only ineffective mechanisms of control, masters were further vulnerable to the clamors of slaves.[17]

If we synthesize all the images we have of Lima's slaves, we must surely include the pictures slaves drew of their multiple connections with this urban society. But first we must ask, how did slaves view themselves?[18] Given their varied positions in urban life and their success at obtaining freedom, did they see themselves as peasants, as small merchants, as water carriers—or did they exist simply as slaves? Most probably, they perceived a combination of roles. On the one hand, slaves had constant and urgent reminders of their duties; on the other hand, they knew that the terms of these obligations rested on their own occupations and that means existed to circumvent a master's control. An occupational honor code existed within slave society along with other reasons that encouraged slaves to interact continuously with those who worked at similar and adjacent tasks. The presence of hierarchies within slave society itself sustained the notion that occupational proximity was linked to slaves' opportunities for social ascent and manumission.

What eased the artisans' mobilization against British imports in Lima after abolition was an occupational placement that emerged from slavery. Without an occupational identity constructed during the previous decades, this incipient demonstration of class interests would have been impossible. Furthermore, the fact that this response was so weak has much to do with the slave system. Before becoming full-fledged artisans, slaves had to invest in their manumission. Thus their first savings did not go to purchase superior tools or to perfect their trade but to pay off slaveholders, giving them a last small victory over their former chattel. In colonial Lima "one could freely buy artisans." Over time a growing number of slave artisans emancipated themselves. Because they were much in demand, Spanish guilds were unable to impose a monopoly or control for "blood purity" (Bowser 1977, 178, 197) on artisanal trades. From a European comparative perspective, the ability to "buy" artisans is certainly an aberrant historical process. Yet among societies in which slavery existed, including the United States, slaves and free blacks existed from the first stages in the formation of artisanal groups. In the United States, white immigrants gradually replaced them; in Lima, free persons of color did. But replacement was just a legal artifice: the people were the same. Race and occupation kept their correlation and—in this case—their measure of disdain. Only after abolition in 1854, and the emergence of an augmented and more sophisticated pattern of consumption, would European immigrants occupy some artisanal rubrics.

All these processes have long-term effects on society at large. The social conditions they create are a focus of research for the United States and, increasingly, one for Latin America as well. Moreover, it forms part of the broader issue of the still very important and overarching construction of national and social identities.[19] The pivotal issue is how racism and a racially determined occupational structure occur and develop; how conceptions of integration and identity may or may not appear. Even the most arduous defenders of liberalism—then and now—are not free from such historically constructed racial prejudices rooted in the systematic marginalization of entire social groups, whether through slavery (as in the case of blacks) or through tributary payments (as in the case of Indians). Even though slaves exhibited their own desires for whitening and great job potential, their racial and economic mobility alike remained in check. As soon as slaves lost their value—as a consequence of economic liberalization in the wake of guano exports—they found themselves on the fringes of the urban economy. "The aristocratic tradition, the essentially castelike way people are grouped and identified, and the paternal concept that the poor must always be poor, that the servant must always remain a servant, has made the gap between 'upper' and 'lower' very great indeed. . . . It is an ingrained part of the total scheme of things" (Tannenbaum 1969, 6).

The structures of domination and the prejudices necessary for the perpetuation of the slaveholding system were the two sides of the same ideological coin, by which the dominant sector sought "to present to itself and to those it rules a coherent world view that is sufficient, flexible, comprehensive, and mediatory to convince the subordinated classes of the justice of its hegemony. If this ideology were no more than a reflection of immediate economic interests, it would be worse than useless, for the hypocrisy of the class, as well as its greed, would quickly become apparent to the most abject of its subjects" (Genovese 1969, 245). The Gramscian "hegemonic trick," the continual willingness of elites to change their power foundations when they perceive that doing so is the best or the only possible way to retain real power in a given context, offers a comprehensive explanation of slaveholders' lack of concern about their slaves' expanding liberty. After all, the abolition of slavery—especially if slaves financed it—opened the doors to British capital, an opening long preceded by British pressures to abolish the slave trade. And while Lima's slaveholders finally conceded that slavery had seen its heyday, they simultaneously robbed slaves of their former means of survival. Abolition became a matter of principle and not part of a consciously constructed policy to incorporate these groups as free persons into a rapidly changing socioeconomic context. Slaves' bitter struggles and ingeniously invented strategies to assimilate into society dropped from sight or drew at best hypocritical interest—in the guise of humanitarianism—and did not translate into improved living conditions for the newly emancipated individuals.

Nevertheless, still on the fringes of "hegemonic tricks," slaves developed amazing alternatives to existing rules and through their actions clearly devised multiple tactics that elites had to counter and overcome in order to assure their own predominance in society. Slaves saw many challenges ahead of them. On the road to freedom, they won decisive human victories that brought them greater recognition. In this sense, and despite the costs, the life of the Lasmanuelos family and the lives of all the other historical characters we have followed illustrate idiosyncratic and wonderful responses to the challenge of constructing identity.

Abbreviations Used in Notes and Bibliography

Archives

AA	Archivo Arzobispal
ADLL	Archivo Departmental de La Libertad
ADP	Archivo Departmental de Piura
AGN	Archivo General de la Nación
BN	Biblioteca Nacional (Lima)

Archival Series

AGG	Auditoría General de Guerra
CCI	Causas Civiles
CCR	Causas Criminales
CD	Causas de Divorcio
CN	Causas de Negros
CO	Causas Ordinarias
CP	Causas Penales
CS	Corte Superior de Justicia
EJ	Expedientes Judiciales
EM	Expedientes Matrimoniales
JC	Justicia Colonial
LM	Litigios Matrimoniales
NM	Nulidad de Matrimonio
RA	Real Audiencia
TM	Tribunal Militar

Miscellaneous Sources

CDIP	Colección Documental de la Independencia del Perú
fs.	fojas (folios)
PUC	Pontificia Universidad Católica del Perú
s.i.	sin indicación (no information)
s.t.	sin título (no title)
s.n.	sin número (no number)
t.	tomo
v.	volumen

Notes

Introduction

1. For a discussion of these figures—particularly the 1.6 million slaves who settled in the Spanish colonies—see among others Ianni 1976, 15; Mellafe 1973; and Fogel and Engerman 1974.

2. For a detailed account of the different political episodes throughout the wars of independence, and of inconsistencies between law and reality, see Blanchard (1992, particularly 37–62).

3. Fenoaltea states (1984, 653) that "given a sufficient number, slaves will be employed even in activities where they have no advantage over free men, and work side by side with them under similar conditions. One expects these to be activities in which the master's dependence on the worker's carefulness and good will makes rewards more profitable than pain incentives; and they appear to include most traditional crafts and trades, commerce and transport, administrative services and at least the nonskilled branches of factory production. These are the activities in which we find slaves living and working independently as if they were free, subject only to a quitrent to their owner." My analysis shows that the balance between pain incentives and rewards depended on very particular situations, rather than the number of slaves, and that bargaining was a part of daily coexistence.

4. Genovese (1974, 450–455) summarizes the new research on slave families: "Largely following the pioneering work of E. Franklin Frazier, the [Moynihan Report] summarized the conventional wisdom according to which slavery had emasculated black men, created matriarchy, and prevented the emergence of a strong sense of family." And yet "almost every study of runaway slaves uncovers the importance of the family motive: thousands of slaves ran away to find children, parents, wives, or husbands from whom they had been separated by sale. From time to time a slave did prefer to stay with a good master or mistress rather than follow a spouse who was being sold away. In these cases and in many others in which slaves displayed indifference, the marriage had probably already been weakened, and sale provided the most convenient and painless form of divorce." My own findings corroborate these assertions for Lima.

For the southern hemisphere Chandler (1981, 112–113) offers evidence of the existence of slave families and their importance. In colonial Colombia "at least 60 percent of all adult slaves had been or were married, most living in nuclear family units, and another 6 percent were single parents who could be considered married, though they were apparently not living with the father of their children"; thus about 65 percent of all adult slaves were married or had a "family" experience. Craton found that 54 percent of English slaves in the Bahamas were living in nuclear family units, and Higman placed 70 percent of English Jamaican slaves in single family households, most of them nuclear units. Conrad found only 10.4 percent of Brazilian slaves married with little family life among them, and Bowser, using an earlier and much narrower sample of largely notarial records, concluded that less than 10 percent of Peruvian slaves were married, even fewer were living in family units, and that Spaniards in Peru actively sought to prevent slave marriages. Chandler concludes that "all these surprising findings challenge many previously held conceptions, not the least of which is that harsh English slavery usually prohibited family life and that benign Latin America slavery usually encouraged it."

1. Major Events and Everyday Life

1. Traversing this long economic cycle were several subcycles (Gootenberg 1990, 28 ff.): (a) a moderate deflation (1800–1814) resulting from the lowering of prices caused by nascent British industrialization and the Bourbon political and commercial crisis; (b) a sharp inflation provoked by the struggles for independence (1815–1824), with a 40 percent increase in prices in 1822 (above all, on basic foodstuff items for domestic consumption); (c) stabilization and deflation (1835–1846). Prices stabilized and fell (on an average of 1 percent annually with 28 percent deflation from 1826 to 1846). The fall in prices affected internal agricultural production as much as it did imported goods. Until 1845 political and military instability brought about a profound economic recession, but the haciendas were able to substitute crops: from cotton and tobacco for export to foodstuffs for domestic consumption. Textile prices suffered most severely from this drop (down 50 percent). After the recession came a slow reflation between 1846 and 1854 with the start of guano exportation. The prices of agricultural products and livestock, nonetheless, remained low until the next crisis of 1854–1855.

2. Cédula Real was issued in Aranjuez on 31 May 1789, reproduced in Clementi (1974, appendix). See also Rout (1977, 87). A case in which we find its application is Archivo General de la Nación (hereafter, AGN; for the remaining abbreviations please refer to the list that precedes the notes) RA,

CCR, L 140, C1727, 1818–1819. Autos seguidos por el Sr. Alcalde del Crimen, Conde de Vallehermoso, contra D. Fco. Gómez, propietario de la panadería del Sauce, a quien se le juzga por el excesivo castigo de azotar a sus esclavos negros Antonio y José (23n).

3. After 1779 the slave traffic route through Panama lost importance and, with the abolition of the slave trade in 1808, slave shipments continued to enter through the port of Buenos Aires (which became the principal port of origin [Haitin 1986, 158]).

4. The distribution of men and women on the haciendas was highly uneven, reflected in each unit of production. An average above this disparity indicated a ratio similar to the one described for the Pando hacienda (2:3). Despite the usual inequalities it is curious that for the three parishes on which we have information in 1792 and 1813, the ratio between men and women on the haciendas is almost even at the parish level and may explain the fluidity of relations between haciendas, which, as will be demonstrated, certainly existed. The statistics for the Pando hacienda come from the AA, Serie Estadística, L 2 (1790) and L 5 (1813). For statistics on the number of slaves on Lima's haciendas between 1826 and 1840, see Aguirre (1993, 51–52).

5. CDIP, XXVII:3:227–235. On the haciendas we examined the average number of children per couple was 0.9; see discussion in chapter 2 of reasons for this very low indicator.

6. On the haciendas whose records we examined, approximately 65 percent of the slaves were married and 58 percent were married to slaves from the same hacienda; see chapter 2.

7. The censuses for the 1812 constitutional elections showed ownership of property as proof of citizenship; those for the parishes we mention noted the presence of *castas* (persons of European and African ancestry, a broad classification including more specific racial mixtures such as *pardos* or *quarterones*) such as the overseers of the two estates.

8. No legal stipulation obligated owners to sell slaves, although an owner's continual abuse was commonly considered the only justifiable reason for a change of ownership. But representatives of the judiciary and the Church disapproved if an owner rejected the sum offered by a slave for self-manumission. Also see Hart (1980, 147) for a discussion of differences between French and Spanish land holdings and enforcement of the Cédula Real. In Brazil slaves could purchase their freedom beyond the margin of their owner's authority only in 1871 (Nogueira da Silva 1988, 71). For a discussion on changing laws and perceptions in Peru see Blanchard (1992, 42 ff.).

9. In some places this final stipulation translated into the creation of municipal licenses so that slaves could obtain permits to "day-labor" and—as Nogueira da Silva suggests was the case for Rio de Janeiro (1988, 22)—the

conversion of slaves into a "good public." But in other places (Lima, for example) these arrangements did not result in actions, and what tended to prevail was the direct master-slave relation. In this paragraph and throughout, translations from Spanish not otherwise identified are those of Alexandra Stern.

10. Document cited in King (1953, 54).

11. CDIP, IV:1:18.

12. CDIP, IV:1:437–438. Report of the Constitutional Commission regarding the proposal of Señor Castilla, heard in the 11 September 1811 meeting.

13. Slavery was abolished without compensation for owners in the United States and Brazil (and evidently in Haiti) (Klein 1986). For Brazil see Karasch (1987, 335 ff.). For a discussion on the pressures exerted by plantation owners in Peru see Blanchard (1992).

14. *Reclamación* 1833.

15. This relation between production on vast haciendas and labor on small-scale plots, as well as labor's adjustments to the extension of the lands of haciendas in response to the fluctuations of market conditions, corresponds to a model devised by Shane Hunt (1975) to explain the transformation of a traditional hacienda into a plantation with wage labor.

16. See the case cited by Vivanco (1990, 49). AGN, L 83, C 1019, 1796.

17. Balmori et al. (1984) describe this type of matrimonial bond (between members of the land-owning nobility and *criollo* merchants) as typical of "notable families."

18. According to Burkholder (1972, 22, 33, 142), during the seventeenth and early eighteenth centuries the military corps had an essentially ceremonial function. This changed in 1765, with the creation of companies along racial lines.

19. See, for example, the accounts of Sales (1974, 68), Vargas Ugarte (1984, 6:165), and General Miller (1829, 1:214).

20. Memoirs by Virrey Abascal and Alexander von Humboldt cited in Haitin (1986, 118–119) discuss the demonstrations.

21. Viceroy La Serna demanded—unsuccesfully because of the opposition of the Cabildo (the municipal council), which argued for peace—the delivery of 1,500 blacks to the royalist army to replace the lower ranks of the corps of Burgos and Arequipa (Vargas Ugarte 1984, 7:165): From 1810 on, under the promise of freedom for blacks, San Martín recruited *pardos*, *morenos*, and *mulatos* (Sales 1974, 68): according to General Miller (1829, 1:214), blacks from the Caucato hacienda in Pisco deserved the nickname "devils" for their skill at infiltrating the royalist troops and for the red caps they wore. These attributes, in addition to a hearty daily ration of meat, had awakened in them "a sincere and enthusiastic patriotic spirit." Conversely

Lima's black artisan population was finally receiving its owed daily wages despite the systematic seizures by royalist authorities.

22. For rumors about Riva Agüero's plan see CDIP, XVI:344. Carta de Marcos de Neyra a un amigo. Lima, 1 de mayo de 1821. With the announcement of the independence of the Peruvian viceroyalty, on 28 July 1821, came these terms: liberty for all children of slaves born hereinafter, the gradual emancipation of those already born, the prohibition of traffic in black slaves (reiterating the measure already decreed in 1808 because of British pressure). An announcement on 11 November 1821 offered immediate freedom for all slaves belonging to Spaniards and to Peruvians who migrated to the Iberian peninsula as part of incorporation into the line of infantry; on 23 November 1821 one promised liberty for all slaves coming from a foreign land who set foot on Peruvian soil; on 27 November 1821 another threatened punishment by death to owners or traffickers who broke these laws.

1823: The Marquis of Torre Tagle decrees mandatory military service in the capital's military garrisons for artisans, menial laborers, students, and slaves living in Lima.

1834: The Council of Hacendados obtains ratification of the 14 October 1825 regulation that consolidates the pro-slavery status quo, prohibits slaves from using any weapons (including axes, machetes, and knives) or from entering towns next to the hacienda without documents signed by the owner, and leaves to the discretion of the owner the decision as to the validity of a previously promulgated manumission (Sales 1974, 103, 109n.).

23. According to the protectorial decree of 1821, *libertos* differed from slaves in that slaves and their earnings remained the owner's property whereas *libertos* could claim a wage of eight *reales* weekly and were the owner's property "only" until they were fifty years old; see AGN, CS, CCI, L 569, 1854. For apprenticeship relations and patronage as transitional stages toward freedom, the Cuban case is particularly interesting (Scott 1985, 172–197).

24. An example occurred in AGN, CCI, L 100, 1830 [s.t.].

25. AGN, Cabildo, CCI, L 26, C 421, 1813, Autos seguidos por Domingo Ordois contra D. José Arróspide sobre su libertad.

26. AGN, TM, L 4 (1826–1870), 1829, Expediente seguido por José María Leizon con su amo D. Mateo Gonzales sobre que se declare su libertad.

27. CDIP, XV:1:127.

28. Charles Walker (1990) asserts that several of these guerrilla groups acted as the armed support of liberal and conservative factions during the period of most political confusion between 1833 and 1836, before the formation of the Peruvian-Bolivian confederation.

29. Twenty-three and twenty-five, for female and male slaves respectively, were the average ages of marriage in the decade of the 1830s.

30. For an itemization of the varied labor performed by slaves and blacks in Lima see Patrón (1935, 28). For Brazil see Karasch (1987, 66–91).

2. From Rural to Urban Life

1. In the United States during the first decades of the nineteenth century the number of blacks, slave and free, in the urban areas increased but decreased after 1840 (see Curry 1981). For a theoretical model to explain this phenomenon see Goldin (1986). But the model is hard to apply to Lima because it supposes that slave owners controlled the allocation of slave labor.

2. The census was recently uncovered and analyzed by Gootenberg (1991, 109–158).

3. Clavero (1885, 48; original emphasis) added more detail about the area, "which forms three zones. The *first* including the area between the mountains and the river; the *second* between the Rimac valley and the boundary starting at the monument of the Dos de Mayo and ending at the Dos de Mayo Hospital; and the *third* between the supposed border and the southern end of the city, 'Circle 5.'" It is very risky to correlate space to population, given that—as Gootenberg also points out (1991)—there were "tricky boundary problems in Lima's censuses." Even so we need a rough idea of the spatial distribution to comprehend countryside-city relations.

4. Haitin (1983, 140 ff.) summarizes the difficulties of specifying the number of production units in estimates of the number of hectares per hacienda.

5. To calculate these figures, I divide the sum of male and female slaves by the sum of Spaniards (citizens of European ancestry) of both genders in barrios and on estates. Citizens (with or without occupations) included indigenous persons, some descendants of free blacks, and *mestizos*.

6. Cushner (1972, 180) reveals that on the Jesuit haciendas, located in Lima's hinterland and stretching from Pisco to Huaura on the northern and southern coasts, the average number of slaves per hacienda between 1665 and 1767 grew gradually, from 98.8 to 256. For the total period Cushner (1975, 180) gives an average of 162.7 slaves per productive unit. Overall, the Jesuit haciendas relied on more slaves than Lima's haciendas.

7. For 1839 a figure of 7,922 slaves was recorded for Lima, divided between 4,792 in Lima proper and 3,130 in the valleys (Aguirre 1990, 178). In these later and more global figures the proportion of urban to rural slaves is lower than the one found for San Lázaro in 1813. This discrepancy is difficult to resolve because of the geographic imprecision in all the censuses. We must

take the figures as rough indicators of long-term trends. Perhaps the San Lázaro parish had a higher concentration of slaves than other Lima parishes.

8. Here is the mix of urban and rural elements in the parish of Miraflores:

> 4 male Spaniards, 4 female Spaniards
> 33 male Indians, 15 female Indians
> 11 *zambos*, 11 *zambas*
> 2 *quarterones*, 1 *quarterona*
> 2 *mestizos*, 7 *mestizas*
> 3 black men, 2 black women
> 0 *chinos*, 2 *chinas*
>
> =total of 97 persons (55 men and 42 women)

In Surco and Chorrillos the rural ingredient, based on an evaluation of the Spanish presence, was even more marked. Only one married Spanish couple lived in Surco, along with 2 single men and 5 *forasteros* (Indians who had abandoned their traditional land and village). But the indigenous presence was significant: 57 married couples, 34 single men, 35 single women, 8 widowers, 9 widows, 54 boys, and 50 girls. In Chorrillos there was not one single Spaniard, but here also the indigenous presence stood out: 174 married couples, 115 single men, 114 single women, 26 widowers, 37 widows, 110 boys, and 111 girls. Both Surco and Chorrillos had an almost perfect balance between the sexes, which is probably an indicator of ethnic endogamy. In Magdalena, 3 individuals were identified by the title *don* (which might mean they were of European ancestry) and the remaining 167 persons were all either *casta*, indigenous, or *mestizo* females.

9. The figures recorded for the Villa hacienda in 1813 contradict the statement its proprietor made after the struggles for independence. In fact this owner, Juan Bautista Lavalle, complained in a letter to Flora Tristán about seeing the number of slaves reduced, from no less than 1,500 to 900 (cited in Aguirre 1990, 144). We might wonder whom Lavalle wished to impress; what we have recorded before the wars of independence is a notable resurgence of the slave population, somewhere on the order of 300—not 900—slaves. Haitin (1983, 141) indicates that around 1773 Carabayllo, Surco, and Bocanegra were among the most productive areas, together producing 50 percent of the total production recorded for Lima. Magdalena, Maranga, and La Legua were the least productive areas, at the other extreme: some fared better than others, discrediting the exaggerations that owners often invoked to bolster the slave trade.

10. For Magdalena's haciendas here are the numbers of married slaves (with percentages in parentheses):

> San Cayetano: 12 out of 40 adult slaves (30.0)
> Maranga: 58 out of 100 (58.0)
> Matalechuzas: 22 out of 42 (52.4)
> Desamparados: 2 out of 7 (28.6)
> Mirones: 4 out of 8 (50.0)
> Cueva: 26 out of 42 (61.9)
> Oyague: 22 out of 36 (61.1)
> Borda: 16 out of 18 (88.9)
> Orbea: 20 out of 31 (64.5)
> Concha: 22 out of 53 (41.5)
> Pando: 4 out of 34 (11.8)
> Ríos: 12 out of 36 (33.3)
> Buena Muerte: 14 out of 23 (58.3)
> Ascona: 2 out of 23 (8.7)

Of Magdalena's two remaining haciendas, Palomino had no female slaves and Aramburú no married slaves. These figures could not be reproduced for the haciendas of Miraflores: marital status was recorded but the slaves were enumerated in a continuous series. In the other parishes the name of one spouse was noted next to the name of the other.

On many haciendas an unmarried adult female slave population appeared, which indicates that the percentage of slave couples was underestimated. An evaluation of the ratio between the sexes, above all in geographic areas that extended beyond the borders of the hacienda, could suggest that, perhaps as a result of the abolition of the slave trade, escapes, and self-manumissions, slave owners on the haciendas tried to contain and augment an increasingly scarce labor force.

11. The percentages of the male and female populations of Magdalena and Miraflores closely correspond to the figure from the census of 1792 that Haitin cites (1986, 167): Lima's hinterland had 4,402 slaves, 63 percent of them men. This statistic would indicate that the situation in Surco and Chorrillos represented an exception—a notorious exception, because within Surco and Chorrillos were the two largest haciendas, the Villa and the San Juan, on which even more female than male slaves worked, both in 1790 and in 1813.

12. One annulment, involving illicit copulation (that is, sexual relations prior to marriage and between individuals of prohibited degrees of kinship) was AA, NM, L 59 (1810–1819), Hilaria Josefa y José Nasario, esclavos de la hacienda San Javier en San Juan Bautista del Ingenio perteneciente al General D. Tomás de Arias. Another case, of parental opposition, was AA, CN, L 35 (1799–1814), Juana Bordon, mulata libre, y Joaquín Lara, sambo esclavo del Director General de Reales Rentas Estancadas, 1803. In this case Juana's mother was the one who opposed the marriage.

13. Several works point out the gradual transition from slave to free labor arrangements (Aguirre 1990, Burga 1987, Engelsen 1977; Flores Galindo 1984; Haitin 1986; Macera 1977). Perhaps the strongest evidence has been put forth by Gootenberg (1991). For Brabón see also the document cited by Vivanco (1990, 49): AGN, L 82, C 1007. In the 1837 listing compiled by Aguirre (1993, 52), 58.6 percent of the haciendas have no slaves (Figure 1).

14. AGN, CS, CCI, L 288, 1842, Josefa Aparicio contra su amo D. Manuel Aparicio por sevicia. Here, we may remember Manuelita's birth as a *quarterona*.

15. This assertion refers to a reading of Lima's recorded wills in the AGN.

16. For a study of differing treatment by size of the unit of production in Martinique see Tomich (1990, 243). For a Brazilian study that contrasts with my analysis see Schwartz (1985, 390).

17. The data in Table 6 show that even in valleys adjacent to Lima (including the Rímac valley), small properties accounted for 53.4 percent of all properties (342), and large ones for 8.7 percent.

18. AGN, Cabildo, CCI, L 16, C 255, 1809, Autos seguidos por Romualda Tavira contra Doña Elena Maldonado sobre su libertad.

19. CDIP XXVII:3:227–235.

20. In the 1820s one dollar was equivalent to one Peruvian peso. The annual income, 55,870 dollars, represented a huge fortune, though some dowries were twice as large; it equaled the purchase price of 186 slaves.

21. The sale of illegitimate slave children would help explain why there were so few minors on the hacienda and also perhaps why some haciendas had fewer male than female slaves.

22. Schwartz describes similar conditions on the properties of the Benedictines in Bahia between 1652 and 1710 (1985, 355–356); it is difficult to assess to what degree Stevenson's description or that of his informants (the *hacendados*) reflects this widespread legal and moral code. Aguirre also discusses the treatment of slaves on Lima's haciendas (1992, 57–74).

23. AGN, Cabildo, CCI, L 33, C 562, 1816, Autos seguidos por José Chala, en nombre propio y de los demás esclavos de Don Manuel Menacho, sobre sevicia y para que los venda.

24. AGN, RA, CCR, L 95, C 1161, 1802, Causa seguida por Don Antonio Ramón de Paranas contra Doña Jacoba Rubio, instigadora de la sublevación de esclavos occurida en la hacienda Punta. Violación de domicilio y otros excesos.

25. AGN, RA, CCR, L 92, C 1129, 1801, Cuaderno incompleto de la causa seguida contra Don Juan E. Theves por suponerle intervención en el suicidio (homicidio) del esclavo Gabriel. For several similar episodes see Aguirre (1990), Flores Galindo (1984, 1990), and Blanchard (1991, 1992).

26. The wife of the administrator of Rentas Unidas in Andahuaylas was indigenous. She ordered a *zambo* to make some candles and out of carelessness he let the dog eat the wick and then replaced it with a stick. "What the said angry zambo replied was that he did not have any reason to obey an Indian woman." Later he stole her jewelry, for which offense he was beaten to death (AGN, RA, CCR, L 97, C 1185, 1802, Causa seguida contra Don José de Campo, teniente administrador de Rentas Unidas de Andahuaylas por la muerte de su esclavo Gerónimo a quien mandó azotar hasta matarlo).

27. With one exception, the administrators of the haciendas of Magdalena that recorded ethnic figures were nonwhites.

28. In 1801 the priests of Nuestra Señora de la Buena Muerte declared themselves ruined, despite the fact that they had several properties. One of these, the most important, the Quebrada hacienda (which the 1803 figures probably refer to), was in secular hands "and headed toward total collapse." In 1808 twenty-five priests remained in this order, and of this number only nine were not incapacitated, as the priests themselves said; this number was not sufficient to fulfill their essential duty of providing spiritual assistance to those dying in jails, hospitals, and private homes. Founded by San Camilo de Luis, the order had obtained an operating license from Gregory XIV and Clement VIII between 1590 and 1591. It appeared in the colonies in 1735 and apparently could never solve its economic problems; impoverishment also affected the order in La Paz, Arequipa, Trujillo, and Cuzco (AA, Sección Convento de la Buena Muerta, L7).

29. AA, Buena Muerte, 1808–1819, letter written by Juan Sánchez Quiñones to the viceroy in Lima, 18 April 1809.

30. AA, Convento de la Buena Muerte, L 7, 1809, Expediente promovido por el Superior Govierno por los PP. de la Buena Muerte sobre que se les conceda permiso para la elección canónica de un prelado interino según lo determinado en sus sagradas Constituciones, y en que incide la solicitud del Provisor Síndico General de la Ciudad de Arequipa sobre remición de quatro o seis Religiosos Agonisantes a dha. Ciudad para el cumplimiento en ella en su Santo instituto, y dos mas para la Ciudad de La Paz. Lima, Octubre de 1808.

31. The slaves of Guaca acted as did many maroon slaves and others who had some "sin" or disobedience looming over their heads to forestall their master's punishment; similarly, Antonio contacted Manuela's former master after she had been put in the *panadería*. On the Gualcará case see AGN, RA, CCR, L 114, C 1382, 1808, Causas seguidas contra José Espinoza y otros salteadores de caminos, Cañete; AGN, RA, CCR, L 119, C 1446, 1810, Autos contra Gavino Zegarra, Juan el Portugez, esclavos del Sor. Marqués de Fuente Hermosa en la hacienda Gualcará, Villa de Cañete por vagos, ladrones y salteadores en el Partido de Cañete.

32. See AGN, Cabildo, CCI, L 36, C 588, 1817. In this case a slave couple fled from the Pativilca hacienda because of maltreatment by the owner, Doña Severina Alfaro.

33. This case corroborates our observation (derived from analysis of the ethnic composition of owners, *mayordomos* and *caporales* on the haciendas of Magdalena and Miraflores) that the whiter and less remote a hacienda's owner, the tighter the mechanisms of control.

34. AGN, EJ, CCI, L 96, 1830, Expediente que sigue Juan Castro con sus Esclabos Pedro José y otro por cantidad de pesos.

35. AGN, Cabildo CCI, L 5, C 51, 1802, Autos seguidos por Tiburcio María, esclavo de D. Vicente Salinas, sobre que lo venda.

36. Reporting similar traffic in Brazil, Karasch (1987, 157) assures us that "some rural slaves moved between countryside and city as frequently as did their owners."

37. AGN, Cabildo, CCI, L 22, C 369, 1811. The granddaughter of Augustina Carrión, slave of Don Fulgencio Guerrero and Vásquez, was Luisa Guerrero, slave of Doña Nicolasa Guerrero y Vásquez. Upon attempting to escape Luisa fell and the female owner, with some assistance, shackled and carried her to the Pescadería *panadería*. The judge decided that Luisa should return to her owner and not delay her owner's journey back to Ica.

38. AGN, Cabildo, CCI, L 22, C 370, 1811, Autos seguidos por Tiburcio Arroserena, parda libre, contra D. José Martín de Toledo sobre procedimiento arbitrario contra su hijo Juan Bautista, esclavo de Fr. Silvestre Durán.

39. See Proctor (1825, 113).

40. Blanchard (1992, 26) also quotes this passage.

41. AGN, RA, CCI, L 70, C 720, 1807, Fransisca Suazo.

42. AGN, Cabildo, CCI, L 11, C 143, 1806, Autos seguidos por Bernardina León, que fue esclava de D. Dámaso Jáuregui, sobre su libertad, dispuesta de su finado amo.

43. AGN, Cabildo, CCI, L 19, C 310, 1810, Manuel Fuente, esclabo de Josefa Chabes solicita herencia de su padre natural Bartolomé de la Parra.

44. AGN, CS, CCI, L 565, 1854, [s.t.].

45. Aguirre (1991, 122) notes that slave children were included in these averages, which helps explain the depreciation in slaves' value over the two decades before the abolition of slavery.

46. This preference for female labor has also been noted by Reddock (1985, 64) for the Caribbean at the end of the eighteenth century and begining of the nineteenth, which she attributes to the higher mortality rate for males, as noted by Patterson (1967), Craton (1978), and Dunn (1972).

47. See for example AGN, CS, CCI, L 162, 1835, Escrito de D. Fco. Chacón, albacea de D. Manuel Reyna y de su esposa Da. Mercedes Mori y tutor y curador de su hija Da. Petronila Reyna.

48. See the proposals of Mintz (1979) and Scott (1985, 31), who interpret the system of day labor not as an indicator of the slave system's collapse but as successive contradictions within it.

49. AGN, Notario Manuel Suárez, Protocolo 881, fs. 920, 1826.

50. AGN, CS, CCI, L 578, 1854, Bartola Cisneros (esclava) contra Da. Isabel Bentín por su libertad.

51. The difference—according to the protectorial decree of 24 November 1821—between patronage and slavery rested in the monthly payment of eight reales a slave received in *patronato* even though the slave was still property, as in slavery.

52. AGN, CS, CCI, L 66, 1840, Patricio Negrón contra Da. Estefa Palacios y D. Carlos Relaysa por azotes inferidos en su persona. See also CDIP XV:1:173, sesión del 2 de noviembre de 1822.

53. This dual situation was recorded for slaves in other coastal cities as well. See ADLL, Justicia Colonial, Intendencia, CCI, L 306, C 273, 1793.

54. AGN, CS, CCI, L 576, 1854, Sebastiana García con el Síndico de la Molina sobre su libertad. For similar cases, see AGN, CS, CCI, L 574, D. Ignacio Palacios sobre libertad de su sobrina Francisca, 1854: AGN, CCI, L 560, Mariano Salazar, 1854: AGN, CCI, L 560, Lorenza García sobre la variación de dominio de su hija Fortunata, 1854.

55. AGN, EJ, CCI, L571, 1854 [s.t.].

56. Ibid.

57. AGN, CS, CCI, L 569, 1854, Variación de dominio del esclavo Francisco Mansilla.

58. Using the 1813 census of the district of Miraflores, we can check the possibilities that women would be the first to leave the hacienda. If we compare the numbers of married men and women to see which group was larger, we find among the collection of haciendas in Miraflores a surplus of fifteen married men and of seven married women. Thus the probability that married women would abandon the hacienda first was approximately 2:1.

59. AGN, EJ, CCI, Autos seguidos por D. Manuel Esteban de Arsola sobre la propiedad de los esclavos Leandro y Ebaristo Arsola. Also of interest in this case is the *mayordomo* of Bocanegra's payment for the breast-feeding of children after the slave mothers had left the hacienda; it shows his determination to keep up the numbers of slaves on the hacienda and marks the boundaries between the responsibilities of master and slave concerning children. The November 1821 decree required owners to feed rather than pay wages to *libertos* during lactation (until they reached the age of three).

60. AGN, Cabildo, CCI, L 35, C 578, 1817.

61. AGN, EJ, L 92, 1830 [s.t.].

62. AGN, EJ, CCI, L 571, 1854 [s.t.].

63. These calculations are based on three charts preserved in the BN, D 8525, Cuerpos de Milicias Provinciales Disciplinadas y Urbanas de Caballería

en el Virreynato del Perú con expresión de los partidos e Intendencias a que pertenecen; D 8526, Cuerpos de Dragones de Milicias Provinciales Disciplinadas y Urbanas; D 8527, Cuerpos de Infantería Provinciales Disciplinadas y Urbanas, Lima 31 de diciembre de 1816.

64. CDIP V:1:250–251, Oficio de Juan Delgado a Bernardo Monteagudo, Secretario de Guerra y Marina, Sayán, 3 de marzo de 1821.

65. CDIP V:1:154–155, Circular enviada al comandante D. Francisco Aldao, Febrero de 1825.

66. AGN, RA, CCR, L 106, C 1287, 1806, Autos de oficio seguidos contra Agustín Guerrero, Juan José Ortiz y otros por los delitos de robo y asaltos en los caminos.

67. AGN, RA, CCR, L 114, C 1382, 1808, Causa seguida contra José Espinoza y otros salteadores de caminos, Cañete.

68. AGN, RA, CCR, L 104, C 1263, 1805, Autos criminales seguidos de oficio por la Real Justicia contra el esclavo Antonio Caballero y otros por los delitos de haberles encontrado en su poder armas prohibidas y por ladrones en el camino de Chillón.

69. Proctor (1825, 215–216).

70. The notarial record books charted the methods of manumission and recorded how slaves had been acquired and where they had been born (and thus whether they had belonged to a hacienda). I consulted all the notarial record books in the AGN for 1830, 1840, and 1850; for 1840 I found only scanty documentation. It is possible that notarial record books were lost, or that during the period's usual political turbulences no notarial records were made; perhaps the transactions actually diminished, since at the end of the 1830s haciendas tried to reimpose control over the slave population.

71. For 1836 the total number of slaves amounted to 5,971, and for 1845 it was estimated at 4,500 (Jacobsen 1974).

72. Between 1560 and 1650, Bowser (1977, 363–364) notes, 33.8 percent of Lima's slaves were liberated unconditionally, and of this population, 92.2 percent were women and children under the age of fifteen. As we have seen, in 1850 (two hundred years later) this type of freedom accounted for only 9.1 percent of the cases of manumission, including conditional grants by owners. In all Latin American slave centers, self-manumission was central. For statistical evidence see Klein (1986, 221 ff.).

73. The cases studied by Flores Galindo (1984) refer to the period 1760–1809, and those by Aguirre (1990) to 1836–1839.

74. For rural-urban relations see the significant analysis by Fields (1985) in her work on nineteenth-century Maryland.

75. Goldin (1976, 51 ff.) records movement in the United States between 1850 and 1860 but in the opposite direction, and largely determined by slave owners' interests.

76. Haitin (1983, 177) claims that the archdiocese of Lima produced 37 percent of the tithes in the viceroy, and that tithes for Lima between 1774 and 1779 amounted to 126,546 pesos per year, and 148,886 pesos annually between 1790–1794. Despite the risks of using information about tithes, we must conclude that not all productive units followed the same destiny over the course of this long cycle.

3. In the City

1. Available information on slaves' lives within monasteries is sparse, despite this statistic on the slave population there, and none of our cases refer to it. Here is a topic for future work.

2. Colonial and, later on, republican authorities and census-takers counted "house entrances" to evaluate population density and exact taxes. Often one "entrance" was used only by slaves.

3. Much debate surrounds the Atlantic trade, and the percentages noted depend on several variables, such as a voyage's size and date, the identity of the trader, and origin and condition of the slaves on departure. See Reynolds (1985, esp. 28–56) for a recent synthesis.

4. Toplin describes this determinate duality (1981, xxiii): "A heritage of color prejudice was passed down, and so, too, was a tradition of economic inequality."

5. Stevenson (1829, 1:304–306). Contemporaries spelled the names of tribal groups such as the Mondongos in various ways: from Stevenson's spelling, "Mandingos," and his burlesque tone, we might infer that he (or the scribe) had little interest in the matter.

6. AGN, Cabildo, CCI, L 23, C 380, 1812, Autos seguidos por María Santos Puente contra Miguel Valdivieso y Manuela Quirigallo sobre que se le nombre reina de la Nación de los Congos Mondongos o se le restituya el dinero gastado.

7. AGN, CS, CCI, L 717, 1859.

8. On this case see AGN, RA, CCI, L 138, C 1684, 1817. For other significant examples of the nearly infinite civil suits about this topic, see AGN, AGG, CP, L 5, C 113, 1812, Autos seguidos por Ma. Rosa Manrique de Lara (negra libre), ama de Ma. Josefa Murga, su esclava contra el sargento N. pulpero de la calle Guadalupe por ser amo de María Dolores su esclava, por maltratos en agravio de la esclava María Josefa Murga; AGN, RA, CCR, L 94, C 1155, 1801, Angela Andrade; AGN, AGG, CP, L 5, C 116, 1813, Autos criminales seguidos por Da. Ma. Encarnación Valverde (parda), contra Pascual Baylón Frias, por maltratos y contuciones en su agravio cometido en su propio domicilio a donde entró violentamente.

9. AA, Estadística 1809.

10. In this special case the state was the owner; I therefore omit it from subsequent calculations.

11. ADLL, CO, Expediente 165, L 301, 1790. See also AA, Particulares, L 2 (1840–1922), Carta de Gregoria Goyburu al Arzobispo. As early as the sixteenth and seventeenth centuries, Bowser (1977, 147) notes, the receipt of daily wages from one slave could represent the difference between a poor owner's comfort or ruin.

12. AGN, AGG, CCI, L 21, C 368, Baraona contra Chacón, 1817. Chapter 5 amply documents the reasons behind the Defensor's perception.

13. ADLL, CO, L 301, Expediente 165, 1790; and AGN, RA, CCI, L 32, C 352, 1803, Autos seguidos por Petronila Sánchez, samba libre, contra Da. Lugarda Márquez, sobre la libertad de su hijo José Andrés.

14. AGN, Notarios, Protocolo 881, fs. 573.

15. AGN, AGG, CCI, L 21, C 368, 1817, Baraona contra Chacón.

16. In the city as on haciendas, owners' wills might include a grant of freedom (total or conditional), and the higher population density made both wills and the notaries to ease their redaction more common. Although life was rather precarious and life expectancy very low, at times an ailing owner would get better and a slave's expectations of freedom would die. See for example, AGN, AGG, CCI, L 23, C 413, Encarnación Albarito, pardalibre, y Bravo Pando, contra la mujer legítima del Mariscal de Campo D. Manuel Gonzáles, sobre la liberación de sus dos hijos Micaela y María Urbana, esclavos mediante la venta por tasación de sus respectivos precios, 1819.

17. AA, CN, L 36 (1817), Fr. Jose Aravjo ae Artobispo.

18. AA, CN, L 35, 1804, Herrera contra Valenzuela.

19. AGN, RA, CCI, L 103, C 1093, Rioja contra Rioja, 1811.

20. AGN, Cabildo, CCI, L 19, C 324, 1801, Autos seguidos por Luciana Josefa, esclava de D. Paula Almogera, sobre su libertad.

21. AA, LM, L 7 (1800–1809), 1806, Palacios contra Teruz.

22. This sum of 12 pesos equaled the allowance that husbands furnished during the divorce process to wives who were relocated to *beaterios*. See chapter 4.

23. Luciana—assuming she was born in 1753—had her first child at the age of eighteen in 1771. When she filed her case in 1810, the noted thirty-nine years had elapsed. In Catalina's case, her wedding in 1791 began the day-labor process of accumulation of fifteen years that ended with the filing of the suit in 1806; we must assume that her price and that of her husband came to 600 pesos.

24. AGN, RA, CCI, L 132, C 1345, Breña contra Iturrizo, 1815.

25. ADP, JC, Intendencia, CCI, L 307, C 317, 1793, Autos que sigue Mathias Sánchez, negra contra Da. Ursula Sánchez, sobre la venta de una samba, hija de dha. negra que dise ser nula.

26. See for example AGN, CS, CCI, L 569, 1854, Vicenta Arzola, liberta con Melchora Barrera, morena libre, sobre la entrega de su menor hija Paula Saldonado, San Lázaro. This case is particularly interesting because it pitted a day laboring black *liberta* against a master who was a free *morena*, and because the new owner intervened on behalf of the *liberta*.

27. AGN, CS, Juzgado Eclesiástico, RPJ 483 (1825–1836), Causa que por vía de fuerza promovió la Madre Sor Isabel del Espíritu Santo y Paters, religiosa en el monasterio de Santa Clara de Lima contra el Señor Coronel Manuel Porras, a nombre de su madre D. Brigida Santoyo, sobre el recojo de una muchacha nombrada María Isabel, hija de Simón Alvarez y de Juana Porras, esclava de la última de aquella, que se halla en dicho convento y a quien pretende hacer esclava.

28. AGN, RA, CCI, L 20, C 213, Pérez y Herrera contra Vidal Bravo, 1802.

29. AGN, RA, CCI, L 159, C 1645, 1819, Da. N. Echenique contra N. Andrea Barrera, su esclava, sobre la esclavitud de los hijos de ésta última.

30. AA, CN, L 35 (1799–1814), 1799, Isabel Sanchez y Baca.

31. AGN, CS, CCI, L 278, 1841, Defensor General de Menores contra Da. Rosa Moreno por querer reducir a servidumbre a Rafael de 17 años, hijo de una esclava suya.

32. AGN, EJ, CCI, 1840, Seguido por el Defensor de Menores con representación de María del Milagro Solórzano sobre libertad de su hija Micaela Bartola con la Señora Da. Juana Murga.

33. AGN, RA, CCI, L 32, C 352, Petronila Sánchez, samba libre contra Da. Lugarda Márquez sobre la libertad de su hijo José Andrés, 1803.

34. AGN, CS, CCI, L 261, 1840, Marcos Esquivel contra Da. Isabel Espinoza sobre que no venda a sus hijas y sobre el Patronato de las mismas. A similar case is AGN, EJ, L 252, 1840, Francisca Solano Palacios contra su ama Da. Manuela Marino.

35. AGN, RA, CCR, L 125, C 1527, Expediente promovido en la vía penal, con el fin de poder esclarecer sobre el suicidio del negro bozal nombrado Antonio, esclavo de D. Ignacio Meléndez a quien se le encontró ahorcado en un árbol de la Alameda del Pino, 1812. On the conditions slaves experienced in the San Bartolomé and San Lázaro hospitals, see Mendieta Ocampo (1990, 20–25, 57–64).

4. Matrimonial Alliances and Conflicts

1. AGN, RA, CCI, L 103, C 1093, Rioja contra Rioja, 1811.

2. Menefee (1981) documents the sale of wives in eighteenth-century England as a symbolic means husbands used to hand over adulterous women to their lovers.

3. AGN, RA, CCI, L 110, C 1161, María Encarnación contra Centeno, 1812.

4. Men's competition for a slave woman occasionally caused badly disguised demonstrations of jealousy, such as the worries of D. Agustín Valdéz (whom his female slave accused of "committing sin daily"): he requested that the slave be returned, because "she could die at the hands of one of those neglectful slaves, who would require her to come up with her own subsistence" (AGN, Cabildo, CCI, L 33, C 561, Adrianzén contra Valdez, 1816).

5. AGN, RA, CCI, L 33, C 368, Neyra contra Balada, 1803.

6. AA, CD, L 87 (1815–1820), Teresa contra Torquera, 1817.

7. AA, CN, L 36 (1816–1855), Juana Manuela Básquez, morena esclava del Señor Regidor del Ayuntamiento, Francisco Alvarado, 1817.

8. Burkett (1975) discusses the experiences of women of all racial groups and the characteristics of their interaction.

9. AA, CD, L 87 (1815–1820) Teresa contra Torquera, 1817.

10. AA, CD, L 87 (1815–1820), 1819, Gutierrez contra Prio.

11. AA, L 1, Comunicaciones, (1765–1818), 1816, Santa María contra Carrillo.

12. AA, LM, L 7 (1800–1809), 1805, Baset contra Guiyón.

13. AGN, RA, CCR, L 102, C 1247, 1804, Comín contra Lamas, C 1247.

14. AA, CD, L 86 (1810–1814), Vargas Machuca contra Sánchez.

15. These figures come from a reading of wills and marriage licenses, in the AGN and AA, respectively.

16. I extrapolate percentages from Table 1, on methods of manumussion in rural and urban areas; see chapter 1. Aguirre (1991) examines *cartas de libertad* from 1840 to 1854 but considers only urban cases; hence my figures for manumission through purchase in 1840 and 1850 differ from his: 69.0 percent in 1840 and 70.0 percent in 1850 versus Aguirre's 58.7 percent and 81.7 percent (my cases for 1840 and 1850 are 139 and 106; his cases, 63 and 60). Aguirre's figures express even more clearly the acceleration of the process of self-purchase in the final decades of the slave system. The discrepancies may reflect different methods as well as areas.

For an assessment of similar indicators for an earlier period, see Bowser (1977, 363; 1984, 375); for a comparison with other Latin American cities, see Aguirre (1993, 218). Lima had the highest percentage of self-manumitted slaves. Aguirre states that of Lima's slaves, 26.2 percent were granted freedom between 1840 and 1854 and the rest made payments to owners (73.8 percent); his findings are close to my own: for 1830 31.3 percent, for 1840 36 percent, and for 1850 30 percent.

17. Reddock (1985, 66 ff.) discusses recent work on the "buy or breed" dilemma by Craton (1978) and Patterson (1967).

18. Islamic slave owners often liberated concubines who bore their children; the practice spread with Islamic expansion to become one of the most common characteristics of slave systems (see Lerner 1983, 188).

19. AGN, RA, CCI, L 131, C 1343, Nuñez contra Dominguez, 1815.

20. AGN, C5 CCI, L 662, Paniso contra Alvarado, 1857.

21. We are dealing with a record in the AA I believe to be complete (see Table 10). Haitin (1983) also uses marriage licenses, and his figures complement my results. My subsequent comparison with the record books of the registry of marriages confirmed the reliability of the data.

22. A caveat is in order here. Most likely, changes in archival criteria within the Archivo Arzobispal explain discrepancies between my figures and those in Haitin's thesis (1983, 217) on marriages during these years (in a graph that is difficult to read). Haitin counts roughly 300 marriages in 1800, 400 in 1810, 250 in 1820, 280 in 1830, and 250 in 1850; only in 1810 and 1820 do his estimates approach mine. Since Haitin's figures are older, I would guess that I have not seen all the records (through lack of opportunity but certainly not of will) but that our final interpretations of the relative importance of marriage between slaves and between slaves and free persons would not vary.

23. The slaves in most of my case studies come from these two parishes: Santa Ana's census statistics in 1813 showed a high number of white residents; San Lázaro was the black parish par excellence and had strong ties to the rural sphere. After the parish of La Catedral (or Sagrario) with 19,619 inhabitants, Santa Ana and San Lázaro had the largest populations (11,432 and 9,711, respectively), followed by San Sebastián and el Cercado (5,444 and 5,122). The record books in the Archivo Arzobispal had information on ethnic descent for blacks, *mulatos*, *morenos*, *chinos*, *zambos*, *pardos*, *quinteronas*, and *quarteronas*.

Of the three record books in the Archivo Arzobispal for the parish of Santa Ana, book 3 referred to *pardos* and *morenos* and recorded ethnic identity for both contracting parties in 93.3 percent of the cases (502 of 538), whereas the other two books listed only a total of fifteen slaves. For this reason I use only book 3 to refer to Santa Ana. Of the two books (nos. 7 and 8) in the Archivo Arzobispal for San Lázaro, only book 8 had information for the years I consider but included no more than four years, from 1817 through 1820. Information about the ethnic descent of both spouses existed in only 49.6 percent of the cases for Santa Ana, and 59.4 percent for San Lázaro. The archives for San Lázaro included a record book for marriages of Indians with members of *casta* groups (eleven marriages between Indians and slaves—three *chinos*, one *zamba*, and two *mulatas*). Neither the record book for Indians nor that for blacks referred exclusively to a single ethnic group.

24. Santa Ana's small sample of slaves married to members of other black ethnic groups coincides with the pattern Haitin (1986, 293) describes in a much bigger sample.

25. These precepts found support in a royal warrant dated 31 May 1789, which ordered the encouragement of marriage among slaves, even if they belonged to different owners, and the display of owners' humanity in finding ways to unite spouses; it declared that slaves were to have the right of free matrimonial choice (Labarthe 1955, 9).

26. AA, CN, L 35 (1799–1814), Barraza contra Arroserena, 1803.

27. AA, Estadística, Parroquia de Santa Ana, 1808.

28. Unfortunately we lack a similar residential census for San Lázaro from which we might infer owners' tactics of opposition.

29. Haitin (1986, 233, 238) calculates 21.7 years as the average matrimonial age of slave women, the highest among all ethnic groups between 1820 and 1840, and 24.0 years as the average of slave men, the lowest among all ethnic groups. The relatively higher matrimonial age of slave women might reflect their attempt to save enough to buy freedom before marriage to a husband of higher social status.

30. AA, CN, L 35 (1799–1814), 1813, Roxas contra Puente. In this case the man was the slave of the marqués of Villafuerte, which perhaps explains the meticulous argument on possible grounds for annulment of the marriage.

31. My reading of all the cases that requested annulment of a marriage in Lima between 1800 and 1860 turned up only four decrees of annulment and none of these involved slaves.

32. AA, LM, L 7 (1800–1809); CD, L 84 (1805–1807); NM, L 58 (1799–1809), Natallana contra Venegas.

33. AA, CN, L 35 (1799–1814), 1808, Torres contra Astorga; emphasis added.

34. AGN, Cabildo, CCI, L 23, C 376, 1812, Autos seguidos por Juan Abril, marido de Rosa Balenzuelos contra D. Alejandro Martínez, amo de la mencionada Rosa, sobre que se le extienda boleta de venta. Rosa was a "white *mulata*," the wife of a black carpenter.

35. AGG, CCI, L 16, C 246, San Miguel contra Salazar, 1810.

36. AA, Particulares, L 1, 1605–1839, 1812.

37. On *panaderías* and sales outside the city see AA, Particulares, L 2 (1840–1922), as well as some episodes noted earlier. On criminal charges see AA, CN, L 35 (1799–1814), Guerrero contra Astorga, 1808. On raising a slave's price see AA, CN, L 36 (1816–1855), Gusman contra Ramírez, 1820. And on reappraisal of a slave's price see AA, EM 1805, Escrito del esclavo José Diaz al Provisor. In this last case, José Diaz was the sponsor of the marriage of two slaves, Joaquín and Juana, and paid Juana's owners 12 pesos for the proceedings. Later he paid the owner 450 pesos for Juana's price, which the owner rejected because he wanted 526 pesos. Finally the godfather requested that the owner accept the money or sign his consent in the marriage license so that the couple could marry. Here again freedom and con-

sent were inextricably linked to a strategy designed to undo the arguments of owners.

38. AA, CN, L 35, 1799–1814, Barrionuebo contra Casillas, 1799; AGN, RA, CCI L 71, C 1093; AGN, RA, CCI, L 66, C 670; AA, CN, L 35, (1799–1814), Mendoza contra Mendoza, 1811; AA, CN L 35, (1799–1814), Catalina contra Querejazu, 1806; AA, CN, L 35, (1799–1814), Vásquez contra Valdivieso, 1801.

39. AA, CN, L 36, (1816–1855), Bellido contra Moles, 1817; AA, CN, L 35, (1799–1814), Encalada contra Mena, 1803; AA, L 36, (1816–1855), F. Jacoba contra Yayo, 1816. And in AA, L 35 (1799–1814), Barela contra Gutierrez, 1805, the owner's claim to ignorance of the marriage did not affect the judgment.

40. AA, EM, Miranda contra del Carmen, 1816.

41. AGN, RA, CCI, L 33, C 367, 1813, Autos seguidos por Da. Bárbara Tixero contra Da. Mariana Noriega, sobre la redhibitoria de un esclavo.

42. AGN, CCR, [s.n.] 1854, Causa criminal contra José del Patrocinio por habérsele sorprendido oculto en la casa del Dr. D. Antonio Arenas.

43. AA, Sección Comunicaciones, 1815, del Cristo contra Carabali.

44. AA, CN, L 36 (1816–1855), Gusman contra Ramírez, 1820.

45. AA, CN, L 35 (1799–1814), Tagle contra Tagle, 1814.

46. AA, CN, L 35 (1799–1814), Espellier contra Marris, 1808.

47. AA, CD, L 86 (1810–1814), —contra Iturrizaga, 1818.

48. AGN, Cabildo, CCI, L 6, C 62, Autos seguidos por Manuel Góngora, marido de María Aparicio, contra D. Manuel Aparicio, amo de ésta, sobre que la venda, 1803.

49. The cases refer to complete sets of the existing documentation from four documentary series (LM, CD, NM, and CN) for the years between 1800 and 1820 and between 1840 and 1860. After 1854 slaves became "servants."

50. Political turbulence probably overrode domestic conflicts, given that between 1840 and 1860, what we find is a diminution of marital conflicts in general, not only of those involving slaves. Between 1800 and 1820, marital conflicts for all of Lima amounted to 409, between 1840 and 1860, they fell to 213 despite demographic growth.

51. AA, LM, L 7 (1800–1809), María Candelaria contra Rosales, 1808.

52. AA, CD, L 86 (1800–1814), Luisa contra López, 1812.

53. AA, CD, L 83 (1802–1804), Nieto contra Bethelem, 1803.

54. AGN, Cabildo, CCI, L 29, C 476, Villaverde contra Bernal, 1814.

55. AA, LM, L 7 (1800–1809), Matallana contra Venegas.

56. AA, CN, L 35, 1799–1814, Juana contra Casanova, 1807; AA, L 36, (1816–1855), Marín contra Romero, 1818; AA, CN, L 35, 1799–1814, Martinez contra Tagle, 1799, in which the husband approved relocation, and AA, CN, L 83, (1802–1804), Nieto contra Bethelem, 1803, in which the woman did the same.

57. For examples of economic arguments between slave spouses, see AGN, Protocolos Notariales, Notaría Julián de Cubillas, Libro 202 (1818–1820) and AA, LM (1810–1819), Texada contra Escobar, 1819.

58. AA, LM, L 8, 1811, Casaverde contra Cuellar.

59. AA, CD, L 86, (1810–1814), Luisa contra Lopes, 1812; AA, L 84, (1805–1807), de la Natividad contra Pacheco, 1807; AA, LM L 7, (1800–1809), María Candelaria contra Rosales, 1808.

60. AGN, CS, CCR, L 116, 1851, Espinoza contra Larrosa (concubinos).

61. Santa Ana's residential census of 1808 stated that only 17.3 percent of the registered slaves were married. Therefore, there was a significant correlation between the number of married slaves in an owner's household and the frequency of conflicts.

62. AGN, Cabildo, CCI, L 6, C 61, Autos seguidos por Mariana Espinoza contra D. Faustino Guerrero, su amo, sobre que la venda, 1803.

5. Slaves and Their Owners

1. Such trials were common among other sectors of society, for example when women accused their husbands of abuse. Slave cases that typify these proceedings are found in AGN, Cabildo, CCI, L 17, C 286, 1809, Autos seguidos por José Valentín Villegas contra su amo, D. Pedro Antonio López Vidaurre sobre sevicia; AGN, RA, CCI, L 10, C 114, Queja de la esclava Jacoba Rubio, perteneciente a Juan Bautista, sobre malostratos y para conseguir amo que le de mejor trato, 1801.

2. AGN, Cabildo, CCI, L 21, C 353, 1811, Autos seguidos por Gregoria Santos, esclava de D. José Ignacio sobre que la venda.

3. AA, Correspondencia, L 1 (1806–1816), Escrito de la esclava Manuela Balenzuela al Arzobispo Las Heras, [s.t.].

4. AGN, Cabildo, CCI, L 99, C 102, 1804, Autos seguidos por Da. Norberta Gallardo sobre insubsistencia del requisito en que fue comprada su esclava Jacoba Román para poder venderla fuera de la Capital.

5. See also Aguirre (1993, 234–237).

6. AA, Particulares, L 2 (1840–1922), Carta de Pablo Calero, esclavo de D. Mateo, residente en Lima al Arzobispo, 1814.

7. An allegation of old age occurs in AA, Correspondencia L 1 (1806–1816), Carta de la esclava Manuela Balenzuela al Arzobispo Las Heras.

8. AGN, CCI, L 14, C 211, 1808, Autos seguidos por Juan de la Cruz Zapata, esclavo de Da. Rufina Trevino, su ama, sobre que lo venda a precio de su tasación.

9. AGN, Cabildo, CCI, L 19, C 324, 1801, Autos seguidos por Luciana Josefa, esclava de Da. Paula Almogera, sobre su libertad.

10. An example is AGN, Cabildo, CCI, L 20, C 330, 1810, Autos seguidos por el R. P. Fr. Domingo Porras contra Da. Atanasia Soriano sobre la libertad de la esclava llamada Manuela.

11. AA, CN, L 35 (1700–1814), Escrito de la esclava Plácida Laynes al Vicario, 17/03/1800.

12. AGN, Cabildo, CCI, L 35, C 578, 1817, Autos seguidos por D. Martín Gonzales contra Da. Jacoba Centurión sobre redhibitoria de una esclava.

13. AGN, Cabildo, CCI, L 17, C 289, 1809, Autos seguidos por Pedro Piélago, Chino esclavo de D. José Ignacio Palacios, sobre que le otorgue libertad, previo pago de los 200 pesos en que lo tasó su anterior ama.

14. AGN, [s.i.], Expediente que sigue el Defensor General de Menores contra Da. Rosa de la Piedra y Lequerica (madre del Grl. Agustín Gamarra) sobre la venta de un esclavo. The case probably dates from 1830.

15. AGN, Cabildo, CCI, L 10, C 121, 1805, Autos seguidos por José Gregorio, esclavo de Manuel Villarán, sobre que lo venda [Da. Manuela Gonzales is the wife of Manuel Villarán]. A similar (but less picturesque) case also shows that things did not change much from the beginning of the century until the abolition of slavery: AGN, CS, CCI, L 577, 1854, Da. M. Concepción Malpartida y Da. Manuela Sanz por redhibitoria de un esclavo. Here the former owner accused the new owner of not furnishing the water-carrying equipment she owed to the slave and thus causing the slave to flee, since he was unable to comply with the daily wage demands. The judgment favored the new owner, who got back the money she had paid for the slave; meanwhile the slave had run away.

16. Such a transaction occurred in a record dated 1800. AGN, Cabildo, CCI, L 11, C 140, Autos seguidos por J.G. de Herrera con D. Felipe Llanos, sobre que se le admita fianza por su libertad. Brokers functioned as intermediaries much as the *cofradías* did.

17. AGN, RA, CCI, L 128, C 1308, 1815; AGN, Cabildo, CCI, L 33, C 555, 1816.

18. AGN, RA, CCR, L 108, C 1301, 1806. See also Córdova y Urrutia (1839, 47) and Mellafe (1973, 125).

19. AGN, Prefectura, L 117, 1827.

20. The tribunal's organization was described by the newspaper *Gaceta del Gobierno*, 22 April 1835; the military decree was issued by Colonel Miguel Angel Bujanda of the national army.

21. BN, D 2218, 1854.

22. Flores Galindo (1990, 63) also quotes the document, AGN, Superior Gobierno, L 26, C 774, 1976, which recorded the following ethnic distribution of a total of 59 prisoners: 15 whites, 12 *mestizos*, 7 *mulatos*, 5 *zambos*, 7 blacks, 7 *chinos*, 6 Indians, 2 *cholos*, and 3 unspecified.

23. AGN, Cabildo, CCI, L 39, C 644, 1819, Autos seguidos por María Ana Murga contra D. Teodoro Murga, sobre que le extienda boleta de venta.

24. Scott (1988, 36) asserts that in Cuba "individual planters often used rented slaves in order to mitigate the problem of fixed labor costs within the

system of slavery. Rental permitted the shifting of the existing slave labor supply to areas of greatest profitability; it did not necessarily weaken slavery as an institution or loosen the bonds of slavery."

25. AGN, Cabildo, CCI, L 16, C 243, 1809, Autos seguidos por Apolinaria Ontañón contra Da. Ventura Espinoza, sobre que le permita buscar ama.

26. BN, Z 713, 1810 [s.t.].

27. AA, CN, L 35 (1799–1814), Petronila de León, 1801.

28. AGN, Cabildo, CCI, L 16, C 242, 1809, Autos seguidos por José Llanos, padre de María del Carmen Marín, esclava de Da. María de la Daga sobre que no la venda para residir fuera de la Capital.

29. AGN, CCI, L 584, 1855, Cuaderno 2do. de los autos seguidos por Da. Fermina García con D. Juan Gualveto Herrero sobre la entrega de una esclava.

30. Labarthe (1955, 7) quotes Mendiburu (*Revista de Lima*, 5:513): "Y esta costumbre se extendió tanto que dichas casas, que no eran pocas, a veces no podían admitir ya más esclavos para conservarlos bajo prisiones."

31. For additional information, see Aguirre (1988; 1993, 251).

32. AGN, CS, CCR, L 124, Expediente iniciado por Manuela Aguirre, esposa libre de Esteban Ita, 1853.

33. AGN, RA, CCR, L 95, C 1168, 1812, Queja de Liberata Sánchez, China esclava de D. José Fariña por defloración con violencia del Abastecedor Juan Espinoza y haberla tenido prisionera en su casa de Abasto. Esto, habiendo sido puesta por su ama en Panadería de Espinoza.

34. AGN, RA, CCR, L 140, C 1727, 1818–19, Autos seguidos por el Señor Alcalde del Crimen, Conde de Vallehermoso, contra D. Francisco Gómez, proprietario de la panadería del Sauce, a quien se le juzga por el excesivo castigo de azotes de sus esclavos negros Antonio y José.

35. As slave labor became more specialized, it brought greater mutual dependence between owners and slaves and suggested more opportunities for sabotage by slaves. On sugar plantations, for example, slaves who oversaw the refining process might add few drops of lemon juice that were enough to ruin the molasses and spoil a substantial share of the harvest (Tomich 1990, 224–225; 248–258). Slaves in a *panadería* could sabotage the production of bread for Lima's inhabitants for an entire day or perhaps longer.

36. AGN, Cabildo, CCI, L 23, C 374, 1812, Autos seguidos por Antonio Lara, esclavo de D. Juan Pérez contra D. Lucas Villa, Administrator de la Panadería de la Plazuela de Santa Ana, sobre sevicia.

37. The "hidden dungeon" image occurs in AGN, Cabildo, CCI, L 21, C 355, 1811, Autos seguidos por María Antonia Jaime, negra liberta, mujer de José Andrés Garcés contra D. Joaquín Miguel de Arnaco, amo de su marido, sobre que lo venda. That of misery and pain, in AGN, RA, CCR, L 105, C 1278, Autos criminales seguidos de Oficio por la Real Justicia contra

Francisco Herrera, negro esclavo de D. Luis de Herrera, por el delito de homicidio que ejecutó en la persona de Patricio, de igual casta y condición, hecho cometido en la panadería de las Animitas con cuchillo según dibujo de fs. 4, 1805.

38. AGN, RA, CCR, L 115, C 1390, 1809, Autos seguidos ante la Real Justicia con motivo del alzamiento de los esclavos que trabajan en la Casa-Panadería de Santa Clara, asimismo se ordena su libertad de Francisco Maldonado, para que satisfaga la deuda que ocasionó su depósito en la Panadería de la calle de La Palma, comunicándolo a su administrator a fin de que si reincide deberá ser corregido severamente con costas; Declaración de Agustín Arana, mulato esclavo de la panadería y de oficio Acechador.

39. Aguirre (1993, 289–291) gives a more detailed description of the conspiracy.

40. This case involved the Animitas *panadería* and, as in the previous one, alcohol influenced the slaves' behavior, AGN, RA, CCR, L 105, C 1278, 1805.

41. AGN, CS, CCI, L 592, 1855.

42. AGN, CS, CCI, L 627, 1856.

43. AGN, CS, CCI, L 562, 1854.

44. See thorough analysis of these events in Gootenberg (1982), Giesecke (1978), and Quiroz (1988).

Conclusion

1. For a broader assessment of "legal" skin color differences also see Lanning (1944) and Moerner (1967).

2. On the implications of these ideas in other areas see Moerner (1967) and Toplin (1981).

3. Bowser comments on the frequency of marriage in the sixteenth and seventeenth centuries. Our sources may not be comparable, but qualitative sources at least show that marriage in the nineteenth century was an important and ever-present argument for slaves.

4. In an analogous interpretation for the United States, Fields (1985, 29–30) writes, "Much more than simple demography worked to keep free blacks in close relationship with slaves. The vagaries of manumission did so as well. Delayed manumission was a widespread practice, embracing just over half of manumissions between 1832 and just under half thereafter. That made for awkward and anomalous family situations. It could result in a family composed indiscriminately of slaves for life, slaves for a term of years, and free people."

5. For a similar assertion in the Caribbean, see Morrisey (1989, 4).

6. By contrast, a slave in the United States who hoped to manumit a relative usually had to obtain and secure property rights in his or her own name; only a freed person could purchase slaves (Genovese 1985). This difference may well explain very different rates of self-manumission in each hemisphere.

7. For example, Schwartz (1982:67) found for the Reconcavo in Brazil that "many of the traditional artisan skills were practiced by the slaves. Engenhos often found it more profitable to train slaves as carpenters, smiths, or coopers rather than pay for the services of free artisans"; the argument suggests an economic rationale for the presence of slave artisans as well as an aversion to manual labor among whites and *mestizos*.

8. Such a paradoxical relationship also occurs in Cuba and Brazil. In Brazil, where the hiring-out system was very prevalent, Mattosso (1986, 123) states, the "possibility of shifting large numbers of slaves from one occupation to another helped to stabilize a market in which demand varied with circumstances and competition. . . . The system was, thus, highly flexible." In Lima owners hoping to shift workers from urban to rural markets often met resistance from their slaves.

9. Contrast the situation for Brazil, where Mattosso states "that it would have been difficult for the slave to save much of what he earned" (1986, 123).

10. In the United States, the hiring-out system was forbidden even by law; nevertheless, it was continued by custom and tradition. "In the towns and especially in the larger cities, many slaves 'hired their own time' and lived away from the masters. Although these practices were generally illegal, they were sanctioned almost everywhere, by custom and in accordance with white business interests. Consequently, free Negroes, whose freedom always was precarious, interacted every day, socially and at work, with slaves who were close to being half-free. A certain amount of intermarriage occurred, and little in the social setting generated antipathy" (Genovese 1974, 406–407).

11. $375 \div 3 = 125$; $125 \times 8 = 2{,}250$ and $125 \times 9 = 1{,}125$. Decrease of the slave population between 1818 and 1836 = 2,798. 2,798:2,250 = 1.24. Similarly, for the second period (1836–1845), the slave population decreased 1,291. 1,219:1125 = 1.14. The simple average of the number of slaves for the three years for which we have censuses is 7,190 between 1818 and 1836 and 5,145 between 1836 and 1845; thus: 2,250:7,190 = 31.3 percent; and 1,125:5,145 = 21.9 percent.

12. For the same period in the United States Hart (1968 [1906], 130 ff.) calculates that in 1850 one out of 2,181 slaves became free; in 1860 it was one out of 1,309.

13. Other slave societies did not share this long-term tendency. In the United States, in the decades between 1820 and 1840 there were higher lev-

els of manumission than between 1850 and 1860. Between 1830 and 1860, "one state after another closed off manumissions altogether and insisted on the removal of freedmen from the state. In the 1850s the position of a free Negro in New Orleans and some other cities rapidly deteriorated through keeping coffeehouses or entering special fields of employment" (Genovese 1974, 399). Until the beginning of the eighteenth century, colonial French slaveholders could do as they pleased, including granting slaves freedom. But thereafter they had to seek special state permission to liberate a slave. In 1775 manumission was taxed, and manumitting a slave woman was doubly taxed (Wirz 1984, 126). Thus, whereas in Lima the process of manumission accelerated abolition, in other areas legal and moral devices hindered abolition.

14. Following Patterson's scheme of analysis (1982), slave formations differ by the nature of their dependence on slavery and by the degree and direction of dependence—or, more simply, by who depended on slavery and what were the conditions and consequences of the relation. My analysis of the distribution of slave ownership shows that slaves occasionally reversed the terms of dependence.

15. Also in Brazil, "hundreds and hundreds of families have one or two slaves on whose earnings alone they live" (Schwartz 1982, 68, based on research done by Ewbank in 1856). Schwartz goes further: "[about] one-third of the households in the urban centers of São Paulo and Ouro Prêto, for example, contained at least one slave. In São Paulo the percentage decreased between 1778 and 1836, but, even at the later date, 46 percent of the free households in the town held slaves. In Ouro Prêto, capital of the old mining district of Minas Gerais, the figure was 41 percent of the households in 1804. This level of diffusion in urban areas is borne out by a published census for the parish of São Pedro in the city of Salvador in 1775, where 47 percent of the households in that central parish contained slaves. The evidence is scattered, to be sure, but it supports the impression given by foreign travelers that slavery was an ubiquitous institution in the cities and towns of Brazil" (1982, 76–77). With less precise indications, something similar seems to have been the case in Costa Rica (Olien 1980).

16. In Rio de Janeiro, state authorities were responsible for punishing slaves. Sometimes, this charge became a pretext to use privately owned slaves for public tasks; slave owners received payment for the slaves' work; but if slaves were sent to prison, owners were asked to pay for part of their upkeep (Nogueira da Silva 1988, 150 ff.; also see Algranti 1988).

17. In this whole setting, Rout's (1977, 93) assertion that in Hispanic America manumission was a gift and not a right, and that those slaves who enjoyed liberty were basically lucky subjects, does not hold true for Lima. There slaves weakened the system and did so not through luck but through a complex set of attitudes and options that grew from their everyday experiences.

18. In following this question, Lombardi (1974, 168, 170) echoes Harris, Elkins, and Klein.

19. In a recent symposium at the University of California, San Diego, Viotti da Costa, Blackburn, and Scott (all 1991) provided new insights on this theme; see also Tomich (1990) and Toplin (1981).

Glossary

Asentista	holder of a long-term contract granted by the Crown, to buy or sell products or services
Barracón	slaves' living quarters on the hacienda
Beaterio	institution resembling convent, administered by nuns, in which girls received education and divorcing women found refuge
Bozal	slave newly arrived from Africa, presumably without knowledge of the Spanish language, religion, or customs
Cabildo	municipal council
Carta de libertad	notarially recorded document in which an owner granted freedom to a slave or explained the conditions for obtaining freedom
Casta	person of European and African ancestry; individuals so labeled included any mixture of European and African ancestors
Chacra	small estate farm
Chino	person of undefined African and indigenous ancestry, a bit lighter than a *mulato*
Cholo	darker-skinned person without clearly defined racial, cultural, or economic features (usually a pejorative term)
Cofradía	mutual-aid society or sodality introduced by the Roman Catholic church and dedicated to the cult of a saint; depending on its specific location, it incorporated aspects of African or Andean culture
Conque	legal document that contained the conditions of a slave's sale and purchase

Criollo	Spaniard born in Latin America
Comadre/compadre	godmother/godfather; ritual kinship ties that expanded social relations beyond the immediate family
Cuartel	quarter or district
Defensor de Menores	the defender who represented legal minors
Gracias al sacar	both the name of a document and concept best translated as "whitening" by which persons of color requested to be considered as having skin lighter than its actual color
Hacendado	owner of a hacienda
Juzgado de menores	the court for litigation of cases involving legal minors (including slaves and Indians)
Liberto	freed slave who was required to stay with his or her master for a certain period of time (often up to the age of fifty) but had a right to demand wages
Limeño	resident of the city of Lima
Mayordomo	overseer or manager of an enterprise, usually a hacienda or estate
Mestizo	person of European and indigenous ancestry
Moreno	person whose appearance vaguely suggested African ancestry
Mulato	person of African and indigenous ancestry
Panadería	both a bakery and a place of punishment where slaves and other individuals were interned
Panadero	owner or manager of a *panadería*
Pardo	person of European and African ancestry (two-thirds to one-third, respectively)
Protomedicato	royally appointed medical body that made judgment for the court
Pulpería	small shop combining functions of grocery store and tavern (the colonial corner store)

Quarterón	person of one-fourth African ancestry, three-fourths European
Quinterón	person of one-fifth African ancestry, four-fifths European
Real Audiencia	highest court of justice and governing body under the viceroy
Sereno	night watchman
Síndico del Concurso	general attorney
Síndico Procurador	public attorney
Tambo	roadside inn for travelers and purveyor of various supplies
Zambo	person of African, indigenous, and European ancestry

Bibliography

Aguirre, Carlos. "Agentes de su propia emancipación: Manumisión de esclavos en Lima, 1821–1854." Paper presented at the 47th International Congress of Americanists, New Orleans, Louisiana, 1991.

———. *Agentes de su propia libertad: Los esclavos de Lima y la desintegración de la esclavitud, 1821–1834*. Lima: Pontificia Universad Católica del Perú, 1993.

———. "Cimarronaje, bandolerismo, y desintegración esclavista, Lima, 1821–1854." In *Bandoleros, abigeos, y montoneros: Criminalidad y violencia en el Perú, siglos XVIII–XX*. Lima: Instituto de Apoyo Agrario, 1990.

———. "Conflicto, resistencia, y adaptación: Los esclavos de Lima y la desintegración de la esclavitud, 1821–1854." Master's thesis, Pontificia Universidad Católica del Perú, Lima, Peru, 1992.

———. "Violencia, castigo, y control social: Esclavos y panaderías en Lima, siglo XIX." *Pasado y Presente* 1 (1988).

Aguirre, Carlos, and Charles Walker, eds. *Bandoleros, abigeos, y montoneros: Criminalidad y violencia en el Perú, siglos XVIII–XX*. Lima: Instituto de Apoyo Agrario, 1990.

Algranti, Leila Mezan. *O feitor ausente: Estudos sobre a escravidão no Rio de Janeiro, 1808–1822*. Rio de Janeiro: Editora Vozes, 1988.

Andrews, George R. *The Afro-Argentines of Buenos Aires, 1800–1900*. Madison: University of Wisconsin Press, 1980.

Balmori, Diana, Miles Wortmann, and Stuart Voss. *Notable Family Networks in Latin America*. Chicago: University of Chicago Press, 1984.

Bastide, Roger. *Las Américas negras*. 2d ed. Madrid: Editorial Alianza, 1969.

Bauer, Raymund, and Alice Bauer. "Day to Day Resistance to Slavery." In *American Slavery: The Question of Resistance*, ed. John H. Bracey, August Meier, and Elliot Rudwick, 38–60. Belmont, Calif.: Wadsworth, 1971.

Berlin, Ira. *Slaves Without Masters: The Free Negro in the Antebellum South*. New York: Random House, 1974.

———, ed. *The Destruction of Slavery*. Cambridge: Cambridge University Press, 1985.

Bierck, Harold A., Jr. "The Struggle for Abolition in Gran Colombia." *Hispanic American Historical Review* 33 (August 1953): 378–385.

Blackburn, Robin. *The Overthrow of Colonial Slavery, 1776–1848*. New York: Verso Press, 1988.
Blanchard, Peter. "The Chicama Valley Slave Rebellion of 1851." Paper presented at the 47th International Congress of Americanists, New Orleans, Louisiana, 1991.
———. *Slavery and Abolition in Early Republican Peru*. Wilmington, Del.: Scholarly Resources, 1992.
Bonilla, Heraclio, and Karen Spalding. "La independencia en el Perú: Las palabras y los hechos." In *La independencia en el Perú*, ed. Heraclio Bonilla and Karen Spalding, 15–65. Lima: Instituto de Estudios Peruanos, 1984.
Bowser, Frederick P. "Africans in Spanish American Colonial Society." In *The Cambridge History of Latin America*, ed. Leslie Bethell, 2:357–380. Cambridge: Cambridge University Press, 1984.
———. *El esclavo africano en el Perú colonial*. Mexico: Siglo XXI, 1977. Originally published as *The African Slave in Colonial Peru, 1524–1650*. Stanford: Stanford University Press, 1974.
Burga, Manuel. "El Perú Central, 1770–1860: Disparidades regionales y la primera crisis agrícola republicana." *Revista Peruana de Ciencias Sociales* 1 (1987).
Burkett, Elinor C. "Early Colonial Peru: The Urban Female Experience." Ph.D. dissertation, University of Pittsburgh, 1975.
Burkholder, Mark A. "Black Power in Colonial Peru: The 1779 Tax Rebellion of Lambayeque." *Atlanta University Review of Race and Culture* 33, no. 2 (1972): 140–152.
Bush, Barbara. *Slave Women in Caribbean Society, 1650–1838*. Bloomington: Indiana University Press, 1990.
———. "White 'Ladies,' Coloured 'Favourites,' and Black 'Wenches': Some Considerations on Sex, Race, and Class Factors in Social Relations in White Creole Society in the British Caribbean." *Slavery and Abolition* 2, no. 3 (1981): 245–262.
Cardoso, Ciro F. S. *Agricultura, escravidão, e capitalismo*. Petrópolis: Editora Vozes, 1979.
———. "The Peasant Breach in the Slave System: New Developments in Brazil." *Luzo-Brazilian Review* 25, no. 1 (1988).
Chandler, David L. "Family Bonds and the Bondsman: The Slave Family in Colonial Colombia." *Latin American Research Review* 16 (1981): 107–131.
Clavero, José. *Demografía de Lima*. Lima: Imprenta de J. Francisco Solís, 1885.
Clementi, Hebe. *La abolición de la esclavitud en América Latina*. Buenos Aires: Editorial La Pleyade, 1974.

Conrad, Robert. *The Destruction of Brazilian Slavery, 1850–1888*. Berkeley: University of California Press, 1972.

Córdova y Urrutia, José María. *Estadística histórica, geográfica, industrial, y comercial de los pueblos que componen las provincias del departamento de Lima*. Lima, Imprenta de Instrucción Primaria, 1839.

Corwin, Arthur F. *Spain and the Abolition of Slavery in Cuba, 1817–1886*. Austin: University of Texas Press, 1967.

Craton, Michael. "Emancipation from Below? The Role of the British West Indian Slaves in the Emancipation Movement, 1816–1834." In *Out of Slavery: Abolition and After*, ed. Jack Hayward, 110–131. London: Frank Cass, 1985.

———. *Searching for the Invisible Man: Slaves and Plantation Life in Jamaica*. Cambridge, Mass.: Harvard University Press, 1978.

———. *Testing the Chains: Resistance to Slavery in the British West Indies*. Ithaca: Cornell University Press, 1982.

———, ed. *Roots and Branches: Current Directions in Slave Studies*. Toronto: Pergamon Press, 1979.

Curry, Leonard P. *The Free Black in Urban America, 1800–1850: The Shadow of a Dream*. Chicago: University of Chicago Press, 1981.

Cushner, Nicholas P. *Lords of the Land: Sugar, Wine, and Jesuit Estates of Coastal Peru, 1600–1767*. Albany: State University of New York Press, 1972.

———. "Slave Mortality and Reproduction on Jesuit Haciendas in Colonial Peru." *Hispanic American Historical Review* 55, no. 2 (1975): 178–199.

Dunn, Richard S. *Sugar and Slaves: The Rise of the Planter Class in the English East Indies, 1624–1713*. New York: W. W. Norton and Co., 1972.

Durand Florez, G., ed. *Colección documental de la independencia del Perú*. Tomo 4, *El Perú en las Cortes de Cádiz*. Lima: Publicación por el Sesquicentenario de la Independencia del Perú, 1974.

Ellison, Mary. "Resistance to Opression: Black Women's Response to Slavery in the United States." *Slavery and Abolition* 4, no. 1 (1983).

Engelsen, Juan R. "Social Aspects of Agricultural Expansion in Coastal Peru, 1825–1878." Ph.D. dissertation, University of California, Los Angeles, 1977.

Febres Villaroel, Oscar. "La crisis agrícola del Perú en el último tercio del siglo XVIII." *Revista Histórica* 27 (1964): 102–199.

Fenoaltea, Stefano. "Slavery and Supervision in a Comparative Perspective: A Model." *Journal of Economic History* 44, no. 3 (September 1984): 635–668.

Fields, Barbara. *Slavery and Freedom on the Middle Ground: Maryland During the Nineteenth Century*. New Haven: Yale University Press, 1985.

Finley, Moses I. *Economía de la antigüedad*. Mexico: Fondo de Cultura Económica, 1974.

Flores Galindo, Alberto. *Aristocracia y plebe, Lima, 1760–1830*. Lima: Editores Mosca Azul, 1984.

———. "Bandidos de la costa." In *Bandoleros, abigeos, y montoneros: Criminalidad y violencia en el Perú, siglos XVIII–XX*, ed. Carlos Aguirre and Charles Walker, 57–68. Lima: Instituto de Apoyo Agrario, 1990.

Fogel, Robert M., and Stanley L. Engerman. "Recent Findings in the Study of Slave Demography and Family Structure." *Sociology and Social Research* 63, no. 3 (1979): 566–589.

———. *Time on the Cross: The Economics of American Negro Slavery*. 2 vols. Boston: Little, Brown, 1974.

Foner, Laura, and Eugene D. Genovese, eds. *Slavery in the New World: A Reader in Comparative History*. Englewood Cliffs, N.J.: Prentice Hall, 1969.

Fox-Genovese, Elizabeth. *Within the Plantation Household: Black and White Women of the Old South*. Chapel Hill: University of North Carolina Press, 1988.

Freitas, Décio. *O escravismo brasileiro*. 2d ed. Porto Alegre: Editora Mercado Abierto, 1977.

Fuentes, Manuel A. *Estadística general de Lima*. Paris: A. Laine, 1866.

———. *Apuntes históricos, descriptivos, estadísticos, y de costumbres*. Paris: Didot, 1867.

García Calderón, Francisco. *Diccionario de la legislación Peruana*. 2 rols. 2d ed. Lima, Paris:Librería Laroque. 1879.

Genovese, Eugene D. "Materialism and Idealism in the History of Negro Slavery in the Americas." In *Slavery in the New World: A Reader in Comparative History*, ed. Laura Foner and Eugene D. Genovese, 238–255. Englewood Cliffs, N.J.: Prentice Hall, 1969.

———. *The Political Economy of Slavery in the Economy and Society of the Slave South*. New York: Pantheon Books, 1965.

———. *Roll, Jordan, Roll: The World the Slaves Made*. New York: Pantheon Books, 1974.

———. "The Treatment of Slaves in Different Countries: Problems in the Application of the Comparative Method." In *Slavery in the New World: A Reader in Comparative History*, ed. Laura Foner and Eugene D. Genovese, 202–210. Englewood Cliffs, N.J.: Prentice Hall, 1969.

———. *The World the Slaveholders Made: Two Essays in Interpretation*. New York: Random House, Vintage Books, 1971.

Giesecke, Margarita. *Masas urbanas y rebelión en la historia: Golpe de estado, Lima 1872*. Lima. Centro de Divulgación de Historia Popular, 1978.

Goldin, Claudia D. *Urban Slavery in the American South, 1820–1860*. Chicago: University of Chicago Press, 1976.

Goody, Jack. *The Development of Family and Marriage in Europe*. Cambridge: Cambridge University Press, 1983.

Gootenberg, Paul. "*Carneros y Chuño*: Price Levels in Nineteenth-Century Peru." *Hispanic American Historical Review* 70, no. 1 (1990): 1–56.

———. "Population and Ethnicity in Early Republican Peru: Some Revisions." *Latin American Research Review* 26, no. 3 (November 1991): 109–157.

———. "The Social Origins of Protectionism and Free Trade in Nineteenth-Century Lima." *Journal of Latin American Studies* 14, no. 2 (1982).

Gunther Doering, Juan, ed. *Planos de Lima, 1613–1983*. Lima: Municipalidad de Lima Metropolitana, Petroperú, 1983.

Gutman, Herbert G. *Slavery and the Numbers Game: A Critique of Time on the Cross*. Urbana: University of Illinois Press, 1975.

———. *The Black Family in Slavery and Freedom, 1750–1925*. New York: Pantheon Books, 1976.

Haenke, Thaddaus. *Descripción del Perú*. 1808. Reprint. Lima: Imprenta El Lucero, 1901.

Haitin, Marcel. "Late Colonial Lima: Economy and Society in an Era of Reform and Revolution." Ph.D. diss., University of California, Berkeley, 1983.

———. "Urban Market and Agrarian Hinterland: Lima in the Late Colonial Period." In *The Economies of Mexico and Peru During the Late Colonial Period, 1760–1810*, ed. N. Jacobsen and H. J. Puhle. Berlin: Colloquim Verlag, 1986.

Hareven, Tamara K. "Family Time and Historical Time." *Daedalus* (Spring 1977): 57–70.

Hart, Albert B. *Slavery and Abolition, 1831–1841*. 1906. Reprint. New York: Negro University Press, 1968.

Harth-Terré, Emilio. "El artesano negro en la arquitectura virreinal limeña." *Revista del Archivo Nacional del Perú* 25, no. 2 (1961).

———. *Negros e indios: un estamento social ignorado del Perú colonial*. Lima: Librería-Editorial Juan Mejía Baca, 1973.

Hayward, Jack, ed. *Out of Slavery: Abolition and After*. London: Frank Cass, 1985.

Hünefeldt, Christine. "Jornales y esclavitud: Lima en la primera mitad del siglo XIX." *Economía* 10, no. 19 (1987): 35–57.

———. *Mujeres: Esclavitud, emociones, y libertad; Lima 1800–1854*. Documentos de trabajo, no. 24. Lima: Instituto de Estudios Peruanos, 1988.

———. "Los negros de Lima: 1800–1830." *Histórica* 3, no. 1 (1979): 17–51.

Hunt, Shane. "La economía de las haciendas y plantaciones en América Latina." *Historia y Cultura* 9 (1975): 7–66.

Ianni, Octavio. *Esclavitud y capitalismo*. Mexico: Siglo XXI, 1976.

Jacobsen, Nils. "The Development of Peru's Slave Population and Its Significance for Coastal Agriculture, 1792–1854." 1974.

Kapsoli, Wilfredo. *Sublevaciones de esclavos en el Perú, siglo XVIII*. Lima: Universidad Ricardo Palma, 1975.

Karasch, Mary. *Slave Life in Rio de Janeiro, 1808–1850*. Princeton: Princeton University Press, 1987.

King, James F. "The Coloured Castes and American Representation in the Cortes of Cádiz." *Hispanic American Historical Review* 23, no. 1 (1953): 33–64.

Klein, Herbert S. *African Slavery in Latin America and the Caribbean*. New York: Oxford University Press, 1986.

Klein, Herbert S., and Stanley L. Engerman. "Del trabajo esclavo al trabajo libre: Notas en torno a un modelo económico comparativo." *Revista Latinoamericana de Historia Económica y Social* 1, no. 1 (1985): 41–55.

Konetzke, Richard. *La época colonial*. 11th ed. Mexico: Siglo XXI, 1981.

———. "El mestizaje y su importancia en el desarrollo de la población hispanoamericana durante la época colonial." *Revista de Indias* 25 (1946): 215–237.

Kriedte, Peter. *Peasants, Landlords, and Merchant Capitalists: Europe and the World Economy, 1500–1800*. Cambridge: Cambridge University Press, 1983.

Labarthe, Manuel. *Castilla y la abolición de la esclavitud*. Revista de publicaciones, no. 2. Lima: Instituto Libertador Ramón Castilla, 1955.

Lanning, John T. "The Case of José Ponceano de Ayarza." *Hispanic American Historical Review* 24 (1944): 432–451.

———. *The Royal Protomedicato: The Regulation of the Medical Professions in the Spanish Empire*. Durham, N.C.: Duke University Press, 1985.

Lebsock, Suzanne. *The Free Women of Petersburg: Status and Culture in a Southern Town, 1784–1860*. New York: Norton, 1984.

Lerner, Gerda. "Women and Slavery." In *Slavery and Abolition* 4, no. 3 (December 1983): 177–191.

Lombardi, John V. "The Abolition of Slavery in Venezuela: A Nonevent." In *Slavery and Race Relations in Latin America*, ed. Robert B. Toplin. Westport, Conn.: Greenwood Press, 1974.

———. *The Decline and Abolition of Negro Slavery in Venezuela, 1820–1854*. Westport, Conn.: Greenwood Press, 1971.

———. "Manumission, *manumisos*, and *aprendizaje* in Republican Venezuela." *Hispanic American Historical Review* 49, no. 41 (1969).

Love, Edgar F. "Marriage Patterns in Persons of African Descent in a Colonial Mexico City Parish." *Hispanic American Historical Review* 51, no. 1 (1971): 79–91.

Macera, Pablo. "Sexo y coloniaje." In *Trabajos de historia*, 3:297–352. Lima: Instituto Nacional de Cultura, 1977.

Mariluz Urquijo, José M. "Victorian de Villava y la pragmática de 1776 sobre matrimonio de hijos de familia." *Revista del Instituto de Historia del Derecho*, no. 11 (1960): 85–105.

Mattosso, Katia M. de Queiros. *To Be a Slave in Brazil, 1550–1888*. New Brunswick, N.J.: Rutgers University Press, 1986.

Mellafe, Rolando. *Breve historia de la esclavitud en América Latina*. Mexico: Sepsetentas, 1973.

Mendiburu, Manuel de. *Diccionario histórico-biográfico del Perú*. Lima: Imprenta de J. F. Solis, 1874–1890.

———. "Ojeada sobre la esclavitud bajo el régimen colonial." *La Revista de Lima*, 5(1862).

Mendieta Ocampo, Ilder. *Hospitales de Lima colonial, siglos XVII–XIX*. Lima: Universidad Nacional Mayor de San Marcos, 1990.

Menefee, Samuel P. *Wives for Sale: An Ethnographic Study of British Popular Divorce*. Oxford: Basil Blackwell, 1981.

Miller, John. *Memorias del general Guillermo Miller, al servicio de la República del Perú*. Translated from the original English version of 1829 by General Torrijos. Madrid: V. Suárez, 1910.

Mintz, Sidney. "Caribbean Marketplaces and Caribbean History." *Radical History Review* 27 (1986): 110–120.

———. "Slavery and Emergent Capitalisms." In *Slavery in the New World: A Reader in Comparative History*, ed. Laura Foner and Eugene D. Genovese, 27–37. Englewood Cliffs, N.J.: Prentice Hall, 1969.

———. "Slavery and the Rise of Peasantries." In *Roots and Branches: Current Directions in Slave Studies*, ed. Michael Craton, 213–242. Toronto: Pergamon Press, 1979.

Moerner, Magnus. *Race Mixture in the History of Latin America*. Boston: Little, Brown, 1967.

———. "The Study of Black Slavery, Slave Revolts, and Abolition: Recent Studies." In *Tijdschrift voor Geschiedenes* 98(3):(1985): 353–365.

Moreno Fraginals, Manuel. *El ingenio: Complejo económico social cubano del azúcar*. 3 vols. Havana: Editorial de Ciencias Sociales, 1978.

Moreno Fraginals, Manuel, Moya Pons, and Stanley L. Engerman. *Between Slavery and Free Labor: The Spanish-Speaking Caribbean in the Nineteenth Century*. Baltimore: Johns Hopkins University Press, 1985.

Morrisey, Marietta. *Slave Women in the New World: Gender Stratification in the Caribbean*. Lawrence: University Press of Kansas, 1989.

Nogueira da Silva, Marilene. *Negro na rua: A nova face da escravidão*. São Paulo: Editora Hucitect, 1988.

Olaechea, Juan B. "El negro en la sociedad hispanoindia." *Revista de Estudios Políticos*, no. 161 (1968): 219–250.

Olien, Michael D. "The Black and Part-Black Populations of Colonial Costa Rica." *Ethnohistory* 27 (1980): 13–29.
Palma, Ricardo. "Las brujas de Ica." In *Ricardo Palma: Tradiciones peruanas*, ed. Julio Ortega, 247–251. Madrid: UNESCO, 1993.
Patrón, Pablo. *Lima antigua*. Lima: Imprenta Gil, 1935.
Patterson, Orlando. "On Slavery and Slave Formation." *New Left Review* 117 (1979): 31–67.
―――. *Slavery and Social Death: A Comparative Study*. Cambridge, Mass.: Harvard University Press, 1982.
―――. *The Sociology of Slavery: An Analysis of the Origins, Development, and Structure of Negro Slave Society in Jamaica*. London: MacGibbon and Kee, 1967.
Pike, Frederick. *The Modern History of Peru*. New York: Praeger, 1973.
Proctor, Robert. *Narration of a Journey across the Cordillera of the Andes, and of a Residence in Lima, and Other Parts of Peru, in the Years 1823 and 1824*. London: Archibald Constable, 1825.
Quiroz Chueca, Francisco. *La protesta de los artesanos: Lima-Callao, 1858*. Lima: Universidad Nacional Mayor de San Marcos, 1988.
Ramos, Demetrio. *Trigo chileno, naveros del Callao, y hacendados limeños entre la crisis agrícola del siglo XVIII y la comercial de la primera mitad del XIX*. Madrid, 1967.
Reclamación de los vulnerados derechos de los hacendados de las provincias litorales del departamento de Lima. Lima: Imprenta de J. M. Concha, 1833.
Reddock, Rhoda E. "Women and Slavery in the Carribbean: A Feminist Perspective." *Latin American Perspectives* 12, no. 1 (1985): 63–80.
Reynolds, Edward. *Stand the Storm: A History of the Atlantic Slave Trade*. London: Allison and Busby, 1985.
Romero, Fernando. *Papel de los descendientes de africanos en el desarrollo económico-social del Perú*. Estudios andinos, movimientos sociales, no. 5. Lima: Universidad Nacional Agraria La Molina, 1980.
Rout, Leslie B., Jr. *The African Experience in Spanish America: 1502 to the Present Day*. 2d ed. Cambridge: Cambridge University Press, 1977.
Sales, Nuria. *Sobre esclavos, reclutas, y mercaderas de quintos*. Barcelona: Editorial Ariel, 1974.
Schwartz, Stuart B. "Manumission of Slaves in Colonial Brazil: Bahia, 1684–1745." *Hispanic American Historical Review* 54 (1974): 603–635.
―――. "Patterns of Slaveholding in the Americas: New Evidence from Brazil." *American Historical Review* 87, no. 2 (April 1982): 55–86.
―――. *Sugar Plantations in the Formation of Brazilian Society: Bahia, 1550–1835*. New York: Cambridge University Press, 1985.
Scott, Rebecca J. "Exploring the Meaning of Freedom: Postemancipation Societies in Comparative Perspective." In *The Abolition of Slavery and the*

Aftermath of Emancipation in Brazil, ed. R. J. Scott, S. Drescher, H. M. Mattos de Castro, G. R. Andrade, R. M. Levine, 1–22. Durham: Duke University Press, 1988.

———. *Slave Emancipation in Cuba: The Transition to Free Labor, 1860–1899*. Princeton: Princeton University Press, 1985.

Seed, Patricia. *To Love, Honor, and Obey in Colonial Mexico: Conflicts over Marriage Choice, 1574–1821*. Stanford: Stanford University Press, 1988.

Slenes, Robert W. "Slave Marriage and Family Patterns in the Coffee Regions of Brazil, 1850–1888." Paper presented at the American Historical Association convention, February 1978.

Smith, Archibald, M.D. *Peru as It Is; A Residence in Lima, and Other Parts of the Peruvian Republic, Comprising an Account of the Social and Physical Features of That Country*. 2 vols. London: Richard Bentley, 1839.

Stevenson, William Bennet. *Historical and Descriptive Narrative of Twenty Years' Residence in South America*. 3 vols. London: Longman Rees, Orme, Brown and Green, 1829.

Tannahill, Reay. *Sex in History*. London: Book Club Associates, 1980.

Tannenbaum, Frank. "Slavery, the Negro, and Racial Prejudice." In *Slavery in the New World: A Reader in Comparative History*, ed. Laura Foner and Eugene D. Genovese, 3–7. Englewood Cliffs, N.J.: Prentice Hall, 1969.

Távara, Santiago. *Abolición de la esclavitud en el Perú*. Lima: Imprenta del Comercio, 1855.

Tomich, Dale W. *Slavery in the Circuit of Sugar: Martinique and the World Economy, 1830–1848*. Baltimore: Johns Hopkins University Press, 1990.

Toplin, Robert B. *The Abolition of Slavery in Brazil*. New York: Atheneum, 1975.

———. *Freedom and Prejudice: The Legacy of Slavery in the United States and Brazil*. Westport, Conn.: Greenwood Press, 1981.

———, ed. *Slavery and Race Relations in Latin America*. Westport, Conn.: Greenwood Press, 1974.

Trazegnies, Fernando. *Ciriaco de Urtecho: Litigante por amor*. Lima: Pontificia Universidad Católica del Perú, 1981.

Vargas Ugarte, Rubén. *Historia general del Perú*. Vol. 6, *Emancipación*. Lima: C. Milla Bartres, 1984.

Viotti da Costa, Emilia. "From All According to Their Abilities, to All According to Their Needs: Slave Day-to-Day Resistance and Notions of Rights in Guyana, 1823–1832." Paper presented at conference, Slavery in a Comparative Perspective, University of California, San Diego, October 1991.

Vivanco, Carmen. "Bandolerismo colonial peruano, 1760–1810: Caracterización de una respuesta popular y causas económicas." In *Bandoleros, abi-*

geos, y montoneros: Criminalidad y violencia en el Perú, siglos XVIII–XX, ed. Carlos Aguirre and Charles Walker, 25–56. Lima: Instituto de Apoyo Agrario, 1990.

Wade, Richard. *Slavery in the Cities of the South, 1820–1860.* London: University of Oxford Press, 1977.

White, Deborah G. "Female Slaves: Sex Roles and Status in the Antebellum Plantation South." *Journal of Family History* 8, no. 3 (Fall 1983): 248–261.

Williams, Eric. *Capitalism and Slavery.* 3d ed. London: A. Deutsch, 1972.

Wirz, Albert. *Sklaverei und kapitalistisches Weltsystem.* Frankfurt am Main: Suhrkamp, 1984.

Index

Abortions, 49, 118
Abuse, 19–20, 60, 63, 77, 80, 156, 184–85, 187, 190–91, 192, 29n32
Abuse trials, 167–69
Agreda, Doña, 20, 25, 73
Agüero, Riva, 26
Aguirre, Carlos, 39, 229n45, 235n16
Albarado, Capt. Don Pablo Josef de, 175
Alcaldes de barrio, 180
Alfaro, Doña Severina, 229n32
Almogera, Doña Paula, 114, 171–72
Alvarado, Cesilio, 142
Alvarado, Don Felipe, 142
Alvarado, Isabel, 142
Amparadas *beaterio*, 162
Andahuasi hacienda, 87
Andrade, Don Manuel, 49
Angelita sugar mill, 209
Angola, 10, 127
Aparicio, Josefa, 49
Aparicio, María, 158
Apprenticeship, 37, 195
Aramburú, Don Isidro, 81
Archivo Arzobispal, 113, 159, 236nn22,23
Archivo General de la Nación, 113
Armero, Don Cristóbal, 81–82
Army, 22, 23, 25, 28, 85–88, 222nn18,21
Arroserena, Doña Teresa de, 67
Arsola, Don Manuel, 65, 83
Artisans: capital accumulation by, 209–11; financial position of, 31–32; nonpayment of, by army, 25; occupational identity of, 213; opportunities for blacks as, 35–36; scarcity of economic opportunity for, 196–97, 213; training of, 37–38; wartime demand for, 22
Asentistas, 99
Astorga, Rafael, 151
Aucallama hacienda, 187
Audiencia Real, 121–22, 123, 126

Bahamas, the, 220n4
Balada, Don Juan, 133–34
Baltasar, Don, 21, 28–29, 30, 34
Baltasara, Doña, 12, 21
Banditry, 16, 62, 85, 88, 89, 90–91, 93, 94, 111
Baquíjano, Dr., 187
Baraona, María, 110
Barracones, 10, 33, 99
Barranca, Peru, 53
Barrionuevo, Antonio, 89
Barrios, slave population of, 39–40
Bartola, Micaela, 124
Basurco, Don Josef, 176
Beaterio, 162, 163, 164, 181
Bellavista, Peru, 113
Biejo sugar mill, 89
Bittar, Don Manuel, 156
Blacks, 6, 14, 98, 180; creation of culture of, 199–200; hierarchies among, 33–35, 98–99, 100, 102–6, 201, 202, 232n3; lack of economic opportunity, 196–97; marginalization of, 213–14; as percentage of total population, 97–98; prejudice against, after abolition, 194–96; racial identity of, 99–100; segregation of, 98; social networks of, 19, 33; social organizations of, 100–105. *See also* Free blacks; Slaves
Blanchard, Peter, 194
Bocanegra hacienda, 19, 82–83, 89, 114
Bocanegra parish, 225n9
Bolívar, Gen. Simón, 3
Bourbon crisis, 220n1
Bourbon reforms, 2
Bowser, Frederick P., 8, 110, 220n4, 231n72, 233n10, 242n3
Bozales: in black hierarchy, 99, 100, 105; earning capacity of, 113, 114, 116–17; importation of, 9, 10, 99; racial identity of, 100
Brabón hacienda, 43, 47
Branding of slaves, 99
Brazil: abolition of slavery in, 222n13; hiring-out system of, 210, 243nn8,9; mobility of slaves in, 229n36; production

Brazil (continued)
  relations in, 68, 209; slavery in, 220n4, 221n8, 243n7, 244n15
Bread production, sabotage of, 191, 241n35
Breña, María del Carmen, 118–19
British slave owners, 168, 169
Brokers, slave, 177–79
Buena Muerte convent: protests of slaves at, 59–60, 61, 62, 63; religious turmoil at, 228n28
Buena Muerte hacienda, 10, 20
Buenos Aires, Argentina, 1, 37,; hiring-out system of, 209; manumission rates in, 92, 139; slave traffic through, 221n3
Bujanda, Col. Miguel Angel, 240n20

Cádiz constitution, 2, 13, 15, 21
Cádiz courts, 13, 14, 168
Calderón, Francisco, 75
Calero, Pablo, 170
Callao, Peru, 37, 87–88, 196
Candelaria, María, 159–60
Cañete, Peru, 60, 61
Canterac, Gen., 26
Caporales, 54, 59, 60
Carabalí, Francisco, 156
Carabali, Josef, 89
Carabayllo parish, 225n9
Caracas, Venezuela, 209
Carmen Seco, Don José del, 125
Caroline code, regulation of slavery by, 13, 168
Carrillo, Don Eusebio, 194
Carrillo, Don Fernando, Marqués de Santa María, 136, 137
Carta de libertad, 17, 18, 23, 25, 30, 70, 73–74, 77, 78, 81, 91, 92, 111, 132–33, 142, 167, 170, 179, 191, 207, 235n16
Casa de la Moneda, 20, 23
Casaverde, Isidora, 164
Casta society, 202
Castilla, Ramón, 5, 72, 77
Catholic church: children in doctrine of, 118, 119; genetic doctrine of, 139; and illness of slaves, 172; moral codes of, 149, 168–69, 200–201; mutual aid societies of (see *Cofradías*); opposition to *hacendados*, 27; and ownership transfers, 185, 186; position on self-manumission, 221n8; and slave marriages, 11, 29, 112, 149–66 passim, 207
Cédula Real, 9, 13
Centurión, Doña Jacoba, 173
Chacarilla hacienda, 45, 47
Chacras, 52, 208
Chala, José, 55

Chancay hacienda, 70, 183
Chandler, David L., 220n4
Chicama rebellion, 194
Children: age of manumission, 83–84, 127; care of, 10, 118–19; concealment of, 119–20; distribution of, in slave population, 42, 43, 44, 118; illegitimate, 21, 132, 138, 139–43; imprisonment of, 187; liberation of, 50, 121, 122, 123, 124–25, 126, 161, 203; maintenance costs of, 16, 17–18, 120–24, 125, 126–27, 203–4, 230n59; ownership of, 12, 17, 120, 123, 125–26; paternity of, 21, 49, 140–41, 142, 201; relocation to haciendas, 185–86; sale of, 10, 49, 54, 114, 115, 119, 123, 124, 126, 227n21; separation from families, 119, 120; training of, 12, 20; value of, 12–13, 114, 115, 126, 185–86
Chillón valley, 89
China, 4
Chincha, Peru, 72, 89
Chocolates, market for, 31
Chorrillos parish, 39, 69, 192; gender distribution of slave population, 43, 45, 46, 226n11; incidence of slave marriages in, 45–46; number of slaves per productive unit, 40, 41, 42, 43; reproduction of slaves in, 47, 48; rural character of, 225n8
Chuquitanta hacienda, 174, 175
Clavero, José, 224n3
Clement VIII, Pope, 228n28
Cofradías, 29, 97, 173; emergence of women in, 205; racial divisions within, 100; racial hierarchies of, 102, 201; role in manumission, 101–2, 169–70; social functions of, 100–101; status hierarchies of, 102–5, 147
Colombia, 220n4
Colonialism, 2–3, 14, 15, 85–86, 88
El Comercio (newspaper), 195–96
Compuertas estate, 52–53
Concubinage, 130, 132–33, 138, 236n18
Congos-Mondongos *cofradía*, 100–101, 102–5
Conque, 11, 20, 74, 75–76, 94, 109, 173, 177, 183, 184, 185, 186, 195
Conrad, Robert, 220n4
Contraception, 139
Corporal punishment. See Punishment, corporal
Cortes de Cádiz. See Cádiz courts
Costa Rica, 244n15
Council of Hacendados, 223n22
Craton, Michael, 220n4
Crime rates, 195–96

Index

Criollo ladinos, 100
Criollos: and black hierarchy, 99, 105; fear of rebellion, 3; protests against colonialism, 2, 14, 15
Cristo, Domingo del, 156
Cruz Zapata, Juan de la, 171
Cuba, 1,, 3, 209, 241n24
Cuellar, Bonifacio, 164
Cuellar, Micaela, 164
Cushner, Nicholas P., 46, 224n6
Cuzco insurrection, 3

Daga, Doña Juana, 185–86
Daga, Juan, 191
Day laborers, 56–57, 62, 63, 82, 83; accumulation of capital for manumission, 110–11, 113–17, 126–28, 209–11, 233n22; "defective" slaves as, 174–75, 240n15; dependence of urban society on, 107–8, 233n10; leverage over owners, 112–13; profitability of, 108–10, 115–16; support of children by, 123, 124, 126–27
"Day-labor" permits, 221–22n9
Defensor de Menores: on hiring-out system, 108–9, 117; representation of slaves by, 64, 65, 75–76, 81, 82–83, 93, 124, 125
De la Vega, Countess, 174
Delgado, Juan, 87
Diaz, José, 237–38n37
Dios Algorta, Juan de, 193
Divorce: in slaveholder marriages, 137–38, 206; in slave marriages, 30, 160, 162–63, 163–64, 181
Domestic service: capital accumulation in, 114–17; illegitimate offspring of, 132, 138, 139–43; master-slave sexual liaisons within, 129–39; status of women and, 205–6

Ellison, Mary, 138–39
Encarnación, Doña María, 132
England. *See* Great Britain
Equality, 5, 200
Escobedo, Jorge, 180
Espinoza, Doña Isabel, 125
Espinoza, Doña Ventura, 183
Espinoza, Mariana, 165
Espíritu Santo Real, Manuel del, 194–95
Esquivel, Marcos, 125
Evangelista Theves, Don Juan, 57

Families: composition of, 10–11; fictive reconstruction of, 6; importance of, to slave life, 4–5, 143, 219–20n4; life of, outside master's household, 122–24, 126; manumission strategies of, 79–85; preserving unity of, 201; prominence of women in, 205; separation of children from, 119, 120; and slave mobility, 46; stresses on, 203–4, 242–43n4; variability in circumstances of, 143–44. *See also* Marriage(s)
Febres, Villaroel, 52
Fenoaltea, Stefano, 219n3
Ferdinand VII (king of Spain), 14
Fertility rate, 49–50
Fields, Barbara, 203, 242–43n4
Flores Galindo, Alberto, 90, 241n22
Frazier, E. Franklin, 219n4
Free blacks: as artisans, 213; care of slave children of, 118–19; in colonial army, 85–86; competition with slaves, 84, 114; economic position of, 244n13; financial hardship of, 30, 31; imprisonment of, 18, 125, 188, 189, 190, 195; indispensability of, 1–2; marriage to slaves, 144–47, 145, 146, 148, 151–52, 153; population of, 38; social status of, 103–5; struggle for subsistence, 18–19; treatment as slaves, after abolition, 194–95
French colonies, manumission in, 244n13
Fuente Hermosa, Marqués de, 61, 133–34

Gaceta del Gobierno, 240n20
Garcia, Doña Fermina, 187
Garcia, Magdalena, 80, 84
García, Simón, 78
Gardening, subsistence, 11, 12, 16, 19, 54, 68–69, 95–96, 202, 205, 208–9, 222n15
Garses, Doña María, 53
Gender, 58–59, 160–61, 228n26
Genovese, Eugene D., 201–2, 219n4
Gómez, Don Francisco, 190
Góngora, Manuel, 158
Gonzales, Doña Manuela, 174–77
Gonzales, Don Martín, 173
Gracias al sacar, 14, 201
Great Britain: competition of imports from, 213, 214; industrialization of, 220n1; pressure against slavery, 197, 214; sale of wives in, 235n2. *See also* British slave owners
Gregorio, José, 174–76, 179, 187, 188, 211
Gregory XIV, Pope, 228n28
Guaca hacienda, 61
Gualcará hacienda, 61, 62
Guano production, 31, 32
Guerrero, Luisa, 229n37
Guerrilla groups, 27, 28, 85, 90–91, 223n28
Guilds, 105, 196–97, 201, 205, 213
Gutiérrez Prio, Juan, 135
Gutman, Herbert G., 200, 204

Hacendados: absentee, 59, 62, 77–78; attempts to reimpose slavery, 27, 28; control of slaves by, 58; fear of revolt, 60–61; killings of, 57; mobility of, 66–67. *See also* Haciendas; Slaveholders
Haciendas, 15, 22, 27, 59; abuse of slaves on, 19–20, 60, 63, 80, 229n32; circulation of slaves of, 46–47, 60, 61, 65–67, 69, 75, 93, 94, 187, 229nn36,37; composition of slave families, 10–11; conversion to wage labor, 222n15; crop substitution by, 220n1; distribution of male and female slaves on, 42, 43, 44–46, 95, 221n4, 226n11; effect of abolition decree on, 77–78; incidence of slave marriages on, 45–46, 225–26n10; land area of, 43, 44, 45, 50, 52; management by slaves, 52–53; migration from, 79–85; monetization of relations on, 96; outplacement of slaves by owners, 37–38; ownership of, 59, 77–78; prominence of women on, 205; recruitment by patriot army on, 87; release of slaves by, 16–18, 32–33, 50, 66–79, 93–96, 202, 204, 205; relocation of slaves to, 28–29, 174, 183–87; reproduction of slaves on, 47–50, 48–49, 54, 84; slave population of, 10, 27, 38, 40, 41–43, 44, 47, 95, 224n6; spheres of production on, 15–16, 222n15; systems of internal control, 58–62, 228n26; transfers of slave ownership from, 19–20, 63–64, 80–82, 83; transition to wage labor, 69–70; value of slave children of, 12–13; working conditions of slaves, 52–58
Haiti, 222n13
Haitin, Marcel, 52, 224n4; on marriage patterns, 148, 236n22, 237nn24,29; on productivity of Lima parishes, 225n9; on rural stagnation, 95, 232n76
Huaito hacienda, 53–55, 58, 69, 96
Huánuco insurrection, 3

Ica, Peru, 26, 30, 31, 65, 67, 76, 165
Ignacio, Don José, 168–69
Ignacio Palacio, Don José, 173–74
Illiteracy rate, 196
Illness, 171–72, 178
Indians, 1, 180, 214; marriages to slaves, 146, 147, 148, 236n23; uprisings of, 2, 3, 14, 15
Infant mortality, 10, 49, 118
Islam, concubinage in, 236n18
Iturrizaga, Pedro José, 157–58

Jamaica, 220n4
Jáuregui, Don Dámaso, 71

Judicia de redhibitoria, 155
Juzgado de menores, 15

Labarthe, Manuel, 193–94
La Camacho, 105
La Legua parish, 225n9
Lambayeque, Peru, 86
Lara, Antonio, 191
Larreguerro, Domingo, 192
La Serna, Viceroy, 222n21
Las Heras, Archbishop, 136
Lavalle, Juan Bautista, 225n9
León, Bernardina, 71
Lesama, Agustín, 89
Lezpus, Doña Juana, 67
Liberalism, 3, 15; opposition to *hacendados*, 27; property rights and, 170; racial prejudice of, 214; view of slaves, 13, 14
Libertos, 26, 80–82, 223n23
Lima, Peru, 1, 5, 26, 37, 59; abolition of slavery in, 2, 31, 77–78, 194–97, 210–11, 213, 214–15; black social networks, 19, 33; black society in, 33–35, 98–99, 100, 102–6, 201–2, 232n3; child (slave) population of, 42, 43, 44, 118; colonial military force of, 85–86; economic opportunities in, 16–17, 31–32, 35–36, 196–97; hiring-out system of, 107–17, 126–28, 209–11; influx of refugees, 15, 16; land area of production units of, 43–44, 45, 50, 52; law enforcement in, 180–82; marketplaces of, 19, 68–69, 208–9; marriage patterns in, 144–48, 236nn22,23, 237n22; methods of manumission in, 24, 51, 91–92, 111, 231n72; migration to, 79–85; movement of slaves between haciendas and, 65–67; number of slaves per productive unit, 40, 41–43, 44; outlaw gangs, 62, 88–91; outplacement of slaves from haciendas to, 37–38; population of, 97–98; prison population of, 187–94; protests of slaves in, 60, 61, 63, 78; rate of manumission in, 23, 24, 51, 91–92, 98, 111, 211, 231n72, 235n16, 244n13; relocation of (former) slaves to, 18–19, 20, 28–36, 67–79, 93–96, 202, 204, 205; reproduction of slaves in, 47–50, 54, 84, 118, 140; rural character of, 9, 38; rural stagnation in, 95, 232n76; rural-urban distribution of slaves in, 39–41, 224–25n7; slave population of, 9, 27, 40, 47, 92, 97, 98, 111, 211; Spaniards in, 14; spatial characteristics of, 38, 224n3; struggle for subsistence in, 18–19; training of slave children in, 12, 20; urban dis-

Index

tribution of slaves in, 106–8; urban expansion in, 95; urbanized slaves of, 37; urban malaise in, 180–81
Llanos, José, 185–86
Lobatón, Doña Nicolasa, 71
Lobatón hacienda, 47
Lottery, 111
Luis, San Camilo de, 228n28

Magdalena, Peru, 11, 16
Magdalena parish, 9, 59; gender distribution of slave population, 42, 46, 226n11; incidence of slave marriages in, 225–26n10; number of slaves per productive unit, 40, 41–42, 43; productivity of, 225n9; reproduction of slaves in, 47, 48
Maldonado, Doña Elena, 52–53
Mansilla, Francisco, 80–82
Manumission, 12, 15; of children, 50, 83–84, 121, 122, 123, 124–25, 126, 127, 161, 203; circumvention of owner's opposition to marriage through, 151–52, 153, 237–38n37; as concomitant of rights of marriage, 157; of "defective" slaves, 173, 177; delayed, 242–43n4; establishment of property rights in, 243n6; as gift, 245n17; link to sexual favors, 131, 132–34, 135, 137, 138, 142; methods of, 24, 51, 91–92, 111, 231n72; and morality, 200; purchase of marital loyalty with, 160, 161–62; rate of, 98, 111, 139, 211, 235n16, 244nn12,13; retractions of, 26–27; as reward for child-bearing, 140, 236n18; as right of illegitimate children, 140–41; role of *cofradías* in, 101–2, 169–70; rural vs. urban, 91–92; terms of, 25; testamentary, 70–73, 233n15. *See also* Self-manumission
Maranga, 225n9
Marchan, Mariano, 89
María, Tiburcio, 65–66
Marín, María del Carmen, 185–86
Maroons, 18, 19, 23, 25, 28, 30, 33, 57, 62, 66, 82, 83, 85, 93, 94, 172, 173, 175–76, 178, 182; activity in independence period, 90–91; imprisonment of, 188, 189; numbers of, 90; objectives of, 88–89
Marriage(s): age of, at, 149–50, 237n29; annulment of, 47, 150, 226n12, 237nn30,31; attempted control by owners, 155–57, 158; celebration of, 11; conflict in, 29–30, 159–66, 207, 238n50, 239n61; consent of owners to, 149–53, 154, 155; dual authority in, 161–64; economic incentive for, 11; enlargement of slaves' rights by, 29, 34, 47, 111–13, 150, 157–59, 204, 207; fertility of, 47–50; free spousal choice in, 149, 150, 151, 237n25; hierarchy within, 33–34; incidence of, in slave population, 45–46, 144, 145, 147, 149, 203, 225–26n10, 239n61, 242n3; nobility-*criollo*, 21, 222n17; paternal authority over, 148–49; preserving unity of, 155, 156, 165; protection of, as institution, 54; and racial hierarchy, 34–35; and slave mobility, 46, 185, 186, 187; types of, 144–48, 145, 146, 236nn22,23, 237n24
Marris, Antonio, 157
Martinique, 143, 208–9
Matallana, Manuela, 161–64
Mayordomos, 11, 57, 58, 75; ethnicity of, 59, 62; mobility of, 66–67; slave protests against, 60, 61, 63; transfer of slave ownership by, 19–20
Mejía, Pedro José, 57
Meléndez, Don Ignacio, 127
Men: departure from haciendas, 33, 81, 83; distribution of, in slave population, 42, 43, 44–46, 95, 129, 221n4, 226n11; in labor market, 84; sexual relations with slaveholders, 137–38
Menacho, Don Manuel, 55–56
Mendiburu, Manuel de, 109, 110
Merced convent, 104
Mercedes Oyague, María, 132–33
Merchants, 89
Mexico City, 37, 92, 139
Milagro Solórzano, María del, 124
Miller, Gen. Guillermo, 25, 90, 99, 222n21
Mintz, Sidney, 8, 199, 200
Miraflores, 59, 225n8; gender distribution of slave population, 44, 46, 226n11; number of slaves per productive unit, 40, 42–43, 44; reproduction of slaves in, 47, 49; transition to wage labor in, 69–70
Mirones hacienda, 11
Miscegenation, 140–41, 200, 201–2
Molina hacienda, 77–78, 80, 84
Monteagudo, Bernardo, 87
Monte de Santa Rosa, 89
Monterrico hacienda, 75, 112
Montesa, Custodio, 152
Mora, Candelaria, 72–73
Mora, Doña Irene, 72
Mulatos, 100
Murga, Ana María, 182
Murga, Doña Juana, 124
Mutual aid societies. See *Cofradías*

Naranjal hacienda, 175
Nazca hacienda, 85
Negreiros, Don Ignacio, 174
Negro, Francisco, 89
Negrón, Patricio, 76–77
New Orleans, 244n13
Neyra, Matea, 133–34
Nieto, María Luisa, 160–61
Ninavilca (guerrilla), 28

Ocharán family, 67–68
Ontañón, Apolinaria, 183–84
Ordóñez, Bernardo, 193
Otero, Francisco Paula, 90
Ouro Prêto, Brazil, 244n15

Palacios, Doña Estefa, 76–77
Palacios, Doña Sipriana, 116
Palmeo, 99
Palomino hacienda, 46
Palpa hacienda, 65–66, 85
Panaderías, 18, 23, 26, 53, 60, 85, 133, 152, 153, 163, 170, 173, 174, 175, 178, 179, 181, 182, 183, 195, 212, 241n35; Animitas *panadería*, 242n40; Caucato *panadería*, 150–51; Nazarenas *panadería*, 184; Paceo *panadería*, 192; Pericotes *panadería*, 77; Santa Ana *panadería*, 176; Santa Clara *panadería*, 191; Sauce *panadería*, 190; Serrano *panadería*, 67, 191; Siete Hormigas *panadería*, 188; Tigre *panadería*, 75
Panama, slave traffic through, 10, 221n3
Pando hacienda, 9, 22, 221n4; abuse of slaves on, 19–20; composition of slave families, 10–11; release of slaves by, 16–18; value of slave children of, 12–13
Paniso, Catalina, 142
Parishes: number of slaves per productive unit, 40, 41–43, 44; rural-urban distribution of slaves in, 39–41, 224–25n7. *See also* under name of specific parish
Pativilca hacienda, 229n32
Patronage, 76, 80–82, 230n51
Patronage decree, 76, 81, 83, 230nn51,59
Peasantization, 68, 95–96, 208
Pedreros, Juana, 127
Peru, 6, 9; abolition of slavery in, 3, 4, 5, 31, 72, 77–78, 139, 142, 194–97, 210–11, 213, 214–15; independence of, 2–3, 9, 21–23, 25–27, 28, 220n1; socioeconomic impact of slaves on, 1–2; sociopolitical instability in, 9–10, 220n1
Pezuela, Viceroy, 23
Piélago, Pedro, 173–74
Pigs, 11, 54, 69

Pisco, Peru, 113, 156
Police, urban, 180–81
Pontejo, Doña María, 169
Porras hacienda, 45–46, 47
Portocarrero, Señor, 156
Price of slaves, 11, 12, 13, 16, 17, 19, 20, 29, 30, 35, 53, 67, 68, 70, 72, 109–10, 126, 127, 153, 237–38n37; abuse and, 80; brokering of, 177–79; of "defective" slaves, 170–77; depreciation of, 73–75, 229n45; effect of abolition decree on, 78; gender differences in, 74, 229n46; increases in, 75–76, 185–86; loan of amount of, to slaves, 76–77; matching of, to accumulated capital, 207, 210
Prices, commodity, 15–16, 22, 220n1
Prisons, 181. See also *Panaderías*
Proctor, Robert, 68, 90–91
Property rights, 169, 170, 186, 200, 204, 243n6
Protomedicato, determination of paternity by, 21, 141
Puente estate, 89
Pulperías, 173, 180
Punishment, corporal, 14, 165; abusive, 77, 80; actionability of, 168–69; illegality of, 167, 168; indemnification for, 195; as means of control, 54, 182; in *panadería*, 184–85, 190–91; of runaway slaves, 46–47, 54

Quarterones, 99
Quebrada hacienda, 60–61, 78, 228n28
Quintanilla estate, 75
Quinterones, 99
Quirigallo, Manuela, 103
Quispico hacienda, 87

Race, 141; in distribution of prison population, 182, 241n22; as factor in control of slaves, 58–59, 228n26; as factor in marital alliances, 146, 147–48, 236n23, 237n24; and occupational structure, 213–14
Racial hierarchy, 33–35, 98–99, 100, 102, 105–6, 201–2, 232n3
Racism, and abolition, 5, 194–96
Ramírez, Don Francisco, 188
Ramirez, Francisco, 156
Ramírez de Arellano, Pablo, 121–23
Rape: master-slave, 21, 131, 156, 190; slave-master, 137, 138
Rentas Unidas hacienda, 228n26
Retes hacienda, 49
Rímac valley, 43–44, 45
Riobo, Don Francisco, 184–85

Rio de Janeiro, Brazil, 37, 79, 221–22n9, 244n16
Rioja, Lorenzo, 130–32
Rosales, Camilo, 159–60
Rosario Velásquez, Doña María del, 72

Sabotage, by slaves, 191, 241n35
Salas, José, 89
Salazar, Pablo, 151–52, 153
Salazar de Monteblanco, Doña Josefa, 53
Saldonado, Don Ramón, 64
Saldonado, José, 64, 65
Saldonado, Mariana, 64, 65
Salinas, Don Vicente, 65
Salvador, Brazil, 244n15
San Agustín plaza, 68–69
San Bartolomé hospital, 30, 124, 162, 190
San Borja hacienda, 45
Sánchez de la Concha, Francisco Bernardo, 137–38
San Francisco plaza, 19, 23, 68–69, 175, 176
San Juan hacienda, 45, 74
San Lázaro parish, 18, 29, 31; as black enclave, 106, 110; black society in, 101; incidence of slave marriages in, 147, 203; land area of production units of, 43–44; marriage patterns in, 145–48, 236n23; movement of slaves between haciendas and, 65–66; residence of ex-slaves in, 82–83, 93; rural-urban distribution of slaves in, 39–41, 224–25n7; working conditions of slaves of, 55–56, 58
San Martín, Gen. José de: freedom for slaves and, 26, 86–87; and guerrilla forces, 90; and Peruvian independence, 2, 3, 23; recruitment of blacks by, 86–87, 222n21
Santa Ana parish, 30; child (slave) population of, 118; continuity of slave ownership in, 179; incidence of slave marriages in, 147, 150, 203, 239n61; marriage patterns in, 145–48, 236n23, 237n24; resistance to slave marriages in, 149–50; urban distribution of slaves in, 106–8, 212
Santa Clara hacienda, 80–82
Santa María, Marquesa of, 136, 137
Santos, Gregoria, 168–69
Santos Puente, María, 103–4
São Paulo, Brazil, 1, 37, 209, 244n15
São Pedro parish (Brazil), 244n15
Sayán, Peru, 87
Scott, Rebecca, 3, 4, 94–95, 241n24
Segregation, racial, 98
Self-manumission, 12, 13, 15, 30, 31, 221n8; accumulation of capital for,

32–33, 37–38, 62–79, 110–11, 113–17, 126–28, 207–11, 233n22; and contacts with urban society, 33, 82–83, 84–85; family relations in strategies of, 79–85; negotiation of, 35, 50, 66–79, 93–96; rate of, 23, 24, 51, 91–92, 111, 231n72; sacrifice of other interests to, 31, 32, 104, 196, 213; terms of, 16–18, 29; transgressions of masters against, 23, 25
Serenos, 180–81, 187
Síndico del Concurso, 80
Sisneros, Don Juan, 175
Slaveholders: (alleged) rape of, 137, 138; attempted control of slave marriages, 155–57, 158; compensation of, after abolition, 194; consent to slave marriages, 149–53, 154, 155; disorganization of, as class, 211–12; divisions within families of, 67–68; illegitimate children of, 21, 49, 132, 139–43; marriages of, 134–38; profits of, 4, 74, 108–10, 115–16, 183, 219n3, 241n24; property rights of, 169, 170, 186, 200, 204; sexual relations with slaves, 129–39, 155, 200–201, 206–7; use of slave wages as capital, 64–65; violation of manumission terms by, 23, 25. See also *Hacendados*
Slave realtors, 20
Slavery: abolition of, 3–5, 15, 31, 72, 77–78, 139, 142, 194–97, 210–11, 213, 214–15, 222n13; disintegration of, 2, 36; inheritability of, 139, 147; legal regulation of, 13, 14, 168, 221–22n9, 223n22; legitimacy of, 169; as social system, 199–202; socioeconomic impact of, 1–2; as survivor of wars of independence, 26–27, 28
Slaves, 6, 10, 37, 201; abuse of, 19–20, 60, 63, 77, 80, 156, 167–69, 184–85, 187, 190–91, 192, 229n32; annulment of sale of, 75–76; in colonial army, 85–86; competition with free labor, 84, 114; control of, 16, 46–47, 50, 52, 54, 58–62, 94–95, 115–16, 179–83, 187, 208, 209–10, 212, 228n26, 244n16; criminality of, 57, 172, 173–77, 188, 189; "defective," 170–77; emancipated (*see* Free blacks); families of (*see* Children; Families; Marriage[s]); fugitive (*see* Maroons); gender distribution of, on haciendas, 42, 43, 44–46, 95, 221n4, 226n11; importation from abroad, 9, 10, 37, 99; imprisonment of, 18, 23, 26, 53, 60, 75, 77, 133, 151, 153, 163, 164, 170, 173, 174, 175, 176, 179, 181–82, 183, 184–85, 187–94, 212; influence of independence movement on, 21–22; initiatives toward emancipation,

Slaves (*continued*)
  4, 5, 6, 28–36, 93–96; job opportunities for, 16–17, 35–36; litigation by, 15, 20, 21, 55–57, 65, 71, 72, 80, 81, 82–83, 101–2, 103–4, 112–13, 114, 121–23, 124, 125, 130–32, 133–34, 140, 141, 142, 157–58, 160–61, 162–64, 165, 166, 167–69, 171–72, 173, 182, 183–85, 186, 187, 239n1; lives during wars of independence, 23, 25; management skills of, 52–53; marriages of (*see* Marriage[s]); mobility of, 46–47, 60, 61, 65–67, 69, 75, 93, 94, 179–80, 187, 209, 229nn36,37; moral personalities of, 200–201, 203; number per productive unit, 40, 41–43, 44, 224n6; occupational identity of, 212–14; participation in wars of independence, 23, 25, 28, 222n21; population of, 9, 27, 38, 47, 92, 95, 97, 98, 111, 211, 212, 244n15; purchase of freedom of (*see* Manumission; Self-manumission); purchase price of, 11, 12, 13, 16, 17, 19, 20, 29, 30, 35, 53, 67, 68, 70, 72, 73–77, 78, 80, 109–10, 126, 127, 153, 170–79, 185–86, 207, 210, 229nn45,46, 237–38n37; racial identity of, 99–100; rape of, 21, 131, 156, 190; relocation to haciendas, 28–29, 174, 183–87; reproduction of, 47–50, 48–49, 54, 84, 118, 140; revolts of, 2, 3, 57–58, 59–61, 85, 87–88, 91, 192, 193–94; rights of, 202–3; rural-urban distribution of, 39–41, 224–25n7; sale of free labor by, 69–70; sale of produce by, 11, 68–69, 208–9; sexual relations with slaveholders, 129–39, 155, 200–201, 206–7; spheres of production of, 15–16, 222n15; subsistence plots of, 11, 12, 16, 19, 54, 68–69, 95–96, 202, 205, 208–9, 222n15; ties to white social groups, 5–6; transfer of ownership of, 19–20, 30–31, 63–64, 72–73, 80, 111–13, 153, 155, 160–61, 167–70, 173–79, 207, 211, 240n15; urban population distribution, 106–8; wages of, 23, 25, 53, 64–65, 69–70, 70–71, 74, 76–77, 107–17, 123, 124, 126–28, 151–52, 159–60, 161, 163, 169, 170, 179, 182, 204, 230n51; working conditions of, 12, 21, 52–58. *See also* Blacks; *Libertos*
Smith, Archibald, 142
Social networks, 19, 33, 82–83, 84–85, 205. See also *Cofradías*
Spain, 2–3, 8
Stevenson, William Bennet, 53, 54–55, 58, 100–101, 103, 104
Suárez, Manuel, 109

Suazo, Francisca, 70
Suazo, Jacinta, 70
Subsistence plots, 11, 12, 54, 95–96, 202, 205; competition with commercial production, 16, 222n15; self-manumission with earnings from, 68–69, 208–9; support of urban relatives by, 19
Suicide, by slaves, 127–28, 159, 182, 204, 210
Supe, Peru, 71
Surco parish, 39; gender distribution of slave population, 43, 45, 46, 226n11; incidence of slave marriages in, 45–46; number of slaves per productive unit, 40, 41, 42, 43; productivity of, 225n9; reproduction of slaves in, 47, 48; rural character of, 225n8

Tacna insurrection, 3
Tannenbaum, Frank, 200
Távara, Santiago, 195–96
Taverns, 180
Tax, military, 86
Teruz, Miguel Geronimo de, 116
Toplin, Robert B., 232n3
Torquera, Francisco, 134–35
Torres, Justa, 125
Torres, Petronila, 151
Torre Tagle, Marqués de, 191, 223n22
Trevino, Doña Rufina, 171
Tribunal de la Acordada, 181
Tristán, Flora, 225n9
Tupac Amaru uprising, 85

United States, 6, 213; abolition of slavery in, 222n13; hiring-out system of, 243n10; manumission in, 243n6, 244nn12,13; movement of slaves to countryside in, 232n75; resistance strategies of slave women in, 138–39; slave families of, 143, 204, 242–43n4; urban black population of, 224n1; wage payments to slaves in, 64

Valdéz, D. Agustín, 235n4
Vallehermoso, Count of, 190
Valverde hacienda, 45, 47
Vargas Machuca, Manuela, 137–38
Venegas, Tomás, 161–64
Vilca, Isidro, 121, 126
Villafuerte, Marqués de, 237n30
Villa hacienda, 42, 45, 53, 74, 225n9
Villar de Puente, Señor Conde de, 175
Villegas, Doña Paula, 161
Vista Florida, Count of, 61
Vivanco, Carmen Lara, 62

Wages, slave, 37, 74, 126, 179, 195; accumulation of capital by slaves from, 69–70, 110–11, 113–17, 126–28, 209–11, 233n22; augmenting of slaves' rights by, 112–13; burden of, 127–28, 204; dependence of urban society on, 107–8, 233n10; division between master and slave, 23, 25, 53, 64–65, 109–10, 127–28, 163; enlargement of marital choice by, 151–52; guarantee of, in ownership transfers, 169, 170, 173, 240n15; as interest payment on manumission loan, 76–77; in *patronato*, 76, 230n51; payment by *panadería*, 182, 187, 212; profits to owners from, 108–10, 115–16; retroactive payment of, after abolition, 78; from sale of free labor, 69–70; as source of capital for slaveholders, 64–65; as source of marital tension, 159–60, 161; support of children from, 123, 124, 126–27; testamentary manumission as repayment of, 70–71

Walker, Charles, 223n28

Wars of independence: guerrilla activity in, 90–91; impact on urban labor, 22–23; involvement of slaves in, 21–22, 23, 25, 28, 86–88, 222n21; lives of slaves during, 23, 25; promises of freedom for slaves, 26, 86–87, 90, 223n22; survival of slavery after, 26–27, 28

Westphalia Treaty, 8

White, Deborah G., 206

Will (testament), 70–73, 111–12, 233n15

Womb assignment, 12, 21, 120, 126, 179

Women, 54; competition for, 155, 235n4; departure from haciendas, 32–33, 80–83, 84, 93, 204, 205, 230n58; distribution of, in slave population, 42, 43, 44–46, 95, 129, 221n4, 226n11; fertility of, 47–50, 48–49; in labor market, 84, 113–15, 116–17, 205; sexual relations with slaveholders, 129–37, 138–39, 155, 200–201, 206–7; social status of, 205–6; subordination in marriage, 159–66, 207

Yauyos, Peru, 28

www.ingramcontent.com/pod-product-compliance
Lightning Source LLC
Chambersburg PA
CBHW021657230426
43668CB00008B/653